DATE DUE		
SE 14 '87		
OC 12 '87		
NO 28 '88		

Native Land

Native Land
Sagas of the Indian Americas

Jamake Highwater

LITTLE, BROWN AND COMPANY
Boston · Toronto

FIRST EDITION

Library of Congress Cataloging-in-Publication Data

Highwater, Jamake.
  Native land.

    Companion volume to the public television program, Native land.
    Bibliography: p.
    Includes index.
    1. Indians. 2. Indians—Religion and mythology. I. Native land (Television program) II. Title. E58.H54111986   299'.7   86-10285
ISBN 0-316-36087-2

Published simultaneously in Canada
by Little, Brown & Company (Canada) Limited

DESIGN: *Mike Fender* ● LAYOUT: *Jean Hammond*
PRINTED IN THE UNITED STATES OF AMERICA

For Joseph Campbell
"There is a world elsewhere!"
—SHAKESPEARE, *Coriolanus*

Contents

Native Land

Introduction:

"This Is the Holy Land"

THIS IS THE HOLY LAND. It is the holy land but it is not Palestine. It is a vast place of exceptional power and unsolved mysteries. It is called America.

It is here in the ancient Americas that the Indian world began. Like the holy land of the Middle East, this place of the American genesis has its own cast of heroic characters. This Indian holy land possesses wide panoramas and a magnitude of time. Here was the first day of the American world. Here, too, were the first great temples and pyramids of America. Like the holy land of Jehovah and Jesus, this American holy land has its own stories and its own songs of destiny. These are some of the stories of the Native Land.

IN THE BEGINNING, everywhere on the face of the earth people with little more than animal intelligence and the need to survive began their perilous ascent to civilization. The subsequent history of the world is a saga of vastly different cultures.

Yet all the people of these different worlds started out by asking almost exactly the same questions: Where did we come from and how did the world begin? What makes their stories fascinating is the fact that most of them came up with different answers, and these answers are the basis of the radically different cultures in which we now live.

In the folktales of ancient people, history was transformed into the metaphoric language that we call myth. It is with these

Monument Valley, Arizona.

myths that all peoples try to answer those fundamental questions that all of us ask. Myths are the foundations on which we build our very different societies. And every aspect of our world is a reflection of that precious mythology that we carry with us like cultural baggage from generation to generation . . . the structure of our societies, our morality, and even our political ideals.

When we speak about mythology in this book, we are not talking about falsity or superstition. Myths are the means by which we make viable and tangible certain basic and ineffable beliefs that are central to our mentality. All cultures have myths about themselves: about their origins and destinies. The world in which we live is determined not only by the way we see ourselves but also by the way we relate to the cosmos. In fact, our mythology is the basis of our cosmology.

For the Aztecs, this influence of mythology on society was quite dramatic. These people of Mexico believed that only human blood could give nourishment to their god, the Sun. To

Shiprock, New Mexico.

assist their god in his eternal struggle against darkness, they created a religion based on human sacrifice.

Brahmans believe that all creatures are slowly evolving toward perfection through a complex process of reincarnation. And so Hindus view all living things as eternal and sacred, and for this reason they prohibit the eating of flesh.

The Genesis of Jews and Christians envisions humans as creatures created in God's image — standing at the pinnacle of nature, the centerpiece of a world that God made for them and for them alone. Therefore they believe that they alone among all creatures of the earth have eternal souls.

Such myths give all of us a sense of purpose and importance. They provide us with a metaphorical language in which we can express the seemingly inexpressible. But if the myths about ourselves don't change, then we cannot change.

Ancient Egypt remained essentially the same for several thousand years and finally perished because it couldn't redefine itself in terms of a world that was changing all around it.

In contrast, our own society has faced immense upheaval because we have persistently reshaped the mythology by which we live our lives. In the most critical sense, we do not exist in the same cosmos that people existed in before the era of Copernicus and Galileo, and we do not live in the same world that people lived in before Columbus and the Age of Exploration. The reality of our day is essentially different from what people meant by reality before Einstein, Freud, and Marx. Such revolutionary awakenings into new worlds of meaning are simply the most obvious twists and turns of Western philosophical history. It is, we must always remember, a history that the West writes for itself. Among non-Western peoples there has always been a reservoir of alternative visions of the cosmos. Their worlds have always been different from ours.

Emerson told us that "the whole of nature is a metaphor of the human mind." The world changes because our vision of it changes. Nothing makes this Emersonian precept clearer than an encounter with an entirely alien culture in which a different kind of history from ours melds with a different kind of mythology. Such are the sagas of the Native Land.

Nomads of the Dawn

IN THEIR MYSTERIOUS, northern homelands, the people of the Sun heard the voice of a bird that spoke to them from a tree, saying: *"Tihui . . .* Let us go. I will call you Mexica and I will lead you to a place where you will become great among many tribes."

And the Mexica left their homeland far to the north of the Colorado River and followed the voice of the bird, taking up their great god Huitzilopochtli and carrying him on a throne of rushes into the wilderness in search of a new homeland. And the war god said to them: "I shall lead you to the place you seek. There you will find me in the form of a white eagle, perched upon a cactus on a rock in the midst of a great lake, a serpent in my beak. And there you shall build a temple which will be my house, my bed of grass. And in that place you shall make your home. And you shall conquer and rule all the land. And your mighty city shall be called Tenochtitlán, and you shall be the people of the Sun!"

Dawn in the Grand Canyon.

And so in the year A.D. 1160, the Mexicans (Mexicas) went in search of the land that was promised to them. It took many seasons, for they spent many years in a place called Tollan before they finally reached Zumpango in the Valley of Mexico in 1216. The ruler of this place, a man called Tochpanecatl, asked the Mexicans if they would choose one of their women as a wife for his son, Ithuicatl. A marriage was arranged, and thus the royal house of Mexico was established. And then the Mexicans traveled onward in search of their promised land.

Eventually the pilgrims came upon a place of dazzling whiteness. There they discovered a white cypress from which a fountain poured, and all around were white willows, white reeds and bullrushes, white frogs, white fish, white watersnakes. It was truly a wondrous place. And the priests wept, saying: "Now we have reached the promised land. Be comforted, O people, for we have now discovered and achieved what our great god promised us."

But the god Huitzilopochtli was not yet satisfied, saying: "You must seek a sacred sign — the eagle and the cactus — and there you will build my temple and my city."

After many hard days, the people finally discovered a small, uninhabited island, which was little more than a heap of rocks rising from the wide marshland. Upon these rocks was a nopal cactus and a white eagle clutching a serpent in its beak. And here they built their city, Tenochtitlán, which means "near the cactus."

THIS ANCIENT TALE of the long and arduous migration in search of a homeland comes from the folk history of the Aztec or Mexica people. The story is an account of at least some of the actual events that took place in the years between 1160 and 1325 — centuries before the arrival of the Spaniards, for in this wondrous tale, history and legend have been transformed into the metaphoric language that we call myth.

The Aztec storytellers recall that they were the original people of the earth, and that all other tribes descended from them and then went off to create their own worlds and their own histories. It is a variation on the tale of genesis that is told by many of the world's peoples.

When the Spaniard Hernán Cortés invaded Mexico in 1519, he and his priest and soldiers brought many of their own stories about the beginning of the world. But nowhere in that Judeo-Christian recounting of genesis was there an explanation for the completely unexpected tribes that Cortés found in Mexico. And thus a major theological puzzle arose: How was it possible for Indians to exist, Europeans asked, if they were not part of the story of creation that is found in the Old Testament? And, since European explorers were certain that Indians were clearly incapable of lofty achievements, who could have produced all the remarkable monuments that were found in the Americas?

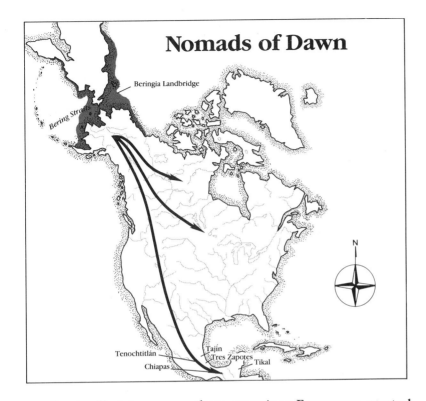

Nomads of Dawn

Beringia Landbridge

Bering Strait

N

Tenochtitlán
Tajín
Tres Zapotes
Chiapas
Tikal

In an effort to answer these questions Europeans created some of their most interesting and also their most irresponsible myths. Robert Wauchope points out that "when Columbus discovered the natives of the New World in 1492, there was no doubt in his mind that they were east Asiatics, and he promptly began referring to them as Indians. He is said to have carried this belief with him to his grave. But long before Columbus died, a number of Europeans suspected that the new lands were not Cathay at all, a suspicion strongly reinforced when Balboa reached the Pacific shore in 1513 and confirmed beyond doubt by Magellan's voyage six years later." Clearly America was not Asia, but a vast land totally unsuspected and unknown by both Occidentals and Orientals. But, in that case, where and how had American Indians originated, and why was their history unexplained in Scripture? And so a great debate began that is still being argued by scholars, theologians, laypeople, and mystics.

One of the wildest tales ever created to explain the origin of American Indians was widely accepted as truth by intellectuals of the seventeenth century. In 1641, a Portuguese Jew named Antonio de Montezinos sailed to South America and reported that he encountered near the city of Quito in Ecuador an Indian who, to his amazement, was Jewish. He also claimed that the man took him to a Jewish/Indian community in the hinterland. And according to the report, Antonio actually heard these people recite the traditional prayer "Hear, O Israel" in Hebrew.

After his return to Europe, he reported his findings to Manasseh ben Israel, the most prominent Jewish scholar of the day. And Manasseh eventually published the spectacular news in a little book called *Spes Israelis* (*The Hope of Israel*), in which he introduced to readers of Spanish, Latin, Hebrew, and English the widely accepted notion that the Lost Tribes of Israel had somehow crossed the ocean to America. This theory that Israelites had wandered into the Americas reached its zenith in the nineteenth century, when Britain's Lord Kingsborough spent his family's fortune and was put in debtors' prison three times in order to publish several splendidly illustrated books proving that the Mexican Indians were descendants of the Lost Tribes.

In yet another flourish of ideas about the Jewish origin of Indians, the Mormon sacred writings refer to two waves of Israelite migrants: an early one undertaken by the so-called Jaredites, who found their way across the Atlantic during the confusion after the Tower of Babel collapsed, and a later journey by the followers of a leader named Lehi, who left Jerusalem about 600 B.C., just before the people of that city were led off into Babylonian captivity.

A good deal of biblical scholarship went into these fanciful explanations. For instance, it was noted that about two centuries before 721 B.C., when the Lost Tribes had presumably disappeared during the conquests of King Sargon II of Assyria, Solomon had "made a navy of ships in Ezion-geber ... on the shore of the Red Sea" which he manned with Phoenicians, the most renowned mariners of the ancient world. With such impeccable nautical and biblical references, the trip was presumably a snap for the Lost Tribes.

In the eighteenth century, the Jews took a second place in the nominations for the most likely ancient émigrés of the Americas. The vote came in heavily in favor of Egyptians. One French adventurer named August Le Plongeon passionately believed that there were so many classical features among American monuments, that he attributed all the wonderful achievements of Mexican civilization to Egyptians — whose presence in Mexico, he innocently claimed, predated the arrival of Columbus and Cortés. According to this long-standing and popular myth, Egyptians used Indian slave labor to build all the monuments of the Americas, and then became bored with their endeavors and unexplainably decided to abandon them and go back home to Egypt. In other words, they simply left their monuments in care of the "ignorant natives," who couldn't cope with their upkeep and therefore let most of them fall into ruin by the time Europeans stumbled upon the Americas.

Another noted writer of the 1860s, the eminent Abbé Charles Étienne Brasseur de Bourbourg, insisted that these same Egyptian builders had not originated in Egypt. Instead, he claimed that they originally came from Mexico itself. There, apparently, they invented great cultures and built huge monuments and cities before abandoning America in favor of their familiar homeland in North Africa.

Almost at once, however, this "Egyptian connection" posed serious nautical problems. The reed boats of Egypt were useful on the Nile, but ancient sailors were smart enough to keep them out of open sea, where they wisely used planked vessels to make runs along the Levantine coast to Lebanon. But unquestionably, such wooden craft were not suitable for journeys between the mouth of the Nile and the Gulf of Mexico. So how could Egyptians (wherever they originated) sail the Atlantic, eastbound or westbound? A popular explanation for this puzzle was found in Plato's allegorical tale of an imaginary continent called Atlantis, which was conceived as the homeland of myriad ancient mariners, including the Egyptians.

Plato recalled a story that was handed down from Solon, who claimed to have met priests in Egypt who had records proving that nine thousand years earlier, when Athens had been the strongest of all states, there existed a vast island called Atlantis, located beyond the Pillars of Hercules (the Strait of Gibraltar). The king of Atlantis tried to enslave his rivals in Greece and Egypt. Athens fought bitterly against this king, until one day great earthquakes and floods destroyed Atlantis, which sank into the sea.

The Greeks regarded the lost continent as an aspect of parable, and were no more inclined to locate it than we are today concerned with geographically locating Utopia. That dubious effort had to wait fully two millennia after the death of Plato. Montaigne and Voltaire argued with conviction and concern about the existence of Atlantis. Norwegian archaeologists, like A. W. Brögger, searched for remnants of the island to no avail.

Yet the debate has never ended, and those who wish to believe in the mysterious lost continent do so undauntedly, despite the fact that no convincing evidence of its existence has ever been substantiated.

Atlantis, after all, made room for every possible fantasy about the Americas. Its massiveness had spread nearly from shore to shore across the Atlantic Ocean, narrowing to a mere channel the thousands of miles of open sea between the Eastern and Western hemispheres. The most widespread theory was that Atlantis itself was the source of all civilizations. There, in a veritable paradise, writing, music, architecture, and all the marvels of the ancient world were supposedly born. Then, during the fateful catastrophe, frantic people leaped into their boats and sailed to safety in America and North Africa, where they reestablished some aspect of their former greatness.

Dissatisfied with only one lost world, other romantics invented the legend of Lemuria, commonly known as Mu — another lost continent, but this one located in the Pacific Ocean. James Churchward, its best-known champion, published his last book on Mu in 1931. Other than its relocation to another ocean, Mu is a close cousin of Atlantis in its history and demise.

Yet another fable about the ancient North Atlantic involves Saint Brendan. According to Irish legend, in the sixth century A.D. he took fourteen monks from the monastery of Clonfert in Galway, and sailed away into unknown seas. Their boat — now called a curragh — was "a very light little vessel, ribbed and sided with wood, and covered with oak-tanned ox-hides and caulked with pitch and ox-tallow." After forty days at sea, Saint Brendan and his monks landed on an island where they found a vast castle in which there was a table conveniently laid with fish and bread. During the next eight years, Brendan continued his remarkable voyage to strange lands, meeting persons such as Judas Iscariot and Pontius Pilate. The legend provides a fascinating candidate for an early visitor to the New World, but unfortunately for those of us who require some tangible basis for our ideas, Saint Brendan didn't leave a single trace of his presence in America.

These European myths and theories have fascinated countless generations. But we must look to the Vikings of the Middle Ages if we are really in search of a serious candidate for the role of the first people to cross the Atlantic. Yet even the Vikings apparently encountered natives already established in the New

World whose habitation much predated their relatively late visits.

For a long time the Viking claim of an American landfall was as misted by legend as those of the Lost Tribes and Atlantis. Viking sagas depict a cast of rather unsavory characters: Eric the Red, his son Leif, Olaf Tryggvesson, and other heartless pirates and mariners who exploited every land and people they encountered. Suddenly, however, during the last few decades, at least some of the events depicted in these grim sagas have been confirmed by archaeological evidence.

All Vikings — Danes, Swedes, and Norwegians — were expert mariners, who had produced the sturdy and graceful galleys that we know from three famous Viking tombs, discovered between 1867 and 1903, in which the dead had been laid to rest in their elegant boats. In such ships the Vikings made their way to the Faroe Island north of Scotland as early as A.D. 800. Within a century they landed in Iceland and established colonies. By 900, a seaman named Gunbjorn, en route from Norway to Iceland, was blown off course and sighted the coast of what is now Greenland, though an actual landing did not take place for almost a century, when Eric the Red made his remarkable voyages, and founded a colony named Julianehab in 982 on the southwest coast of Greenland. Danish archaeologists excavating Julianehab have uncovered Eric's very house, a typical Viking long house.

It was Eric's son Leif who became famous for his remarkable travels. He left Greenland for Norway, where he was converted to Christianity. He was sent home as a missionary, but his father was not anxious to accept the Christian faith. By about 1000, Leif Ericson (literally the "son of Eric") gave up proselytizing and turned instead to exploration with a boatload of thirty-five seamen. According to now-substantiated legend, they came upon a rocky island and then a wooded coast, and in another two days they sighted an island with abundant grass. On the mainland opposite the island they discovered vines heavy with grapes — fruit entirely alien to all of these Vikings from an icebound homeland, except for one of their company who was from Germany, where grapevines were plentiful. In honor of this fruitfulness, Leif called the place Vinland. In the spring they sailed home. Sometime later, Leif's brother, Thorwald, returned to Vinland, where he spent two years in Leif's abandoned huts. Eventually Thorwald encountered difficulty with a large party of Indians in skin boats. He was killed by an arrow. But even after the death of Thorwald, two more Viking expeditions reached Vinland and spent time there before returning home.

Even among conservative scholars there is no doubt that the Vikings landed in the New World; they tend to place the landfall as close to Greenland as possible, in Baffin Island or the vicinity. A Danish archaeological team conducted excavations from 1961 to 1968 at l'Anse aux Meadows on the northernmost tip of Newfoundland, unearthing unquestionably Norse artifacts dating to about A.D. 1000.

Less conservative scholars are willing to extend the range of the Viking landings to the east coast of the United States, as far south as Virginia. And a few highly controversial experts, like Barry Fell and Hjalmar R. Holand, have insisted, despite immense objection from scholars, that various runic inscriptions and European Bronze Age structures have been identified not only in the Northeast of the United States, but as far west as Minnesota.

Meanwhile, Professor Ivan Van Sertima of Rutgers University has summarized a long-standing but much contested theory that black Africans arrived in the Americas before Columbus, a view based upon navigational and shipbuilding research, cultural analogies "found nowhere else except in America and Africa," similarities between Native American and African languages, and evidence of the transportation of plants, cloth, and animals from Africa to the Americas. Unfortunately, Van Sertima's argument is also based upon the apparent Negroid physical and facial characteristics of certain American groups such as the Olmecs. This "look-alike" method (i.e., "the people depicted in ancient Indian art look Negroid, therefore they must have been Negroid") is much criticized for its naïveté.

Even more fascinating and audacious than Professor Van Sertima's black African voyagers are the unexpected "Homo sapiens" found in the work of anthropologist Jeffrey Goodman, who believes that modern human beings (Cro-Magnon) made their world debut in North America instead of Europe. Goodman also insists that major skills were not brought to the Americas by waves of Asian nomads; rather, such skills and innovations that were transmitted by cultural contact were those of Indians, who traveled from the New World to the Old, and not the other way around. The premise is that Neandertal may have originated in Africa and then migrated into Europe, but Cro-Magnon arose separately in the Americas, eventually migrating into Asia and Europe and bringing with them all the "refined culture" usually associated with Cro-Magnon. Obviously, this is a highly controversial thesis.

Today it is generally accepted that American Indians originated in Asia and migrated into the Americas by way of Alaska. Though there is abundant evidence to support this theory, some nagging questions nonetheless remain about alien influences which seem to have occurred in the Western Hemisphere long before the arrival of Columbus. A multitude of scholars and amateurs have been fascinated by the possibility that certain horticultural, religious, and artistic influences were somehow transmitted across the Pacific Ocean and profoundly changed the course of American Indian civilizations. There are tales of Buddhist monks who landed on the west coast of the Americas in the fifth century A.D.; of Koreans who inadvertently sailed to America while escaping Chinese tyranny; and survivors of the storm-tossed fleet of Kublai Khan, and another fleet, of Alexander the Great — both of which are rumored to have drifted into the New World.

These stories grew in their implications during the nineteenth and early twentieth centuries, as data seemed to reveal some curious coincidences: Maya visual motifs that "seemed" to resemble Chinese motifs; Ecuadorian pottery that "looked" very much like pots produced in Japan; certain architectonic inventions found in Yucatán that "appeared" to be very similar to elements in Cambodian architecture. All of these coincidences *seemed* to support the Diffusionist stance that invention is so exceptional that it only occurs once and then necessarily spreads (diffuses) widely to other regions, no matter how distant. To prove the Diffusionist point, a great deal of evidence was assembled: Chinese bronzes of the Shang and Chou periods that were similar to the so-called Tajín style of ancient Mexico; the lotus motif in Buddhist art and its treatment in the sculpture of Yucatán. But, as Lionel Casson points out, the trouble with this evidence is that the dating of the various cross-cultural similarities simply do *not* make sense. For instance, a Chinese bronze of the Shang period (1000 B.C.) and a remarkably similar pot (dated A.D. 1200) found near the mouth of the Amazon are separated by more than two thousand years. Certain iconography of the Chou period of China does have strong resemblances to monumental reliefs in the Tajín style found near Veracruz, but the Chou period closed about 200 B.C., while the Tajín examples date from A.D. 350. A famous Maya temple at Tikal in

Guatemala does indeed resemble one in Cambodia, but the Maya structure was built fully five centuries earlier than its Cambodian counterpart. And even the most substantial evidence of transpacific contact — the unmistakable correlation between Valdivian pottery of Ecuador (3000 B.C.) and Jomon pottery produced in Japan at exactly the same time — has fallen out of favor due in part to the fact that the Ecuadorian pots are probably much later than originally assumed (about 1000 B.C.), and researchers, such as Donald Lathrap, have uncovered Ecuadorian pottery which predates the Japanese style and clearly demonstrates the gradual Native American invention of the style, which only seemed to have been borrowed from Japan.

"Moreover, no Chinese or [East] Indian object — or any object at all from the Old World — has been found in the New World in archaeological levels that date to pre-Columbian times." (Casson) If there was regular contact between American Indians and traders from China or India, they left no trace whatsoever of their visits. Nor, importantly, did they contribute to the Americas any of their highly useful discoveries, such as the working of iron, the domestication of animals like cows, pigs, and horses, the planting of wheat, or the complex technology associated with the invention of the wheel (which was used only for toys in the Americas).

As Casson notes: "The winds and currents of the North Pacific trend eastward. Any craft caught helpless in their embrace can easily be carried across the ocean; in fact, there are records to show that, for example, between 1775 and 1875 about twenty Japanese junks were blown, against their will, to the west coast of America and deposited at various points between Alaska and Mexico. If Japanese vessels in the last century, why not Chinese or Indian or Malaysian during all the long centuries that preceded the arrival of Columbus? There must have been a certain number that ended a storm-tossed journey on this side of the Pacific. Perhaps a few of the hardier spirits among their crews risked the long sail back home, but most must have chosen to live on where they landed. Eventually they either died out or became wholly absorbed, leaving behind only tantalizing, indirect reminiscences of their presence such as art motifs, pottery shapes, and the like."

At the conclusion of a 1968 conference in Santa Fe, New Mexico, on the topic "Man Across the Sea," a scholar declared: "Those who used to believe that there is botanical evidence of significant pre-Columbian contacts between the Americas and the rest of the world can carry on in their belief; those who doubted it may remain disbelieving. Agnosticism has not yet been put to flight by revelation." As a matter of fact, when all sides had been heard at that conference, the balance had clearly tipped in favor of the disbelievers. Any crossing before Columbus, whether of Japanese fishermen, Peruvians on their balsa rafts, or Polynesian mariners, at the very best had only the slightest effect on the agriculture, botany, art, religion, and society of either the New World or the Old World. "In other words," Casson points out, "if there had been such crossings, from the point of view of history, they were hardly worth the fuss made about them."

American Indians retain the honor of being the true discoverers of the New World. And they also invented the myriad technologies, social structures, arts, and architecture of the Americas.

Despite these distinctions, there is still a good deal of debate about the exact origin of American Indians because of a number of factors, the most important of which is the fact that archaeological data have been profoundly reshaped by the discovery of new and more precise methods of attributing dates to finds, opening the era of the "new archaeology." Methods, such as carbon 14 dating, have shattered a number of strongly ethnocentric preconceptions that were long popular among Europeans. Thus the Leakeys moved the cradle of human beings from Asia and the Near East to Africa; while, at the same time, Colin Renfrew and his colleagues demonstrated that the first great masonry works were not produced in Egypt and Mycenae, but among the illiterate "barbarians" of Western Europe, who built monumental stone structures like Stonehenge. Such drastic rethinking of cultural ideas that we once took for granted has thrown the entire subject of chronology as well as the demographics of cultural achievement into turmoil, altering our views of the ancient societies of both the Old World and New World. This ideological and historical open season finds a great many startling new theories and a good many preposterous old notions vying for our attention and belief. But despite some drastic revision and the attendant confusion of new perspectives, there remains a substantial premise for the origin of American Indians, which is accepted by most Western scholars, and there is little doubt that the great achievements of Indians were the result of their own insights, efforts, and inventions.

It is ironic that the accepted theory concerning the peopling of the Americas is remarkably similar to many Indian folk histories, which depict a long and difficult journey from a distant place of origin to a new American holy land. That story takes us back in time and space, to an immense and fertile land that is filled with huge animals, but in which no human being has ever set foot. No human face has ever been seen in this vast Eden, and no human hand has left its traces upon the land. Then, some fifteen to forty-five thousand years ago, an unfamiliar sound is heard, as small bands of primitive people begin to wander into a strange new world. It was they who truly discovered America, for they were the first people in history to see this incredible American hemisphere.

But what drove them to make such a long and difficult journey?

Of course, they did not know that they had left their homeland or that they had quite literally *walked* into the Americas. They were simply searching for food, following the huge beasts of the Ice Age into a perilous new landscape. What they found was an enormous sea of ice engulfing much of Siberia, Alaska, and Canada. The ice had frozen so much of the earth's water that the sea level had fallen as much as three hundred feet, making a windy and cold thousand-mile-wide landbridge across the Bering Strait between Asia and North America.

These ancient Paleo-Indians, as they are called, followed their shaggy prey into the early dawn of the American world, discovering an unspeakably expansive terrain, rolling from the frozen ice cap in the north to the lush tropics of the south. As the animals slowly moved from feeding ground to feeding ground, the hunters followed at a rate of movement that may have averaged no more than a few miles per generation. It is estimated that it took countless generations for Indians to find their way to Tierra del Fuego, the southernmost tip of South America — a journey of more than ten thousand miles. They conquered the longest frontier ever traversed. The French prehistorian François Bordes has pointed out that not until we occupy another planet will we explore a domain so vast. Yet, once beyond the barrier of ice in the Arctic, there were few barriers in those primeval days to hold back the adventurous Paleo-Indians who came to this land of saber-toothed tigers, mammoths, giant sloths, elephants, panthers, and huge wolves ... creatures that eventually vanished from the Americas. It was upon the flesh of these animals that Paleo-Indians kept themselves alive, and from whose hides and bones they made clothing and implements. They even used their dry dung to make campfires that kept them warm and safe in their freezing and savage new world.

It is the dawn of America — perhaps forty-five thousand years ago — and the land is bountiful. The climate in the north is cold and wet, with wild winds blowing off the solid mile-thick mantle of ice that covers most of what is now Canada. Of these first American pioneers there are only faint traces to be found, and a persistent debate surrounds the chronology of their lives.

According to Dr. Dennis Stanford, director of Paleo-Indian Research for the Smithsonian Institution, "Our understanding is in a state of transition. The last big breakthrough occurred in the 1920s and 1930s with the discovery that Paleo-Indians were here toward the close of the Ice Age, nearly 12,000 years ago, hunting giant bison and mammoths. Now the cumulative evidence from a host of sites convinces most of us that man was here many thousands of years earlier. But so far we haven't found that unarguable site that establishes to everyone's satisfaction just who these people were or when they came."

Scholars who support the "early arrival" theory, like Dr. Alan L. Bryan of the University of Alberta, date human presence in heartland America from at least forty thousand years ago. Dr. Bryan believes that these very first Americans may have been members of *Homo erectus*, a human type predating modern man, who underwent substantial evolutionary development in the Western Hemisphere. In a report in *National Geographic*, Thomas Y. Canby lists several tantalizing but much-disputed clues which might substantiate Dr. Bryan's position. For instance, the anthropologist Louis S. B. Leakey believed that crudely fractured stones found in the Calico Hills of California indicated an ancient human presence. Further examination, however, suggested that the stones were "geofacts" — objects shaped by natural forces rather than human hands — but the investigation continues. Fire pits on Santa Rosa Island off California were the source of stone tools and the bones of dwarf mammoths, indicating the possibility that Paleo-Indians killed and cooked the horse-size elephants on the site more than forty thousand years ago. Along the California coastline, archaeologists have found human bones that have been dated to be forty-eight thousand years old. But there is considerable professional skepticism about the dating technique used to determine the

Art from 28,000 B.C. scratched on a mastodon bone: images of camels, tapirs, and other creatures now extinct in the Americas.

age of the finds. Near Taber, Alberta, the skeletal remains of an infant were unearthed, with a possible age of fifty thousand years, but once again the date of the so-called Taber Child is much disputed. There is one object that may prove to be the most remarkable of all finds of ancient America. It is a fragment of mastodon pelvic bone unearthed in Mexico.

More than thirty-five years ago a Mexican paleontologist named Juan Armenta Camacho was attracted by a rich deposit of bones of extinct animals in a riverine area called Valsequillo. Among this trove Dr. Armenta uncovered primitive stone artifacts, along with mastodon bones on which some ancient artist had scratched crude sketches of Ice Age beasts. At about the same time, at a nearby site in Tlapacoya, a team of archaeologists led by Dr. José Luis Lorenzo discovered signs of human activity rivaling in age those of Valsequillo. The bones of black bear and two types of deer were uncovered in association with twenty-two-thousand-year-old hearths.

Most experts agree that the finds at Valsequillo and Tlapacoya are authentic, but — nonetheless — they are two lonely outposts in an otherwise desolate human history. It is more than two thousand years later that we find convincing evidence of human presence in Mexico.

Many questions remain. Who were these prehistoric Indians of the Americas and where exactly did they originate? Despite many uncertainties and debates, some facts are widely accepted about the ancestors of Indians. For example: Human beings are not native to the Americas. No early forms of mankind existed in the Americas. No human ancestors — such as Java Man, Peking Man, Neandertal Man or any of the other apelike predecessors from which modern people apparently evolved — have ever been found in the Western Hemisphere. In fact, there are absolutely no apes of any kind — living or fossilized — in the Americas. And so it seems to scholars that Indians had to have come to America from somewhere else. The dominant theory, associated with the landbridge across the Bering Straits (called Beringia), assumes that Paleo-Indians came from Asia. They already possessed many Asian traits, such as coppery pigmentation, dark eyes, straight black hair, wide cheekbones, and distinctively curved incisors, which anthropologists call "shovel-shaped." And yet these pioneers who walked or, perhaps, sailed to America were not true Mongoloids, like the people of China and Japan, for apparently Mongoloids in the modern sense of that word had not yet evolved in Asia at the time of the first great Indian migration. Only much later, with the arrival of Aleuts and Innuets (Eskimos), did true Mongoloid people settle in North America.

Paleo-Indians were probably very much like us, of the subspecies *Homo sapiens sapiens*, with full-size brains and the ability to communicate with spoken language. Whether they came within a limited time span in one massive migration, or in several migrations over a vast amount of time, we do not know for certain, but they have been in the Americas long enough to account for a remarkable amount of diversification in custom, physical stature, and unique languages, which are often as dissimilar from one another as German is from Chinese.

There is no question that they were people of the Stone Age, yet their tools were not crude and their hunting skills were exceptionally advanced. Thousands of years before the American invention of the bow and arrow, Paleo-Indians apparently carried spear-throwers capable of plunging a stone-tipped projectile deep into a mammoth's body. Whatever culture and technology they eventually possessed had to be discovered by themselves, for they came to the Americas with very little in the way of cultural baggage, before the invention of the wheel, before the evolution of any of our modern Asian or European languages, even before the development of agriculture. They had no metal tools and relied entirely on implements chipped from stone or bone. They knew nothing of weaving or basketmaking, and they had not yet invented pottery. Even the oldest animal friend of human beings — the dog — was apparently not yet domesticated when Paleo-Indians came to the Americas. In fact, they came away from their old world when it was indeed *very* old. And, thus, they had to invent just about everything for themselves.

Eventually the sixty-thousand-year Ice Age ended, and the climate changed drastically. The ice cap began to melt. The oceans rose, submerging the Bering landbridge, and forever cutting off these Asian hunters from their old world in Siberia.

Now they found themselves completely isolated . . . literally orphaned from the human race. But despite the technological poverty and isolation of these ancient Americans, they gradually began to produce some of the most remarkable civilizations in world history. One of the earliest of these cultures was founded by a mysterious and now vanished people called the Olmecs.

Coda: On the Road to Civilization

Olmec ceremonial ax from La Venta, Mexico.

IN THE DEEP JUNGLE of southeastern Mexico, in the states of Tabasco and Veracruz on the tropical Gulf Coast, is one of the cradles of civilization in the Americas. Among the humid and rain-drenched undergrowth are huge stone carvings, looking very much like decapitated heads. These curious sculptures have long outlasted the remarkable people who carved them some two to three thousand years ago.

We know very little about these immense stone heads with their perplexing and unexplainable Negroid features — though they were carved fully seven hundred years before blacks officially arrived in the Americas. These colossal sculptures are some of the only traces left by a society of extraordinary Indians known as Olmecs. Their world has been recovered from the jungle in ancient centers that we now call Tres Zapotes, La Venta, and San Lorenzo, although we have no idea what the Olmecs called them. In fact, we don't know what the Olmecs called themselves, what language they spoke, or precisely what kind of lives they lived. Few people inhabit this hellish region today, but in the past few decades archaeologists have discovered a great deal of evidence that here, in this most unlikely setting, a grand culture somehow arose and eventually dominated most of Middle America for more than a thousand years.

The creators of this grand Gulf Coast culture are of unknown origin, and their mysterious ascent to grandeur is often compared to the history of the Sumerians. Thousands of years of gradual technological and cultural development preceded their rise to a civilization. By the first century B.C., the people of Mesoamerica lived in small agricultural villages where they had flourished from Mexico to Costa Rica for centuries. In this modestly productive milieu, the Olmec world rose to greatness. Besides their remarkable invention of highly advanced agriculture and horticulture, they possessed good pottery and cotton cloth.

Ancient poems in Nahuatl, the language of the much later Aztecs, recall a land on the eastern sea that was settled so long ago that "no one can remember" its history. Its name, Tamoanchan, is not Nahuatl but Maya and means "Land of Rain." The word *Olmec*, however, does derive from the language of the Aztec people, meaning "the rubber people," so named, we suspect, because of the characteristic rubber ball they used in their ritual ball game, a ceremony of which we know very little except that it was a very serious game of life and death, played in a

two-sided court with goal hoops on the elaborate stone walls.
The game was apparently invented by the Olmecs and spread,
like many other Olmec influences, throughout Mexico. Clearly,
the Olmecs were very important to the development of civilization in the Americas. And despite strong evidence that Maya and
even Amazonian sites are as old as Olmec settlements, it is certain that the Olmec people were essential to the growth of
American cultures. Whatever the origin of the Olmecs, there is
no doubt about the impact of their unique art style and religious
ideals. Typical Olmec rock carvings, figurines, and sculptures
have been discovered not only in their native Gulf Coast homeland but as far north as Mexico City and as far south as Honduras. No one knows if these influences were carried by Olmec
colonists, war parties, merchants, or missionaries.

Their known history is hardly more than a sketch. As
George C. Vaillant wrote, the Olmecs "move like shadows
across the pages of Mexican history; a few notices that there
were such people, a few delineations of a physical type foreign
to the racial features of known people like the Maya, and a handful of sculptures out of the known artistic traditions comprise
the testimony of their existence." It was only by accident that
their grandest achievements have come to light.

In 1862, the Mexican scholar José Maria Melgar y Serrano
was visiting southern Veracruz. Sugarcane workers told him
they had come across a very strange "kettle" — a huge object
buried upside down in the jungle. When the object was dug
from its ancient grave, it proved to be a ten-ton head carved in
volcanic basalt. The head had what Melgar thought to be "Ethio-
pic features." This observation led him to assume that Africans
had once been in Mexico. These events and opinions were the
basis of a modest report that he wrote for a bulletin published
in 1868 by the Mexican Society of Geography. José Melgar y
Serrano had discovered an Olmec head, now known as the
Colossal Head of Hueyapan. But little notice was taken of his
report.

It was not until 1925 that the major Olmec complex at La
Venta was discovered. Danish-born archaeologist Frans Blom
and New York writer Oliver La Farge found a colossal head at La
Venta, which they unfortunately ascribed to the Maya. Matthew
W. Stirling, of the Smithsonian Institution, was certain that the
La Venta head was Olmec, for he had made a connection be-
tween several archaeological finds of the past, commencing
with the Colossal Head of Hueyapan, along with a curious stone

Olmec portrait in jade.

Olmec clay figurine of a male.

ax with a jaguar mask carved upon it that had been described by the Mexican scholar Alfredo Chavero in 1883, and a small image of a jaguar carved in jade that a North American engineer had found at a dam site in northeastern Puebla, Mexico, in 1909. Stirling's evidence was sufficiently impressive to win the confidence of the National Geographic Society, which agreed to finance an expedition. Field work began in 1938 — fully seventy-six years from the date that Melgar had discovered the first colossal head of the Olmecs.

In 1940 Stirling began digging in La Venta, a swamp-locked "island" near the Gulf Coast of Mexico. The excavation soon made it clear that La Venta was not a city in the ordinary sense of the term. In fact, there is no trace of an ancient residential zone. Apparently this jungle complex was purely a ceremonial center, a shrine to which the people of a vast agricultural district provided food and labor, coming to the center only to take part in religious rites. It was in this rarefied atmosphere of a religious center that Stirling discovered what is still considered to be the greatest of all Olmec sites, an elaborate ceremonial center with an imposing pyramid, temple platforms, plazas, huge carvings, and tombs filled with exquisite jade. The pyramid, constructed of clay, was 110 feet high and, according to expert calculations, took some 800,000 man-days to build. Stirling found four more colossal heads, a fourteen-foot-high monolith, called a stela, weighing over fifty tons, and several huge altars.

As a result of Stirling's efforts, which did not end until 1946, the Olmecs were finally credited with being the masters of a unique civilization that anticipated and greatly influenced all its successors down to the Aztecs, who dominated Mexico at the time of the Spanish invasion of Hernán Cortés in 1519. In fact, it was long believed that the fabulous Maya civilization was a successor to Olmec culture. That chronological relationship has become very complex in recent years. Because of work by archaeologist Norman Hammond in Belize, it now appears that the Olmec may have had some kind of complex direct relationship with the Maya during the last period of the long decline of the Olmec centers. It also seems more than likely that the Olmec had influence not only on the Maya but on all the cultures of Mesoamerica. Hammond has posited an *Olmec-Maya complex* — a hybrid culture that developed at the end of the Olmec and the earliest establishment of the Maya cultures. According to Hammond, the Olmec-Maya complex was the original source of the complex written language later developed and refined by the Classical Maya (A.D. 400–800) in their Central American homeland. From this same Olmec-Maya complex seem to spring the major deities, cosmology, numerology, and astronomy of the later Mesoamerican world. In fact, we find striking examples of Olmec-Maya iconography throughout the Mesoamerican world.

In what kind of a society did these ancient and mysterious Olmec live? And how did they spend their days?

It is difficult to guess what the Olmec people looked like, because their sculpture, as Karl E. Meyer points out, was un-

Classic Olmec heads from La Venta, Mexico.

questionably idealized. Despite a lack of substantial information that might provide a picture of the Olmec face and stature, we do have many recently emerging profiles of the kinds of lives the Olmec lived.

A wealth of information about the Olmec life-style has emerged from San Lorenzo, located in the tropical lowlands of southern Mexico, not far from La Venta. This rain-drenched location was excavated in 1966–68, by the renowned Mayanist Michael D. Coe. The greatest triumph of the exploration at San Lorenzo took place in March 1967, when Coe found a great trove of stone figures buried on the western side of the complex. To his amazement, all of these stone figures had been willfully mutilated and then carefully buried. "The amount of pent-up hatred and fury represented by this enormous act of destruction must have been awesome, indeed," Coe wrote. "These monuments are very large, and basalt is a very hard stone. Wherever possible, heads were smashed from bodies, 'altars' were smashed to pieces, and strange, dimpled depressions and slots were cut into Colossal Heads. . . . Why was this done? Because the Olmec monuments must have stood for the class of leaders that held the tributary populace in such a firm grip, forcing from them incredible expenditures of labor. These stones must have been the symbol of all that had held them in thrall, and they destroyed these symbols with as much fervor as the Hungarian revolutionaries toppled the giant statue of Stalin in Budapest in 1956." Remarkably, Coe adds, the Indians must have feared the power of the carvings, because after mutilating them, the statues were dutifully buried.

Only slowly and just in the last couple of decades have we been able to piece together some notion of the Olmec world. Commencing about 1200 B.C., when the Golden Age of Greece was still seven hundred years in the future, in an utterly inhospitable region where no one would normally imagine the rise of a great civilization, a region with rainfall reaching 120 inches annually, the mysterious Olmecs produced a society that prevailed unchanged for more than a thousand years. Here, in this place of sluggish rivers and unbroken jungle and swamp, where the air is filled with mosquitoes and where monkeys howl in treetops, a glorious culture evolved so long ago that it survives only in lovely jade carvings, clay figurines, and the Colossal Heads, carved in stone that isn't native to the region and therefore had to be quarried some eighty miles away, and then dragged to the nearest river, loaded upon rafts, and floated to the tropical ceremonial centers on the Gulf Coast.

The Olmecs invented American civilization. They created the prototype of American architecture: elaborate ceremonial centers as distinct from residential complexes, including structures such as earth mounds and pyramids, as well as an accent upon monumentality and grand theocratic design. They also created Middle America's first formal religion: the cult of the jaguar. Everywhere in Mexico and Central and South America there are echoes of the image of a jaguar that was persistently depicted by the Olmecs. Mythologists believe that a legend central to the Olmec cosmology concerned a woman who mated with a jaguar, giving birth to a race of were-jaguars, in which human and animal features were combined. Countless depictions of such were-jaguars have been found — invariably asexual in gender and with the curious mixture of the chubby features of a baby and the snarling mouth of a feline.

The Olmecs were a people that lived its mythology. All scholars agree that the jaguar was the primary mythic figure of the Olmecs. Jacques Soustelle notes that "what appears almost certain is that this 'were-jaguar' . . . was a great divinity, perhaps the principal one, of the Olmec pantheon." But what did it represent? A number of experts regard the jaguar god as a "rain god." Michael Coe is of the opinion that the feline monsters bearing maize symbols correspond to a god of agriculture.

The possible influence of this jaguar cult has been noted as far south as Peru, where the Chavin culture, appearing at about the same date as the Olmecs, was also preoccupied with feline deities. It is not unlikely that the Olmec civilization was not only an influence upon Andean societies, but the point of departure for a fundamental attitude found in all the cultures of Mesoamerica: an intense religiosity that was the driving force behind every activity and ideal. This dogma resulted in the Olmec creation of a system of religious leadership that became the political basis of most Middle American civilizations. An element of that religion was the practice of blood sacrifice, which was a widespread Mesoamerican ritual.

The Olmecs are doubtlessly responsible for the most widely used system of writing calendrical information, and — by extension — for the origination of the only true form of written language in the Americas. At Tres Zapotes, Stirling unearthed the broken piece of a large Olmec monument, its face carved

Seated baby-jaguar made by the Olmec.

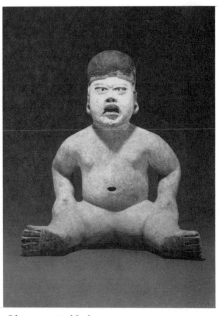

Olmec seated baby.

with the likeness of a jaguar. On its reverse side he found a date in the style of the Classical Maya, who used bars and dots to record dates. The date on the monument was 31 B.C. — not only three hundred years prior to the earliest known Maya date, but also the oldest calendrical inscription ever found in the Americas ... suggesting that the Preclassical Olmecs might have been Mayas who later moved eastward to Yucatán. The relationship between the Olmec and the Maya has yet to be established. Michael Coe suggests "a paradoxical solution ... namely, that the Olmec were the Maya." More specifically, they were pre-Maya. At the date of the Olmec decline, Coe suggests that certain groups began to emigrate eastward, "into the forested lands of the Peten-Yucatán Peninsula, and some up the river valleys into the oak- and pine-covered mountains of Chiapas and Guatemala. What had once been Olmec civilization eventually transformed itself into the Maya civilization."

The flowering of San Lorenzo took place between 1200 and 900 B.C. This makes it the oldest known Olmec site. But it was at La Venta, not at San Lorenzo, that some of the most brilliant achievements of the Olmec civilization took place. Then, quite suddenly, about 400 B.C., unknown invaders attacked the Olmec centers, and their world began to collapse. As Coe pointed out, this work of destruction must have involved tremendous fury — the laborious mutilation of sculpted monuments that were first assaulted as if they were living gods and then buried deep in the ground.

By the time the Aztec people made their fabulous migration into the Valley of Mexico and founded their great city of Tenochtitlán, nothing remained of the Olmecs but echoes of their legends and their broken and buried monuments. The people themselves had either vanished or had been militaristically overpowered and assimilated by their invaders.

Centuries later, the Aztec poets sang their praise. They were the rubber people — they who took rubber from the trees. They who lived in a distant land near the sea, where the Sun awakens each morning. There, among the flowers, a great people ruled all mankind; until they vanished suddenly, leaving no trace of their names or of their faces except those which speak to us from the stones.

Lords of Yucatán

WHERE THERE WAS NEITHER HEAVEN NOR EARTH there sounded the first word of the great deity, who is called Itzamma, "Lizard House." And he unloosed himself from the stone and declared his divinity so that all the vastness of eternity shuddered. And his word was a measure of grace, and he broke and pierced the backbone of the mountains. And he took a wife who is called Ix Chel, "Lady Rainbow," the Moon, who gave into the world all the gods and all the days.

So Time was born and walked alone, for there were no people. Then when he reached the East, he said, "Someone has passed this way, for here are his footprints!"

Then he measured the footprints that had been left by the great god Itzamma, and each imprint became a fragment of Time, which was the way the days came into the world. Then Time created the heaven and earth in the form of a ladder. And he created water, earth, rocks, and trees. He made all things of the earth and of the sea. Then the first candle was made and cast into the sky, and thus it was that light was created where there had been no sun. On the final day, he took into his hands water and clay and shaped the bodies of people. But with men and women another thing fell from the fingers of the great deity, and it was called pain. And in remorse at the birth of pain, the god Itzamma invented death.

All moons, all years, all days, all winds, reach their completion and pass away. So does all blood reach its place of quiet, as

Classic Maya head from the Temple of the Inscriptions, Palenque, circa A.D. 700.

it attains its power and its throne. Measured is the time in which we may know the sun's warmth. Measured too is the time in which the stars may look down upon us. The gods are forever distant, trapped within the stars where they look down upon us and our days.

And Itzamma took shape in the void where there was neither heaven nor earth, and he turned himself into a glittering cloud which became the cosmos. And his immense power and majesty shook the heavens to the farthest speck that glows in the night sky where the gods live.

THIS TALE ENVISIONS the world of the Maya, recounting the mythic origins of one of the most fascinating civilizations in history.

With slight variation from place to place, and time to time, the Maya saw the world as a flat square of layered earth upon which people lived. At its four corners — the cardinal directions which are so prominent in Native American cosmology — stood the Bacabs, the bearded gods who held up the skies. Below them, standing in the Underworld, were four Pahuatuns who supported the layered earth. Each cardinal direction and its associated god was symbolized by a color: red for the east (the most significant direction); black for the west; white for the north; and yellow for the south. At the very center of the earth stood the Tree of Life, a sacred tree called the ceiba — which grows in great abundance in Central America today. Its roots descend into the depths of the Underworld, while its vast branches reach into the heavens. The symbolic color associated with the ceiba in the center of the cosmos was *yax* — green, the color of all precious things: new corn, jade, and water.

One of the sacred books of the Maya, the *Chilam Balam of Chumayel*, provides a richly poetic description of the cardinal directions of the world in which the ancients lived — the sacred stones, the birds, the seeds, the cosmic ceiba trees, and the powerful beings that correspond to each quadrant of the earth:

> *The red flint stone*
> *is the stone of the red Mucencab.*
> *The red ceiba tree of abundance*
> *is his arbor*
> *which is set in the east.*
> *The red bullet-tree is their tree.*

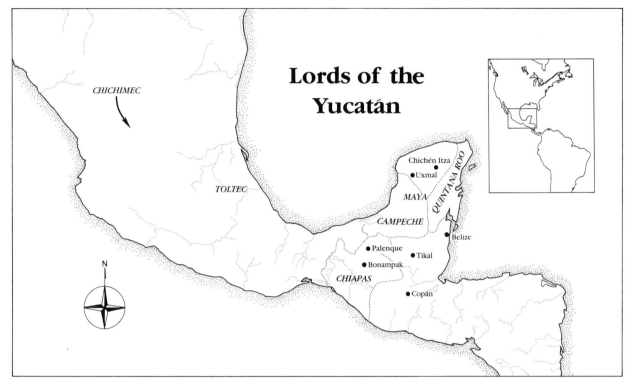

Lords of the Yucatán

The red zapote . . .
The red vine . . .
Reddish are their yellow turkeys.
Red toasted corn is their corn.

The white flint stone
is their stone in the north.
The white ceiba tree of abundance
is the arbor of the white Mucencab.
White-breasted are their turkeys.
White Lima beans are their Lima beans.
White corn is their corn.

The black flint stone
is their stone in the west.
The black ceiba tree of abundance
is their arbor.
Black speckled corn is their corn.
Black tipped camotes are their camotes.
Black wild pigeons are their turkeys.
Black akab-chan is their green corn.

Black beans are their beans.
Black Lima beans are their Lima beans.

The yellow flint stone
is the stone of the south.
The ceiba tree of abundance,
the yellow ceiba tree of abundance,
is their arbor.
The yellow bullet-tree is their tree.
Colored like the yellow bullet-tree are their camotes.
Colored like the yellow bullet-tree
are the wild pigeons which are their turkeys.
Yellow green corn is their green corn.
Yellow-backed are their beans. . . .

"Madrid Stela," a Classic Maya relief, Palenque.

THE SACRED TREE joined two different realms of power: sky and earth. The sky consisted of thirteen layers, each related to gods of various rank and aspects. Reigning above all of these deities was Itzamma, the supreme being of sky and earth. His symbol, the two-headed iguana, defined the four corners of the heavens. Far below were the nine layers of the Underworld, where numerous horrifying deities presided. One of these great lords was the fearsome Jaguar God of Night, whose spotted coat represented the starry sky.

The idea of cyclical creations and destructions — rather than an eternal motion toward perfection — was typical of Mesoamerica, as it is in the Orient. There was in the Maya mentality a persistent anticipation of the end of time — the failure of life to renew itself. The world was surrounded by countless dangers and an equal number of deities to protect supplicants against disaster.

Exceedingly little is known about the Maya pantheon despite the survival of various instructive holy books from the Spanish Colonial period. More, by far, is understood about ritual practices. The Maya clergy, for instance, was not celibate. Sons succeeded their fathers to religious office. The priest was assisted in human sacrifices by four old men, called *Chacs* in honor of the rain god, who held down the victim, while the breast was opened up by another individual who had the title *Nacom*. Another high religious figure was the *Chilam*, a visionary shaman who received messages from the gods while in a drug-induced state of trance.

Behind every religious act of the Maya were the dictates of the calendar. The Maya were obsessed with time. No other people in history were so concerned with the passing of time. The priests imagined it as an endless procession of numerical gods, pacing eternally, bent under the weight of the burdens they carried upon their backs: the animals and birds which were the patrons of individual days or multiples of days. This complex and mathematically bound procession moved relentlessly through the Maya eternity. Each day was marked by the passage of Kinich Ahau, "Sun-faced Lord," on his journey through all the layers of the sky and Underworld. The daily passage of Kinich Ahau was the basis of two calendric schemes (one sacred and one secular) that were probably inherited by the Maya from their Olmec forebears. The first of these calendars, called the Sacred Round (the Short Count), was 260 days long, mathematically composed of the combination of thirteen numbers (1 through 13), along with a sequence of twenty different day-names. These sacred days were endlessly repeated through all time.

The second temporal cycle (the Long Count) was very similar to the calendar as we know it in the West, consisting of 365 days; made up of eighteen months of twenty days each, with a brief final period of five "free" days called *Uayeb*.

Elegant Jaina clay figurine from the Classic Maya.

These two calendars interlocked like gears, so that each day of the short calendar connected with a day in the long cycle, although the same day-names interlock only every 18,980 days.

As George E. Stuart notes, "For the ancient Maya, the naming of days, and the reckoning of the number of them that had passed — by means of the Long Count — were not mere mechanisms. Each day number, each name, and each month had its own immutable associations with good, bad, or indifferent fortune. Thus time itself, for the Maya, became an arena for the battles of fate."

Intrinsic to Maya calendrical theory was Maya mathematics. A notable achievement in their numerical thinking was the invention of the principle of zero. This abstract concept, which is essential to all complex calculations, was discovered by only two other peoples in world history: the Babylonians and the Hindus. Even the Greeks and Romans had no knowledge of the zero, and it was not introduced into Europe until the Middle Ages.

One of the major accomplishments of scholars has been the correlation of Maya calendrics with our own measure of time, the Gregorian calendar, which places Mayan history in the context of Western chronology. Yet many problems still remain in regard to the Maya past, largely because no one has succeeded in the full decipherment of Maya hieroglyphs, the only true writing known in the Indian Americas. This situation is exceptionally frustrating since the Maya covered every monument and building, as well as four surviving fanfold books (called codices), with written messages that we cannot read.

Charles Gallenkamp has summarized this enticing linguistic puzzle: "Granted that most of the inscriptions involving calendrics, astronomy, and mathematics can now be easily read, only a small portion of those glyphs presumably dealing with such matters as history, religion, or mythology are presently understood."

Obviously no comprehensive insight into Maya civilization can be achieved until we know the content of the innumerable inscriptions from which the Maya seem to call out to us. That goal remains elusive. Epigraphers quickly recognized the system of writing used by the Maya as both unique in pre-Columbian America and totally unrelated to Indo-European scripts, leaving them with no precedents to follow in deciphering it. "Only through painstaking efforts on the part of many students using a variety of approaches [including computers] has any progress at all been made toward this end — and that has been disappointingly limited." (Gallenkamp)

Despite frequent reports of major archaeological finds and interpretative breakthroughs, there is currently no satisfactory explanation of how Maya civilization originated or how it managed to evolve to great refinement in an environment totally hostile to human habitation. There is almost no fully accepted

Maya pyramid on the Main Plaza, Tikal.

Classic corbeled arch, Palace of the Governors, Uxmal.

and substantiated information on the origin of the Maya calendar, hieroglyphic writing, and mathematics. Most perplexing of all, even the horrendous catastrophe leading to the abrupt abandonment of the greatest Maya centers during the ninth century A.D. — surely one of the most baffling of archaeological puzzles — remains largely unexplained. Undoubtedly, this very elusiveness adds a unique fascination to the exploration of the mysterious lords of Yucatán.

THE EARLIEST KNOWN Maya inscription is found on a monolith (stela 29) at a major ceremonial center known as Tikal, located in the jungle lowlands of present-day Guatemala. The date inscribed on this stela corresponds to our date A.D. 292. The tropical setting of monumental Tikal is in many ways similar to the world of the Olmec, to whom many scholars attribute the controversial origin of the Maya. Whatever their origin, it was here in the inhospitable lowlands that Maya civilization attained its greatest refinement and complexity.

It is impossible to imagine a less favorable environment for such remarkable achievement. Poor soil, excessive heat and humidity, high rainfall (90 to 120 inches annually), armies of biting insects, rampant disease, and exceedingly limited natural resources plagued the lowlands. Here, in Tikal, architects invented an aesthetically superb masonry technique — using the

House of the Magician, Uxmal: Toltec-Maya culture in Yucatán.

rather primitive corbeled arch (without the keystone of the "true arch") to build structures on a heroic scale. All the intellectual and religious pursuits of the Maya flowered at Tikal: mathematics, hieroglyphic writing, astronomy, and calendrics. The arts triumphed: stone and wooden sculpture, brilliantly elaborate reliefs, exquisite architectural detail, and painted ceramics and murals. Fundamental to this artistic inspiration was a pervasive religiosity. Even the great architectural centers were not true cities, but gigantic shrines. "Despite regional variations in certain aspects of Maya culture — particularly art and architecture — the fundamental precepts of cosmology, ritualism, iconography, hieroglyphics, and calendrics remained essentially alike throughout the lowlands, a fact suggesting a high degree of orthodoxy and single-minded devotion to spiritual ideals." (Gallenkamp)

Maya society displayed a rigid structure based on class distinction. The most dominant persons were *almehen* — nobles — a hereditary elite, with close association to the priesthood. But the Maya appear to have lived in a secular society despite the austerity and authority of their religion. The nobility possessed private lands and held the most important offices — ranking warriors, merchants, and clergy. Peasants were free workers. Slaves were mainly commoners taken in war (ranking prisoners of war were sacrificed). Slavery was hereditary, but menials could buy their freedom. Under the authority of the Maya nobility, the life of the peasant and slave was entirely devoted to cultivating the soil, to constructing and repairing public spaces, and to the strict observation of religious life: prayer, offerings, homage, and sacrifices.

Agriculture was the foundation of Maya civilization. Maize, beans, chili peppers, cotton, squashes, and various root crops and fruit trees were widely cultivated. In the lowlands the farmer prepared his plot by the slash-and-burn method, though it is unclear how trees were felled without the use of metal tools. (Copper axes were not used until the Post-Classic period, circa A.D. 900.) Every Maya household had a garden in which fruit trees and vegetables were grown: papaya, avocado, custard apple, sopodilla, and breadnut were cultivated. Livestock consisted of several breeds of dog; the barkless strain was fattened on corn and eaten or sacrificed. Both wild and domesticated turkeys were eaten. The Maya farmer also kept the native stingless bees. Larger prey, such as deer and peccary, were hunted with

bow and arrow, with the aid of hunting dogs. Fishing was accomplished with nets and hook and line in the sea, while in the
streams stupefying drugs were introduced into the water, and
fish floated to the surface where they were collected by hand.
The resin of the copal tree was used both as chewing gum and
as a much-venerated incense: "the odor of the center of
heaven."

Life began for the Maya with ceremonial disfiguration: immediately after birth, Yucatecán mothers washed their babies
and fastened them to a cradle with their heads compressed between two boards, so that after two days a permanent fore-and-
aft flattening had taken place, which the Maya considered a
mark of great beauty. Between the ages of three and twelve a
baptismal rite was conducted in the dwelling of the town elder.
Boys and young men lived away from their families in special
communal houses where they learned the art of war and were
given religious instruction. They also amused themselves with
gambling and games. In virtually every Maya center was a ball
court in which a ritualistic game known as *pok-to-pok* was
played. The communal boys' house was frequently visited by
the community prostitutes, indicating the considerable sexual
license of males. Girls, on the other hand, were brought up
strictly by their mothers, and suffered grievous punishment for
premarital sexual activity. A double standard was pervasive in
Maya society. Though monogamy was the general custom, important men often took more than one wife. Adultery — a term
applied almost exclusively to women's sexual activity — was
punished by death.

Personal grooming was an important activity among the
Maya. Young men painted themselves black until they married.
Tattooing and decorative scarification began after marriage for
both men and women. Slightly crossed eyes were considered an
attribute of beauty for both sexes, and parents often hung a
small bead over the nose of their child to promote this
condition.

Death was intensely dreaded by the Maya. Their scheme of
an afterlife was dismal and unrewarding. Peasants were buried
beneath the floors of their homes, their mouths filled with food
and a jade bead. The elite were cremated, and funerary temples
were sometimes placed above their urns. At an early period,
burial in sepulchers beneath imposing temple/mausoleums was
the right of the greatest nobles.

Classic ball court at Copán
in the Maya region of Honduras.

In contrast to what we know about the nobility of Maya society, archaeology has revealed little concerning commoners. The remains of their ancient "house mounds" provide a meager picture of daily life among peasants — the *yalba uinicob* (lower people), as they were known in Yucatec. And yet they were the work force of Maya civilization, and without them the nobility, the priests, scholars, and rulers could scarcely have had time for their study of astronomy, calendrics, mathematics, and art. Nonetheless, so little survives of the lives of peasants that scholars must rely upon the early observations of Spanish padres, who, like Diego de Landa, were obsessed with both the destruction and the detailed written preservation of every aspect of the Maya world. Through such historical records of the sixteenth and seventeenth centuries, we can only imagine the daily life of the vast and elaborate ceremonial centers that were lost for centuries under heaps of debris and foliage within the most remote jungles.

There are few truly "lost worlds" in the annals of archaeology. Usually, even the most inaccessible ruins are known by the people who live within their location. This rule does not hold, however, for many of the Classic Maya centers. They were truly lost until the beginning of the nineteenth century, when brief reports of crumbling cities in the midst of impenetrable jungle began to appear. Almost without exception, such stories were dismissed as reckless rumors and sheer nonsense.

One of the rare surviving examples of Classic Maya wood-carving: a detail from a lintel at Tikal.

Tikal was a giant among Classic Maya centers, the largest site in the Maya realm, and one of the greatest "cities" in the Americas. Its six temple-pyramids rise into the clouds, literally skyscrapers among buildings of their kind. From the plaza to the top of its roof, Temple IV — the most impressive of all — measures 229 feet in height. The plaza was the heart of Tikal, flanked by two massive pyramids on the east and west, and on the north by the acropolis. The deities of the Maya must have been pleased by such an exquisite architectural homage . . . the steep temples rising incredibly into the sky, the vast "palaces" where the priests or the nobility resided, the noisy marketplace, and the tiered courts where mysterious games of "high skill and deadly risk were played."

Tikal was a triumph of Maya art and technology in its heyday. We can only wonder what it might have been like to enter its protective walls in its time of splendor — the year A.D. 650.

It is early morning, and the horizon bursts into flame, as Kinich Ahau, Lord Sun — his crimson headdress burning brightly — triumphantly emerges from the darkness of the Underworld and tosses his brilliant cloak over the shoulders of Tikal. Beyond the walls of the city and among the pole-and-thatch dwellings of the peasants comes the sound of morning: dogs barking and the relentless rhythm of women grinding breadnuts for the day's supply of tortillas. The smoke rises from the cook fires as the women work and the men make their way to their fields. Rain clouds hang heavily in the sky, promising an abundant season for the plots of maize, squash, chili peppers, and beans which nestle upon the narrows strips of land that have been wretched from the surrounding jungle.

We make our way among the crowds of peasants who have come from their humble dwellings, bending under heavy bundles of produce and firewood, ceramics, salt, and tobacco, on their way toward the marketplace of Tikal. Once beyond the gateway shrines of the nobility, we suddenly step onto a remarkable, paved causeway, eighty feet wide, leading directly into the heart of the great city. It is a truly awesome sight: gleaming, brightly painted towers rising abruptly from the miles upon miles of unbroken, deep green tropics. As we make our way along the causeway we pass the plastered reservoirs that supply water during the dry winter season. Birds of many colors screech and flutter over these captive lagoons.

Now we enter the magnificent East Plaza, teaming with people. Just ahead of us lies the Central Acropolis, with its palaces and priestly schools and dormitories. The sun climbs higher as we walk, piercing the rain-filled clouds and sending rippling streams of light over the North Acropolis, where a temple to the rain god stands in splendid relief against the stormy sky. A mighty ruler, a descendant of deities, is interred in an ancient tomb, which is the foundation of this even greater shrine that has been built upon the old structure.

Now out into the Great Plaza we go, where scaffolding and thatched shelters surround the ceremonial space, and where people are beginning to assemble for the rites of office that will soon be held for the new ruler who has ascended to the throne. As Lord Sun reaches the highest peak of the Sky World, all preparations for the ceremony are at last completed, and the crowd murmurs expectantly. The nobility, in lavish costumes, assembles in the shade of the shelters. Visiting ambassadors and priests are given favored places upon the observation stand, while the impersonators of the gods line the flank of the North Acropolis, dressed in their phantasmagoric garb. They move in their strange, trancelike manner, transformed into the deities whose costumes they wear. They have spent the entire night in the most sacred chamber of the central temple of the acropolis, praying and purifying themselves by piercing their lips, ears, penises, and tongues with the spines of stingrays, and letting their blood flow upon strips of paper. Now they wait expectantly for the appearance of their new ruler.

One of the two great pyramids of the Central Plaza of Tikal in Guatemala — Classic Maya.

At last the procession comes into sight, moving solemnly into the plaza as the wooden trumpets, the conch shells, the turtleshell rattles, and the drums make their fantastic music. In the lead are men carrying large wicker parasols, decorated with spectacular plumage. Following the parasols are wave upon wave of colorful banners, flying in the breeze that sweeps into the Great Plaza with the procession. Now we see the nobles, clad in precious jaguar skins; and behind them the litter-bearers, upon whose shoulders floats the wooden chair in which the ruler rides beneath a canopy of dazzling, iridescent green feathers. A jubilant shout goes up as the sunlight catches his figure and his oiled, black hair glistens.

Now he steps from the litter as it is lowered to the ground before the red temple where his predecessor is entombed. His body is covered with massive jewelry of jade, and on his chest is an elaborate ornament of spectacular beadwork. The great ruler pauses only momentarily as an old priest places his palm upon his shoulder in a formal gesture of greeting. Then the new monarch slowly climbs the steps leading to the throne, as the tall and regal headdress of quetzal plumes is brought forward.

In utter silence the new ruler is crowned.

Then the dancers begin their slow ritual gestures, stepping with dignity to and fro as the priest chants words from the ancient book. Now clouds of copal incense pour from the temple doorways. The young ruler rises and, with delicate fingers, makes an offering to the great mystery that is hidden from our eyes in the days that are not yet born. And with this gesture, a joyful shout rises all around us from the assembled crowd. The music roars in our ears for just a moment, and then it is silent. And the ceremony is ended.

We come away in a delighted stupor, amazed by the events we have witnessed. Among a throng of happy people we make our way toward the vast marketplace, stopping momentarily to peek into the patio of a noble family that reposes before the midday meal in celebration of the enthronement of their ruler. Two men relax upon a stone ledge, covered with the skins of jaguars. They are eating fruit as they talk about the new king.

Just beyond these noblemen, hidden by a cotton drape that partitions her section of the dwelling, the woman of the house comforts her child and then arranges her family's prize possessions on shelves and in net bags that she hangs from the walls.

She pauses momentarily to give directions to several servants who are pouring water, grinding maize, and making gruel for the meal of celebration.

Then we continue on our imaginary way.

As we enter the marketplace, there is a burst of chattering voices. People shout and laugh as they bargain and barter their goods. The long galleries are filled with wonderful things: fine textiles, flint tools, pottery, beeswax candles, baskets, fine animal skins, turkeys, rabbits, dried fish, salt, tobacco, and blades of obsidian. In the central court sacred paraphernalia is sold: herbs, incense, masks made of paper, plumes, clay figurines, and tiny jade offerings.

The bartering continues until sunset, with agreements sealed by the symbolic gesture of drinking together in public. Small purchases are made with cacao beans that serve as money. Everywhere there are people haggling. Everywhere there is prosperity and the curious joy of the merchant, for as Padre Diego de Landa reported: "The occupation to which [the Maya] are most inclined is trading."

The day of commerce and regal ceremony is climaxed by the shouts of spectators and the resounding thump of a hard rubber ball striking the stone walls of the ball court, where players in elaborate, padded costumes lunge for the hurtling ball and smash into one another. No one knows for certain when this sacred game began, but every spectator knows that its outcome is a serious matter, for the game is played in order to rescue the stellar gods that have vanished from the sky. It is a battle between life and death, drought and fertility, day and night, heaven and earth.

The ball game has probably been associated with ritual human sacrifice from its beginnings among the Olmecs. For symbolic reasons, various zones within the ball court are marked: point zones and foul zones, depending on where the ball falls. To define these zones the court is painted with different colors and lines are drawn on the masonry floor. Stone markers are placed in the center and at the ends of the Classic Maya court; these markers are carved in animal forms. The people of Tikal are intensely taken up by the game, for they understand it as the eternal life-and-death battle of the heavens. Two gods rage against one another: the black god represents the west, place of the dead and of darkness, and the red deity signifies the east, place of flowers and dancing. These gods compete against each other in a contest that must end in sacrifice. The players have dedicatedly trained for many months. Before the game, they purified themselves in the ritual sweatlodge, praying and seeking the blessings of the priests. Now the players hurtle through the air, leaping high to intercept the elusive ball, which they may not strike with their hands, but must send ricocheting about the court with a thrust of their hips. Their desperate but precise gestures express a determination to win, to keep the ball from dropping to the paved floor, for if they lose, their leader will be sacrificed.

(In the *Popol Vuh* of the Quiché Maya, a line celebrates the abundance of nature that the blood of the sacrificial victim brings to the land: "This tree which has never given fruit, was now covered with fruit after the head of Hun-Hunahpu was placed among its branches." These words come to life in the bas-reliefs at the ball court of Chichén Itzá: the players of two teams, wearing their typical costumes and protective paraphernalia, witness the decapitation of a player who kneels with one knee on the earth. From his neck flows blood in the form of seven serpents, one of which is transformed into leafy foliage that covers the scene with symbolic fertility imagery. Marcia Castro Leal has suggested that "it is possible the colossal stone heads, marvelous examples of Olmec sculpture, represent decapitated ball players" from the mysterious era that saw the origin of the sacred game in Veracruz.)

In this game at Tikal, the nobles shout and cheer from their privileged places atop the walls of the court, while peasants line the steps and platforms of the Central Acropolis. Rich or poor, they all gamble heavily upon the outcome of the game, wagering their most precious possessions, their homes, even their children and themselves as slaves. The violent and bloody game is intriguing and revealing, for it contradicts many of the notions we have about the peaceful and humane Maya. Despite a long-held picture of the Maya as an intellectual and nonaggressive people — "the Greeks of the Americas" — we have come to realize that, in fact, the Maya were obsessed with violence, human sacrifice, and war. Their plebian captives were forced into slavery, while the nobles and great warriors "either had their hearts torn out on the sacrificial stone, or else were beheaded, a form of sacrifice favored by the Classic Maya." (Coe)

Despite abundant indication of violence in Maya society, archaeological evidence paradoxically suggests that there were

probably only rare instances of sustained and large-scale warfare during the Classic period, for "most of the ceremonial centers were situated in terrain vulnerable to attack from all
directions, and [yet] fortifications of any type are conspicuously
absent. . . . But this does not imply the complete absence of war.
Raids and skirmishes constantly took place, touched off perhaps
by territorial disputes, feuds between rulers of neighboring
cities, or the need for sacrificial victims and slaves." (Gallenkamp)

Just such confrontation is vividly depicted in the famous
murals of Bonampak, which were unknown until rather recently, when, unexpectedly, an ancient temple in the Mexican rain
forest of eastern Chiapas was rediscovered. For years this battered structure had been used as a secret shrine by the Lacandon Maya — a little-known tribe that has kept its whereabouts
secret since the time of the sixteenth-century Spanish invasion,
when they retreated into the wilds. They remained secluded in
the jungle until the mid-1900s, when regions of Chiapas were
exploited by oil prospectors and mahogany cutters. The Lacandon persisted through this new invasion. Although their identification with the Classic past is slight, the Lacandon still
conducted rituals in the long-deserted temples amid the lost
Maya sites, such as Bonampak. Even as the world of the ancients
was gradually rediscovered by Europeans, somehow Bonampak
remained safely forgotten in the deep humid jungle of Chiapas.

Then, in the spring of 1946, a photographer named Giles G.
Healey came to Chiapas to photograph the Lacandon for a documentary film. While working in the location of the Lacanha River, Healey noticed that the Indians made secret pilgrimages into
the jungle. For a long time they resisted his requests to be led to
the ancient shrine where they still worshipped, but eventually
the Indians agreed. Gallenkamp has reconstructed this remarkable adventure: "He was led deep into the rain forest along narrow trails hacked out of the bush with machetes. In places no
direct sunlight penetrated the overhanging vegetation, and one
could easily have passed within a few yards of an entire city
without suspecting its existence. Finally, they reached an area
enclosed by barely discernible ruins — temples, palaces, platforms, and monuments, rising like chalk-white phantoms out of
a sea of jungle green.

"In a courtyard at the foot of a terraced acropolis lay a
massive sculptured stela broken into several pieces. Its central

figure, etched in bold relief, depicted a dignitary laden with jade ornaments, holding a ceremonial staff, and surrounded by columns of hieroglyphic inscriptions. Flanking the stairway ascending the acropolis were two more elaborately carved stelae.... On a platform near the northeastern corner of the acropolis stood an unpretentious flat-roofed building which, despite a thick mantle of trees and vines, had remained in a remarkably good state of preservation. Its three doorways opened into small interior chambers, and above each entrance was a niche containing fragments of seated stucco figures. Visible on the upper façade between two of the doors were remnants of a weathered relief showing a standing human, and the outlines of an ornate mask still adhered to a section of the wall.

"Entering one of the doorways, Healey found himself in a narrow vaulted room. When his eyes adjusted to the chamber's dim illumination, he suddenly became aware of faces peering at him from the walls; gradually they assumed sharper delineation and muted colors, and he could see figures of richly costumed priests, nobles, musicians, and strangely masked impersonators surrounding him on all sides. In the next room he came upon a tableau of opposing armies locked in a furious battle, while on an adjoining panel prisoners of war were being judged by haughty chieftains. Magnificent paintings of dancers in exotic costumes, an orchestra, and scenes of human sacrifice adorned the third room, along with a group of nobles attended by retainers. What Healey had stumbled upon was a dazzling array of murals completely covering the walls of the building's three chambers."

Quite by accident, Healey became the first outsider to view the most extensive murals yet discovered anywhere in Mesoamerica — a veritable gallery of pre-Columbian paintings. The unique site was given the name Bonampak, a Maya term meaning "painted walls."

A team of scholars and artists descended upon Bonampak, and for months they painstakingly copied the eleven-hundred-year-old murals, reconstructing them in their original vivid colors. The result of their labor is a rare portrait of a group of ancient Americans as they actually looked and lived at the height of their power and refinement.

A continuous mural wraps around the sloping ceiling of the first three chambers of Bonampak's main building, revealing a scene of diverse activities, as the Maya prepare for a ritual procession in honor of their fertility and agricultural gods. Four-teen white-robed aristocrats stand in a row beneath a margin of abstract depictions of various animal-like god-masks. The rul-er — *halach uinic* — sits in casual dress on top of a stone table, looking back and giving orders to a servant holding a child — probably the chief's son, who has apparently been brought by a nurse in order to witness the scene. Sharing the dais of the chief is his consort on his right. Another aristocratic woman sits on his left.

In the next panel, servants are dressing three of the chief's war captains, who stand on the low platform that runs through the entire scene. Already costumed in jaguar skins, heavy jade

The victors and the vanquished: reproduc-tion of the Maya murals of Bonampak.

necklaces, and earrings, these elegant men are being groomed for a momentous event. In yet another panel, the same three captains are seen in the midst of a splendid procession.

In the second room, we see a continuation of the pictorial narrative upon which the creators of the murals devoted great creative effort and skill. After the procession, the warriors are shown in the midst of a surprise raid upon an enemy village. Wielding clubs and blowing trumpets, the warriors fall upon their enemies, whose lack of weapons indicates that they are entirely unprepared for the attack. The chief clutches a captive by the hair, while three captains stand nearby, ready to protect their lord with spears.

In another panel of the murals, we see the chief standing atop the steps of a ritual platform, passing judgment on his captives. A naked prisoner at the chief's feet raises his arms and seems to implore mercy. Just below this figure is another prisoner: gracefully sprawled unconscious or dead upon the steps, his eyes closed and his head thrown back — a tragic posture that has persistently evoked the acclaim of those who have studied the murals, for this is surely the most emotionally charged single image to be found in the remarkable visual arts of Mesoamerica.

Three other prisoners are shown with blood spurting from their fingers, a ritual wounding that may be the preliminary to sacrifice — a death by decapitation, which seems to be symbolized by the disembodied head on a cushion of ceremonial leaves depicted in the center of the lowest step of the platform.

In the third and last room, the visual drama draws to a close: the prisoners are led away to their sacrifice while the chief is seated on a dais and commemorates the blood-ritual by pricking his tongue and thus adding his own blood to the sacrificial offering to the gods. The triumphant moment is marked by a recessional, led by standard-bearers carrying banners of brilliant plumes. Musicians march across the scene, blowing their long wooden trumpets and shaking gourdlike rattles. And thus the drama ends.

What most distinguishes Bonampak's murals from the highly stylized and abstract frescoes found elsewhere in Mesoamerica is their uncommon realism. For this reason, the images of Bonampak have added immeasurably to the knowledge of Maya culture, providing hitherto unknown details about costume, musical instruments, warfare, human sacrifice, and ritual procedures. The interpretation of the murals, however, is highly conjectural, especially since the significance of certain details can only be guessed and some sections are permanently destroyed by erosion. The hieroglyphic inscriptions indicate that the murals date from about A.D. 800, the height of the Classic Maya world. The French anthropologist Jacques Soustelle notes that "Bonampak is a sort of pictorial encyclopedia of a Maya city of the eighth century; the city comes to life there again, with its ceremonies and its processions, its still and solemn-looking dignitaries weighed down by their heavy plumed adornments, its warriors clothed in jaguar skins. Lively and violent scenes are displayed side by side with gracious, familiar pictures of daily life. A complete cross-section of society — women, children, servants, musicians, warrior chiefs, dying prisoners, and masked dancers — that is what these painters succeeded in depicting on those walls, lost today in the depths of one of the continent's most impenetrable jungles."

The murals of Bonampak may have been created by artists who were pressed by a sense of urgency. Mayanist Tatiana Proskouriakoff notes an intimation of fear which pervades the images: "As far as we know, this was the last brilliant chapter in the history of the region. We see at Bonampak its full pomp, its somewhat barbarous and elaborately designed ritual. . . . There is a bare hint, a mere suggestion in the dramatic scenes, and in the excitement of line foreign to the serenity of the Maya style, of an emotional tension which might have presaged a crisis; but there is, unfortunately, no sequel to the scenes. . . ."

Not long after A.D. 800, when the murals were created, the crisis to which Proskouriakoff alludes descended upon the lowland, and the remarkable civilization of the Maya began to falter and to decline. When the haunted murals of Bonampak were painted, most of the great centers of the lowland region had only a few years left before they would turn into ghost towns, lost for centuries in the shadows and humidity of an unbroken sea of foliage.

Six hundred years before Columbus, early in the ninth century, a catastrophic series of events crushed the people of the Maya lowland. Tikal and Bonampak became dying cities. One after another the ceremonial centers ceased construction, and in some sites buildings and monuments were left half-finished, as if the great architects had been swept away in the midst of their marvelous work. Even the practice of regularly erecting dated, commemorative stelae came to an abrupt end. Within a hundred years — from A.D. 800 to 900 — all of the once-populous centers of worship and government were abandoned. The great monumental cities were left deserted and silent. Incredibly, the buildings were entirely untouched, without any sign of invasion, insurrection, or natural calamity — almost as if the people had been carried away ... as if, at any moment, the inhabitants might return to their monuments and plazas.

But they did not return. Instead, an immense decay from which they would never recover descended upon the cities. The rains came, and after them came the suns of many summers. The regal, ornate stucco and stone figures atop the pyramids stared out into the deserted plazas where countless seedlings began to sprout through the eroding plaster pavements. Succulent vines crawled without restraint over the sculptured stonework. Saplings were born in the dust of centuries, which piled upon the high ledges and terraces, and trees gradually sank tiny tendrils between the handsomely carved stones, taking hold and then growing into massive roots that eventually shattered the walls and threw down the stones in great silent heaps.

The silence also grew, until it was eventually broken by roaming monkeys and parrots that came to explore the new jungle which had piled, layer upon layer, upon these mighty works of humankind. Wild figs climbed the towers and intertwined among their own branches until they made a leafy tomb for the abandoned stone people of the monuments and stelae. Then came the giant fruit bats, attracted by the putrescent ponds and the stench of rotting leaves, and clouds of mosquitoes and gnats. The copious rain sent rivulets of mineral-rich water over the walls, encasing whole buildings in delicate crystalline cocoons. Ficus raced to the tops of the temples and brought down their lofty summits like fallen birds. Time devoured Tikal and spat out its precious bones, scattering stones and bits of monumental debris across the bottom of a great, deep sea of vegetation. Time ate Bonampak and licked its memory clean, leaving nothing but the shadow of its faded murals in a place where there were no eyes to see them. And after the feast of time was over, there were only the piled bones of a people's whole world, blotted out and broken ... buried alive and forgotten. All they had known and said and done, all they had built, all the gods they had praised and the ideals for which they had died sank beyond reach to the bottom of a vast deep sea of human dream and memory.

Then one day in 1839, John Lloyd Stephens, an American attorney turned explorer, and his friend, the British architect Frederick Catherwood, rediscovered a world so lost in time and space that no hint of its existence had been seriously considered for several centuries. Despite countless hardships and calamities, Stephens and Catherwood made their way to several Maya centers, recording their observations in vivid prose and pictures. Their travels were among the most remarkable adventures in history.

It was on their second exploration of Yucatán that they came upon the glorious Maya settlement now called Palenque. Against a constant spray of a windy drizzle, they cut their way through the underbrush, slowly climbing the stones of a pyramid until they came upon the temple at the top. Plants wound through the latticework of the roof, and trees with great naked roots dug into the masonry and tried to dislodge the stones. Though the building had suffered greatly from the invasion of creepers and roots, this marvelous structure, the Temple of Inscriptions (which Stephens called "No. 1 Casa de Piedra"), was the most awesome and best preserved of the outlying temples of Palenque. The front of the temple, facing north, was entered by five doorways and was decorated by four handsomely crafted stuccoed reliefs, though all the figures had lost their faces to the ravages of the centuries. Yet Stephens and Catherwood felt that the elegance of the art was unmatched for its detail. They had been to the Holy Land and to Egypt and Greece, but they had never seen any art that vaguely resembled the forms and styles they encountered among the Maya ruins.

When they entered the vault of the Temple of Inscriptions, they stopped and peered into the blackness of the interior. Again there was the familiar stench of decay. The jungle was silent except for the subdued hiss of the light rain on countless leaves and the screech of the bats, which hung from the ceiling of the dark, fetid room. The chamber was entirely empty except for two great limestone slabs on one of the side walls, completely covered glyphs that were barely visible through the thick slime and moss that covered them. One of the expedition's helpers was put to work with a scrub brush, trying to remove the deep verdure of centuries. Catherwood and Stephens watched with great excitement as the glyphs came through the dissolving slime. Slowly, almost magically, the carving was becoming visible — row upon row of complex signs that shouted out to them in a language entirely unintelligible, like nothing they had ever seen before. There was absolutely no mistaking these sculptured characters. Stephens was certain that they were the same as those he had found at other Maya sites. And he instinctively felt that these hieroglyphics told the history of Palenque. If only they could be read, they might answer the thousands of questions that were raised by the mysterious ruins: who had built them, where had these people come from, and what had become of them?

In the hope that scholars might be able one day to find these and many other answers, Stephens asked Catherwood to

Classic Maya ceremonial center: Palenque in Chiapas, Mexico.

copy every glyph as accurately as possible. As the artist worked
in the light of pine torches, which filled the vault with smoke,
he paced incessantly back and forth, coming very close to the
glyphs and then backing away to try to grasp the overall design
of the enormous slab upon which the peculiar writing was incised. His footsteps rang out resoundingly, but neither Catherwood nor Stephens could possibly have realized that
immediately under their feet was hidden one of the most exceptional secrets of the ancients who had built these astounding
temples. That secret would not be uncovered for one hundred
and ten years, when, in 1949, the Mexican archaeologist

Stairway of the Inscriptions at Copán, Honduras, containing twenty-five hundred incised glyphs — one of the most celebrated
Classic Maya sites.

Detail of a stone relief from the East Court of the Palace at Palenque.

Alberto Ruz Lhuillier noticed that the slab floor of the vault of the Temple of Inscriptions was drilled with what seemed to him to be "finger holes." These indentations were entirely unexplainable. The floor, Ruz noticed, was not finished with stucco as in most Maya buildings, but with carefully fitted flagstones. With intense curiosity, Ruz began to clear the area of debris. It was then, he recalls, "that I found the cigarette butt of the criminal . . . the architectural detail that gave me the clue I needed." The wall of the temple continued beneath the floor. For some reason the floor slab was fitted with perforations so that it could be moved. In a moment of revelation, it occurred to Ruz that there must be something *under* the slab.

Raising one of the stones, he was disappointed to find nothing but a debris-filled hole. Ruz and his workmen dug downward beneath the flagstone with little expectation. But then their shovels struck something: a huge stone crossbeam. The

men worked with a good deal more excitement, quickly digging through the packed rubble and clay. Six feet farther their spades clanged as they struck something solid. They looked down into the hole in amazement, for they had found the straight edge of a step — a concealed staircase that led into the core of the massive pyramid.

"So difficult was the work — the breaking up of the rubble packing and the lifting out of the stones with ropes and pulleys," Ruz recounts, "that in the first season's labor, we got only 23 steps down — about eight steps a month."

Working from late April to July each year, Ruz and his crew finally descended forty-six steps, reaching a stone landing at the end of July 1950. Expectation was high, for the landing seemed to signal that they had finally reached their mysterious destination. To their amazement, they discovered that the corbeled tunnel did not end, but turned 180 degrees and continued downward. The labor resumed, and by the end of 1951, the crew had descended another thirteen steps.

"By then we knew we were close," says Ruz, "for we were only about ten feet above the level of the plaza outside."

Late in May of 1952, the workmen reached a great slab poised horizontally against what might be a doorway located sixty feet within the pyramid. Just in front of this sealed doorway were skeletons of six retainers, who had apparently been left as the guardians of the stairway. Cautiously the excavators applied their tools to this barrier. Suddenly one of the workmen's crowbar sank into emptiness. After almost three years of effort, Alberto Ruz Lhuillier anxiously pressed his face against the hole and, putting a light through, stared into the void.

"To my amazement, out of the shadow arose a vision from a fairy tale. . . . First I saw an enormous room that appeared to be graven in ice. The walls were covered with a brilliant calcareous layer, stalactites hung from the ceiling like curtains, thick stalagmites resembling huge tapers rose from the floor, all limestone formations caused by the filtration of rain water through the body of the pyramid for more than a thousand years. The chamber was so perfectly constructed that the centuries had not affected it even though it supports the entire weight of the pyramid and temple. The walls of the interior glistened, and on them marched relief figures of great size. Most astounding was the colossal monument that occupied most of the chamber — a great sculptured tablet resting upon a monolithic block. Our first impression was that it might be a solid ceremonial altar,

Tomb of a high priest, discovered in 1952 deep within the Temple of Inscriptions at Palenque.

preserved in this secret place far from the public eye. In the dimness I could see that the near-side of the altar was covered with hieroglyphs in red paint, while on the upper surface only the fact that it was entirely carved could be made out in the darkness."

Three days later, Sunday, June 15, 1952, Ruz and his crew turned aside the great triangular stone that sealed the chamber and descended the final five steps that led into the crypt.

"I entered the mysterious chamber with the strange sensation natural for the first one to tread the entrance steps in a thousand years. I tried to see it all with the same vision that the Palenque priests had when they left the crypt; I wanted to efface the centuries and hear the vibrations of the last human voices beneath these massive vaults. . . . Across the impenetrable veil of time I sought the impossible bond between their lives and ours."

The immense carved slab that dominated the chamber was in pristine condition. Twelve by seven feet, its exquisite relief work depicts the figure of a male reclining in the mouth of a monster. Behind this figure is the sacred ceiba — the tree of life — in which a bird is perched. The relief is framed by a row of fifty-four glyphs. The stone lay upon an even larger base, a massive rectangular block estimated to weigh about twenty tons. The block, in turn, rests upon four carved pedestals. Ruz conjectured that "if it were an altar, then the monolith under the tablet had to be solid and its function was merely that of a base. But there was also another possibility: that it might be hollow and therefore not an altar. I decided to bore a tiny hole in the base to determine if it were solid or hollow. The first probe reached the center of the block without finding anything but stone. In another attempt, however, the drill penetrated a cavity, and a wire that was threaded through the hole showed traces of red paint.

"The moment in which I verified that the base was hollow was one of tremendous excitement. It might have been a huge receptacle for offerings, but the size and form of the monument, as well as the presence of red paint, promised something else. In the Maya cosmology, red is associated with the East and almost always appears in tombs."

The mere possibility that he had discovered an ancient tomb that had not been opened for a thousand years was so unlikely that Ruz attempted to restrain his growing excitement. He knew, however, that he somehow had to find a technique to lift the huge lid from the hollow base, no matter how difficult such a task would be in the confines of the crypt and at such a depth. Raising the five-ton slab was one of the most laborious tasks, but also one of the most intriguing.

"The slab had to be raised despite the difficulties and dangers. Using truck jacks placed under logs just below the four corners of the tablet, we lifted it. Introducing the truck jacks into the crypt, their proper placement, and the delicate operation of raising the tablet took twenty-four consecutive hours which I spent in the crypt without leaving it, from 6:00 AM November 27, 1952 to the same hour on the 28th.

"As the tablet began to rise, I could see there was a cavity carved out of the heart of the huge monolith . . . a polished stone slab sealed it perfectly. This inner slab had four perforations, each sealed by a large stone plug. As soon as space permitted, I slid into the narrow space between the tablet-cover and the slab inner-seal, lifted out one of the plugs, and flashed my electric torch into the opening. A few inches from my eyes appeared a human skull covered with pieces of jade.

"By passing ropes through the holes we removed the slab in a maneuver that must have been similar to the one used by the priest in placing it. Now the mortuary cavity appeared with its impressive contents, in a setting of vivid vermilion, for the walls and floor of the cavity were covered with cinnabar. The skeleton rested in a normal position, arms and legs extended, face up. The bones crumbled to the touch due to the humidity, but were still in place. We were able to determine that the skeleton was of a man of 40 to 50-years-of-age; tall, robust, and well proportioned, without apparent pathological lesions. The state of destruction of the skull prevented our being able to tell if it had been artificially deformed as was the custom among Maya nobles and priests.

"At the moment of burial his face had been covered by a jade mosaic mask, the pieces being stuck to a thin layer of stucco applied to the face. He had also been buried with all his jade jewels: diadem, earplugs, necklace, breastplate, bracelets, and jade figurines. It is to be assumed that the dignitary interred was the same person who planned and ordered construction of the gigantic mausoleum. After he was buried, the sarcophagus was sealed and the sculptured lid lowered into position. The priests then placed on the tablet other symbols of his office: a belt adorned with three tiny jade masks and nine slate pendants in the form of hatchets; a shield with a figure of the sun god; and what was probably a scepter, with a mask of the rain god. The crypt was then closed, and six young men, in all likelihood sons of nobles, were sacrificed to accompany the prince to the other world. Finally, they filled up the stairway to the level of the floor of the temple, depositing various offerings along the way. But even if access to the tomb had been sealed off forever, a spiritual bond remained, for we discovered a stucco serpent undulated along the steps from the sarcophagus to the temple threshold — a kind of molding that was at the same time a hollow conduit and a magical means of maintaining communication with the illustrious deceased.

"Discovery of the Royal Tomb in the Temple of Inscriptions caused a sensation for various reasons: its unusual location under the pyramid; its dimensions, solidity, and excellent construction; burial of a high-ranking personage with all of his jewels. This discovery demonstrated for the first time that the American pyramid was not necessarily and exclusively a solid base to support a temple, as previously believed, in opposition to the Egyptian pyramid which served as a massive mortuary monument."

Who was this distinguished man, buried with such splendor? Two archaeologists — David Kelley and Floyd Lounsbury—have interpreted the name glyph of the corpse as "Pacal," or Shield. Peter Mathews and Linda Schele place the birth of the man at A.D. 603. He lived, they agree, for eighty years before his death and interment in A.D. 683. Alberto Ruz Lhuillier does not agree with these interpretations, and continues to place the man's date of birth earlier and his age when he died at about forty. These conflicting opinions and interpretations underscore the persistent research, questioning curiosity, and scholarly renewal that surrounds the study of Pre-Columbian civilizations.

SIXTY FEET ABOVE the famous tomb and one hundred and twelve years earlier, in 1839, Frederick Catherwood was carefully copying the same row of glyphs which are today the sources of debate. He worked in the last light of the evening, his fingers swollen and his eyes fatigued, totally unaware that the grave of some unknown and ancient royal person lay far beneath his feet. Today those who have spent a lifetime in the search for answers to the mysteries of the Maya know comparatively little more about the Maya than Stephens and Catherwood did in 1839.

As these irrepressible explorers who had rediscovered the world of the Maya stood at the summit of the pyramid, they trembled with the intensity of their ignorance. "Who built these fantastic temples? Where did they come from, and where did they go and who were they?"

More than four centuries after the arrival of Columbus, almost none of the really fundamental questions concerning the indigenous peoples of the Americas have been fully answered. And of unanswered riddles, those of the Maya are surely the most puzzling. No one has satisfactorily explained where Maya civilization began or exactly what earlier cultures influenced it. No one has explained the origins of the Maya world or exactly how it managed to evolve in an extremely hostile environment, where conditions of weather and landscape made the construction of large complex social units almost unthinkable. There is

The Classic Maya acropolis at Copán, Honduras; reconstruction by Tatiana Proskouriakoff.

Chacmool — a Toltec-Maya stone carving associated with the ceremonial centers of Yucatán.

no reliable information on the origin of the Maya calendar, their hieroglyphic writing, and their mathematics. We do not know what they called themselves or their ceremonial centers, despite the fact that living on exactly the same land where the ancients lived for centuries are the descendants of the Maya.

It was Columbus who had the first reported contact with these mysterious people in 1502, near the island of Guanaja off the northern coast of Honduras. His ships came upon a canoe carrying Indian traders who reportedly came from a place called *Maia* or *Maiam*, the name from which the word *Maya* was subsequently derived. But that was not the name by which they knew themselves.

There is overwhelming irony in the fact that a people who spent much of their energies leaving careful records of their lives and times left them in inscriptions that are unintelligible to us. Those who made the inscriptions and knew their meaning vanished long before the arrival of the European invaders, leaving few clues for people who have spent their lives trying to understand Maya writing.

Probably the most pressing mystery of all concerns the decline of the Maya world. Even the catastrophe that led to the abandonment of the greatest of Maya ceremonial centers during the ninth century is still totally unknown except for highly debated and contradictory conjectures about natural disasters, insurrection of the peasants, plague, and famine. At the close of

The descendants of the Maya still build the thatched, oval dwellings in which they lived in the Classic period, some thousand years ago (Guatemala).

the twentieth century, despite all of our technology and re-search, the fate of the Maya remains one of the most baffling archaeological puzzles. In our day, the Maya world is one of the last great frontiers of exploration, and the great cities are some of the last places on earth which are still sources of profound mystery and wonderment. And so we can understand the fasci-nation and the frustration of John Lloyd Stephens and Frederick Catherwood as they stood atop the Temple of Inscriptions and gazed in silence over the broad, jungle-covered hills of Palen-que. They could see the wide plazas which were once covered with brightly painted plaster. They gazed upon the gleaming pyramids on which processions of bejeweled priests in great feathered headdresses had once made flamboyant patterns on the steep gleaming stairways as they presided over marvelous rites of passage: of war and peace, of time and death, of fertility and eternal renewal.

The winter moon rises, and in its pale light comes a faint echo of trumpets as the splendid figures vanish into the rainy wind that whirls through deserted chambers. Now the jungle embraces the silent ruins like a groom on his wedding bed.

WHAT BECAME OF THE PEOPLE of the lost cities? Had they vanished or moved away from their decaying settlements, seek-ing a new land? Or had they stayed on, falling into ignorance generation by generation as they forgot how to read and write,

The Toltec-Maya culture at Uxmal, Yucatán: Palace of the Governors.

how to construct the remarkable structures of their ancestors — descending unknowingly into an American dark ages?

These questions are not as easily answered as they were a few decades ago. But one fact is clear: the Maya are not a lost race that vanished entirely. There are approximately two million Indians of Maya descent still living in their ancient homeland today, the largest group of surviving aboriginal peoples in the Americas anywhere but in the Andes of South America, where the Quechua descendants of the ancient Inca Empire are even more numerous. At its height, the Maya world consisted of a federation of loosely associated city-states not unlike those of classical Greece; consolidated culturally more than politically. They dominated much of the southernmost sector of Mesoamerica: 125,000 square miles of predominantly tropical lowland and highland, ranging widely from southeastern Chiapas, Tabasco, Yucatán, Campeche, and Quintana Roo in what is now Mexico, through the Petén region of Guatemala, and then extending into Belize, the western frontier of Honduras, and western El Salvador. The disastrous event that brought about the collapse of the Maya civilization was once regarded as the turning point between an "Old Empire" and a "New Empire" — the decline of the Classic Maya sites such as Tikal, Palenque, Bonampak, and Copán in the southern lowlands, and the rise of hitherto nonexistent Maya centers at Uxmal, Chichén Itzá, Kabah, and many other cities in the northerly Maya region, mainly in Yucatán. This simplistic picture of Maya history has proved to be inaccurate. Granted, the Classic centers declined. For reasons not yet understood, the lowland in which the greatness of the Maya had triumphed became the setting of a decline in population from the end of the tenth century onward, resulting in only a small and rather insular scattering of Maya descendants. Gallenkamp notes that "every aspect of their existence reflects at best a weak imitation of former glories, an almost desperate effort to preserve rapidly fading links with their past without the benefit of an educated elite or strong political authority. At Tikal these survivors were so culturally impoverished that they had sometimes reset monuments upside down or backward, as if their hieroglyphic texts could no longer be read."

Research has also shown that settlements in Yucatán do not represent a sudden flowering of Post-Classic Maya culture — a "New Empire." Yucatán had not been a Maya backwater or a barbarous province during the Classic period. "Archaeologists now believe that all but a few of its cities flourished at the same time as those of the Central Area. No longer do they look upon such ruins as Uxmal, Chichén Itzá, Labna, and Sayil as crowning jewels in a 'renaissance' wrought by survivors of the 'Old Empire.'" (Gallenkamp)

But these findings compound rather than explain the mystery of the Maya decline. If there wasn't a massive exodus from the lowland region and an accompanying migration of survivors into Yucatán, then what became of the Maya population? As Michael Coe points out, "not only the demise of the Classic centers must be explained, but also the disappearance of the Maya people throughout most of the Central Area." All the potential causes for such a disaster were reexamined: agricultural collapse, epidemic diseases like yellow fever, invasion by foreigners from Mexico, social revolution, forced evacuation by the early Toltec rulers from the Valley of Mexico, who invaded Yucatán, and even earthquakes and an unbalanced sex ratio! But there is little or no proof that any one or any combination of these factors was the cause of the Maya collapse. "An increasing number of Mayanists look to the most probable of such causes as social revolt, with destruction of the elite and their architectural and monumental symbols — a revolt that inexorably spread from one center to another." (Coe)

A Toltec-Maya stela from the Yucatán center of Chichén Itzá.

Whatever actually happened in the lowland area, we know that only a few groups stayed on, wandering among the deserted ceremonial centers and living in the wilds or in the chambers of forgotten palaces — peoples like the Lacandon, who had no cultural claim to the learning and refinement of the Maya, but who retained a shadow of its influences; making half-understood offerings of copal incense among the ruins and living in awe of the ancients, who had become gods.

For reasons we do not understand, the story of the Maya moved northward, to the arid Yucatán Peninsula, where the so-called Post-Classic period flourished. Into this region of small Maya settlements, in the same state of decline as those of the lowland, came a new people, the Nahua-speaking Toltec, whose origin in the far north and whose settlement in the Valley of Mexico are substantiated by their legendary kinship with the nonagricultural nomads called the Chichimec, from whose barbarous ranks evolved both the Toltec and the Aztec peoples. The story of the invasion of the Maya of Yucatán by these descendants of the Chichimec is fascinating to the point of incredibility; and we will investigate this intriguing folk history when we explore the world of "The Giants of Mexico."

For now, let it suffice to say that historical sources in Yucatán folk history speak of the arrival from the west of a man calling himself Kukulcan (*kukul*, "feathered," and *can* "serpent") in A.D. 987. This stranger overwhelmed the people of Yucatán and established his capital at Chichén Itzá. As Maya scholar Ralph Roys has shown, unfortunately the accounts of this important event are seriously confused with the history of another, later people of Yucatán called the Itzá, who moved into the region in the thirteenth century and gave their name to the formerly Toltec site of Chichén. Such confusion aside, the Maya claim Kukulcan and his retinue as the overlords of Yucatán, and credit them with the introduction of many alien artistic, political, and religious traits. The predominantly Mexican chroniclers of this event have pictured it as benign and peaceful. "The archaeological record tells us that the conquest of Yucatán by the supposedly peaceful Topiltzin Quetzalcoatl [as Kukulcan was better known in Central Mexico] and his Toltec armies was violent and brutal in the extreme." (Coe)

The legendary drama is depicted in murals found in the Temple of the Warriors at Chichén Itzá. It opens with the invasion of the Toltec forces by seas, most likely along the Campeche shore, where they reconnoiter a coastal Maya town with whitewashed houses. The Maya suffer the first of their defeats in a marine battle in which they come out on rafts to meet the Toltec war canoes. Then the scene changes to the mainland, where the natives are again defeated in a great pitched battle fought within a major Maya settlement. The pictographic history ends with the heart sacrifice of the Maya leaders, while the Feathered Serpent himself hovers above to receive the bloody offerings.

Under the rule of the Feathered Serpent (Kukulcan/Topiltzin Quetzalcoatl), Chichén Itzá became the supreme metropolis of a united Toltec-Maya kingdom, a splendid recreation of the city of Tula in the Valley of Mexico from which the legendary Quetzalcoatl had been exiled, and from which he and his retainers went by sea in search of a new kingdom. Novel architectural styles and techniques were introduced by the Toltec and amalgamated with the existing Maya forms: the use of colonnades, interior courts divided by columns which expanded the traditionally small Maya rooms (necessitated by the limited stress-bearing capacity of the corbeled arch) into much larger and open chambers, and a construct of exterior walls known as *talud-tablero* — rectangular and upward walls alternating with outward-sloping panels. Other Toltec influence may be seen in the construction of square ceremonial platforms and so-called skull racks, on which the heads of sacrificial victims were publicly displayed. Architectural detail emphasized both militaristic and serpentine motifs: warriors with exposed genitals carved in relief, spears, shields, and elaborate incised patterns inspired by the skin of the diamondback rattlesnake. Elsewhere we find strongly anthropomorphic sculpture: the Atlantean figures (familiar in Tula) which depict warriors with their arms upraised, used to support altars and door lintels. Also characteristic of the Toltec influence was the introduction of a unique graven figure: the so-called *chocmol:* a reclining male with raised head and knees, holding a shallow basin on his abdomen.

The Toltec dominated the Yucatán of the Maya, not only architecturally and artistically, but in terms of government and religion. "[Mexican] Jaguar and Eagle knights rub elbows with men in traditional Maya costume and [Toltec] astral deities coexist with Maya gods. The old Maya order had been irreversibly overthrown, but it is obvious that many of the native princes and priests were incorporated into the new power structure." (Coe)

A Classic Maya stela from Copán, Honduras.

The history of the Americas, like most human chronicles, seems to be the tale of a succession of societies that evolve toward great achievement and then decline and vanish. The Toltec were no exception to this irony of time. All evidence indicates that in about A.D. 1224, their mighty capital, Chichén Itzá, was abandoned. And, quite suddenly, the Toltec vanish from history, and are heard of no more.

The corbeled arch key-pattern decoration of the Palace of the Governors, Uxmal, Yucatán.

Rulers of the Andes

IN THE LONG LEAN DAYS before the beginning of history, the Great Sun strolled each day along the golden pathways of heaven, beaming with delight and contentment. But his radiance dimmed one morning as he climbed into the sky, for as the clouds separated, to make way for him, Great Sun glanced down upon a rock in the sky where savages lived in a dreadful state. Tears came into the eyes of the Sun as he looked upon the pathetic situation of the people of the earth. So great was his pity that he sent his two children Manco Capac and Mama Ocllo, brother and sister, to an island in the midst of Lake Titicaca, telling them that they must instruct the hopeless barbarians of the earth in the arts of a good life. In his hand, Manco Capac carried a golden staff which his father, the Sun, put in his charge, telling him: "When you reach a land where the soil is so fertile that this staff sinks out of sight into the earth, then and only then will you have come to a good land for the people of the earth. There you shall found a city."

Manco Capac and his sister came among the savages of the place called Peru, and these brutish people fell to their knees at the sight of the golden twins, so great was the brilliance of their majesty. Then they listened to the instructions sent to them by the Sun, commanding them to change their violent ways and to follow the heavenly children to a new land where they would build a great city. And so they left the deep jungle, and they

The throne-niche of the Inca in Coricancha, Cuzco, once studded with gems and covered with gold.

climbed the great mountains, following in the footsteps of
Manco Capac and Mama Ocllo as they ascended toward heaven.

Each morning, as his father the Sun came into the sky,
Manco Capac would summon all his might and thrust the golden
staff into the ground. But the land was so sterile that the staff
remained in full view, hardly sinking into the soil. Then, at last,
when the pilgrims had almost reached the top of the world
where the air is very thin and the clouds gather around the
snowy peaks, Manco Capac shouted with joy, for when he threw
the golden staff to the ground, it vanished into the fertile earth,
signifying that he and his followers had finally reached their
promised land.

Now Manco Capac raised his eyes and with deep humility
asked the Sun to favor him, providing the vision which would
allow the barbarians of the earth to build the greatest of all
cities, where the children of Manco Capac and his sister would
rule many generations of a great nation. Then Manco Capac
watched the birds as they swept through the sky, and he observed the figures made by the stars in the night . . . awaiting
the good omen which he sought as a sign to begin to build a city.
At last, all the indications were right, and in the name of the Sun
and of the other gods, he placed a stone upon the ground, and
this stone became the foundation of a new city.

The first dwelling had walls of earth and a roof of straw,
and it was called *Coricancha* — The Place of Gold. The people
gasped in amazement when they saw the house that Manco Capac
and Mama Ocllo had built, and they rejoiced and drew close to
the heavenly twins, honoring them. And so it was that Manco
Capac founded the city of Cuzco and built the first humble
structure that would eventually become the celebrated Temple
of the Sun, where the gods were worshipped and where Manco
Capac became a great king and the father of the long line of
rulers of the Andes.

Then the Sun gave these commandments to Manco Capac
and Mama Ocllo: "When you have reduced these people to our
service, then you shall keep them in reason and in justice with
devotion, tenderness, and fairness, being at all time their loving
father and mother, as I, the Sun, am father and mother of all
creatures. For I look to the well-being of the world, since it is I
who give people my light by which they see and by which they
warm themselves; which makes their pastures thrive, their fruit
trees to bear abundantly and their beasts to multiply. I am the
light of the world. I bring rain and fair weather in their season,

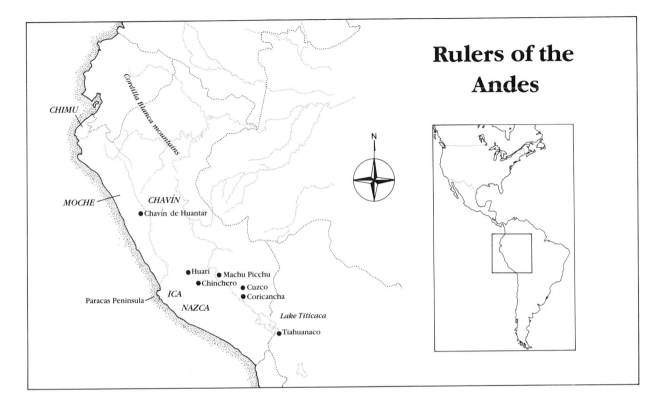

and each day I come into the sky and look down upon the earth in order to know the needs of the world to succor and to provide for my children as father and mother. And so, Manco Capac and Mama Ocllo, my children, I name you lords of all races whom you thus benefit with my instructions and with the blessings of the sky."

Having declared his will, the Sun took leave of his children. And Manco Capac stood in the midst of the people and said: "It is in this valley that Our Father the Sun commands us to make our abode in accordance with his will. Therefore, Queen and sister, it behooves each of us to do his wishes and bring the people of the earth to him in order to instruct them and to care for them as our Father the Sun has commanded."

From the height of the mountain where Coricancha arose from its humble foundations, the King and Queen went, each in a different direction, to gather together all the people of the land. Manco Capac went to the north, and Mama Ocllo journeyed southward. To all the people they came upon in the barren regions they told how their Father the Sun had sent them from the sky to be lords and benefactors of a new nation. The people bowed, seeing that in their words and demeanor and in their glistening robes Manco Capac and Mama Ocllo showed themselves to be truly the children of the Sun. And thus the word passed from one person to another until great throngs assembled before them, wanting to follow wherever the children of the Sun might lead them.

Seeing the great number who flocked to them, Manco Capac ordered some of the people to gather food from the fields lest hunger disperse them, and Mama Ocllo instructed workmen to build dwellings for each family, that no person be without shelter. It was in this fashion that the children of the Sun and their followers began to build their imperial city, dividing it into two parts which they called Haman Cuzco ("Upper Cuzco") and Hurin Cuzco ("Lower Cuzco").

As the great city grew, Manco Capac sat upon a throne and was called *Inca* — ruler — and he taught the male Indians the duties of men: how to break and cultivate the rich soil, how to sow grain and vegetables. He taught them how to make plows, instructed them in the digging of irrigation channels from the streams which flow through the valley of Cuzco. Queen Mama Ocllo gave the women of Cuzco their womanly offices, sewing and weaving cotton and wool, making garments and caring for children.

"How many years ago the Sun Our Father sent these his first children, I cannot tell you exactly," the Indian chronicler Garcilaso de la Vega ("el Inca") wrote. "It was so long ago that it was not possible to retain the memory: we believe it was more than four hundred years. Our Inca was called Manco Capac and our Mama Coya was called Ocllo Huaco. As I have already told you, they were brother and sister, children of the Sun and the Moon, our heavenly ancestors."

THUS THE GREATEST EMPIRE OF THE ANDES BEGAN. "We know, curiously enough, no more about the origins of the Incas than that which they tell us of themselves in their 'remembered' history and mythology . . . what part is history and what part is myth, we do not know." (Hagen) The folk historians of the Inca insist that their vast empire originated in the Cuzco Valley, where they gradually evolved from a brutish way of life into a remarkable civilization, centered in the capital city of Cuzco.

Today Coricancha is the most fabled ruin of the Incaic capital. An eyewitness description, written in 1551 by Pedro de Cieza de León, expressed the astonishment which the ceremo-

Tamboymachay, grand Inca ruins near Cuzco.

nial structure aroused in all the Spaniards who saw the Temple of the Sun (as it is now called) before it was buried alive under the Santo Domingo Church: "There is a garden in which the earth was of pieces of fine gold, and it was sown with corn of gold, stalks as well as leaves and ears ... more than twenty gold sheep [probably llamas mistaken for sheep by the early padres], with their lambs, and the shepherds who guard them, their staffs and slings, were all made of this precious metal. There were many huge jars of gold and silver and emeralds [probably turquoise], vessels, bowls, and all manner of vases, all of the finest gold. On the very walls were sculptured other great things of gold. All around us there was nothing but gold. It was, in fact, one of the richest temples anywhere in the world!"

Coricancha was the brilliant architectural center of the Inca Empire, a vast and utterly remarkable society that rose and fell in a span of less than four hundred years. Manco Capac, the first and most fabled of a line of thirteen hereditary rulers, founded the Inca dynasty at Cuzco in about A.D. 1200. During the brief life of the empire, Coricancha was built, the most splendid edifice constructed by the Inca, who were renowned for the brilliance, invention, and beauty of their structures. The Temple of the Sun (Coricancha) served as the model for similar ceremonial buildings throughout the domain — *Tahuantin-suyo* — "Land of the Four Quarters," as the empire was known to its own people. Coricancha, both in legend and in historical reality, was the geographical center and the political and religious heart of Tahuantinsuyo, the mythic navel and the legendary foundation upon which Manco Capac built Cuzco and his empire. About three centuries later, in 1532, with the tragic assassination of Inca Atahualpa, the Spanish conquistadores under Pizarro brought the Inca world to a disastrous end.

When Cuzco was being divided up among its Spanish invaders, Juan Pizarro, a relative of the conqueror, was given the Temple of the Sun, which he ceded to the Dominican Order. During the Inca revolt under Manco — an Indian puppet-ruler who refused to be dominated by his Spanish overlords — Coricancha was sacked and burned. Little of the original structure survived this siege of April 1536. Soon after, the Dominicans began to erect the Church of Santo Domingo on the Incaic foundations. The glory of Coricancha became a vague memory of splendor lost forever under the imposing European church.

Two cultures: Santo Domingo Church rests upon the famous parabolic foundation of Coricancha, Cuzco.

Then on March 31, 1650, the most devastating event in the three centuries of Spanish rule very nearly shook the consecrated Colonial edifice from its pre-Columbian superstructure. Sixteen hundred earthquakes shook Cuzco during the early months of 1650, and by the end of March, the only major buildings that remained standing in Cuzco were two of its churches and its cathedral, which was still under construction. The survival of the Church of Santo Domingo, built on the foundations of the most sacred of Inca temples, was looked upon by the padres as a victorious sign from heaven.

Three hundred years later, the message from on high changed abruptly. In May of 1950, another violent quake shook Cuzco. As American writer Miriam Beltran has pointed out: "The 1950 quake seemed an attempt by nature to obliterate colonial Cuzco." Towers twisted and toppled; façades and domes cracked and slipped into empty space; roofs and balconies collapsed. From the dust and debris Incaic Cuzco — massive and low to the ground — withstood the trembling of the earth, emerging shaken but victorious. UNESCO sent a technical team to assist in the painstaking reconstruction of the ancient capital of the Inca Empire. And in 1960, with the cooperation of the Peruvian government, UNESCO's experts undertook a ten-year comprehensive program for restoration of both the Incaic and Colonial structures of the region. Gradually the wreckage was cleared and the glorious city of the remote past arose once again.

Today we may reach Coricancha by taking a short stroll down Loreto Street, about ten minutes from the Plaza de Armas, which is the modern center of Cuzco. As we walk, we pass a broad expanse of meticulously constructed walls — the exterior of the Acllahuasi — "House of the Chosen Women," a sanctuary for virgins in pre-Columbian times and today part of the cloister of Santa Catalina Church. Originally Acllahuasi was a spacious enclosure, reaching from the Plaza de Armas halfway to Coricancha itself. As many as one thousand women once resided here, among the gardens, dormitories, and work quarters. Some of these women were trained as domestic servants for the royal household, while others were designated as prospective imperial brides. Still others, called "Virgins of the Sun," were dedicated to the Great Sun deity, and were treated with reverence, doing no work of any kind. Even the Inca himself was not allowed to look upon the Virgins of the Sun.

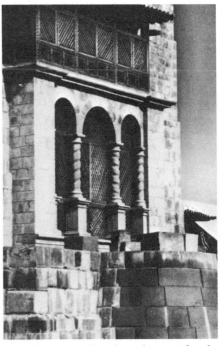

Santo Domingo Church — the west façade showing the famed curving wall of the former Inca Coricancha ("Temple of the Sun"), Cuzco, Peru.

The semiparabolic wall of the Inca temple Coricancha, Cuzco.

As we continue along our way, about a block beyond Aclla-huasi, we encounter the rear view of the Church of Santo Domingo. Here we see a remarkable sight: just below the baroque apse of the church a retaining wall of brilliantly fashioned stones curves gracefully beneath its immense Colonial burden. This is our first glimpse of ancient Coricancha: a semiparabolic wall from the original Incaic structure which now serves as the church's foundation. This cultural layer cake is a constant experience in Hispanic America, but at Coricancha its ethnic and political impact is overwhelming. The sight of this duplicity of cultures asserts with poetic impact the fact that history will not be silenced. From the distance come the ancient voices. From the ground rise the magnificent ruins of an unending past.

Though called the Temple of the Sun by the Spanish invaders, the precise translation of Coricancha is "Golden Enclosure," insofar as this was not a temple to the Sun alone, but a place also to worship the Moon and the Stars, Thunder and Lightning, and the Rainbow. In fact, Coricancha was a temple dedicated to all the deities of the Incas.

Originally the temple rose from the terraced ridge between two small rivers named Huatanay and Tullumayo. It faced the small plaza which is still called by its native name, Intipampa — "Square of the Sun." At the height of the Inca Empire, people did not dare enter this sacred place without first removing their sandals and covering their heads. The impact of the Temple of the Sun must have been overwhelming: it is traditionally believed to have been entirely paneled in gold sheathing, some of which was reportedly removed for the ransom of Atahualpa, whom the conquistadores held prisoner before murdering him — even after his full, unbelievably rich ransom had been paid by his devoted subjects. Three Spanish soldiers, on their visit to Cuzco to supervise the collection of this ransom, are said to have stripped large gold sheets from the walls of Coricancha. Today the gold is gone, but what remains is perhaps equally awesome: the remarkable masonry of the Incaic architects and artisans.

As we enter the cloister of what is now the monastery of Santo Domingo, we stand where the grand courtyard of Coricancha was originally located. In the center of this space, there was once a stone fountain carved from a single block of stone and entirely plated with gold. In this fountain was kept the corn potion used in rituals. The history of this ceremonial place rings out from the writing of Pedro Sarmiento de Gamboa's *Historia indica* (1572): "Embellishing the city of Cuzco with buildings and streets and many wonderful things, the ruler Pachacuti Inca Yupanqui told us that from the time of Manco Capac none of his Inca successors had enhanced Coricancha. Therefore he decided that he would undertake a glorious renovation of the building and of its famous oracle, to stun ignorant men and entice them to follow him meekly when he set out with his armies to conquer all the land of the four quarters of the world. This great work of renovating Coricancha he began. And to this purpose, he had the mummies of the seven deceased Incas, from Manco Capac to Yaguar Huaca, disinterred; and all of them were laid out in Coricancha. He had these mummies adorned in gold; he had masks of gold put upon their faces; also discs, bracelets, scepters, called *yauris* or *chambis*, as well as other precious objects of gold. Then he ordered feasting and he presented play-acting that depicted the lives of the great rulers. The feasting, called *purucaya*, went on for more than four months. And great sacrifices were also offered up to each Inca's mummy at the end of the ritual-plays. So it was that ruler Pachacuti Inca Yupanqui imbued his predecessors with such awesomeness that they became gods, being adored by every person who came to look upon them where they sat in state. The mummies were held in great veneration, remaining thus on display until the coming of the Spaniards to this land of Peru."

Writing at a later date, Garcilaso de la Vega ("el Inca") recalled many vivid details about the temple: "The roof of wood was very high, allowing air to circulate. The material covering the roof was straw because tile-making was then unknown. The four walls of the temple were coated from ceiling to floor with plates and stripes of gold. On what we would call the main altar stood the likeness of the Sun, fashioned from a sheet of gold that had double the thickness of the metal that lined the walls. On either side of the Sun's image were arranged the corpses of deceased kings, in order according to their succession as sons of the Sun. They seemed to be quite alive, so accomplished was the method of embalming that no one now remembers. These mummies occupied chairs of gold. Past the temple stood a cloister with four facades, one of these belonging to the temple itself. All around the cloister, above the walls, ran a frieze . . . a gold sheet more than a yard in width crowning the whole. Off from the cloister were five large square cubicles, none of them interconnecting, and each one was covered over in a pyramidal pattern. They made up three walls of the cloister. One of these cubicles was dedicated to the worship of the Moon, wife of the Sun. The doors and the entire interior of this room were lined with sheets of silver; and by the pallid glimmer of this metal it was understood that this was the proper dwelling for the Moon, whose image was also found there — a disc like the Sun, but of silver, sketched with the face of a woman. To either side of the image of the Moon were arranged, in order of their succession, the cadavers of deceased queens. Other cubicles were dedicated to the planet Venus, known as *Chasca*, which is the word used to describe persons with long, curly hair. Another room was dedicated to *Illapa*, the personification of Heat-Lightning, Thunder, and the Rainbow."

As we have seen, the architectural detail of Coricancha was lost in the centuries — until suddenly in May of 1950 an earthquake shook loose four-fifths of Cuzco's buildings, shattering the modern layers of the city and laying open the ancient terrain. In that horrendous quake Coricancha was set free from the Dominican overlay that had buried it. This destruction of Santo Domingo was so complete that, for a while, it was hoped that the church would be entirely eliminated, so Coricancha might be fully restored to its past glories. But a bitter battle ensued between historians, church officials, archaeologists, and politicians. It was argued that there was no valid hope of reconstructing Coricancha exactly as the Incas had left it in 1533. In that year, the Incas themselves had destroyed the temple during a revolt against the Spaniards. There are no extant plans for the building, not even an amateur sketch by one of the conquistadores. For a time, the authorities maintained a curious compromise between pre-Columbian and Colonial architecture: a combination of the Incaic and the Dominican structures, side by side. But as the restoration proceeded, through the 1950s and 1960s, a trend became gradually visible: more and more of Coricancha emerged as the church surrendered to the picks of the workmen. Today the compromise is an unsettling juxtaposition of two utterly different cultures.

Moving clockwise from the central cloister, we walk along the east side of the quadrangle, where there are the remains of two rectangular rooms, originally identical, separated by a "ceremonial patio." The first of these two rooms is not complete: its north wall was knocked down in order to enlarge the reception hall of the Dominican's structure. In the three remaining walls there are the handsome trapezoidal niches so characteristic of Incaic architecture. One of these recesses opens onto the connecting alcove. The second room is almost complete; the back wall now forms part of the enclosure wall facing Ahuacpinta Street. The plaster that was used to cover the south wall in Colonial times has now been removed. The exposed stonework of the Inca artisans is remarkable for its balance, technique, and line.

On the west side of the cloister, we see a long wall of marvelous Incaic stonework. In this wall is a large niche: shallow, carved, and channeled: backed on the inside of the same wall by a duplicate niche. Both of these niches are believed to have served as thrones or seats for the great Inca. Cieza de León wrote a description of them in 1551: "There were two seats in that wall, which the Sun struck as it rose, and the masonry interior of the niche was cleverly pierced, and many precious stones and emeralds were set in the holes. In these seats the kings of the Inca sat, and if anyone else did so, the punishment was death."

The long-standing efforts fully to restore Coricancha have moved forward very slowly because of religious friction. Bit by bit, the church has nonetheless given way to its predecessor. An arched doorway cut into the original Incaic walls in Colonial times (as an entrance into the Dominican capitulary hall) has now been obliterated. Today, upon entering through one of the two elegant portals, we find ourselves in the best-preserved and most-restored rooms of Coricancha.

Other remarkable Incaic features are discovered as we continue northward toward the remains of the church: a door with a double-jambed lintel in the purest Incaic manner, and next to the door are the remains of yet another room.

There is still considerable dispute about the location of the main shrine, which was dedicated to the Sun. Historians speculate that it is now buried beneath the remains of the church, a notion supported by the tradition among early missionaries to build their churches directly on top of the sanctuaries of the gods they deposed. In oral tradition, there are many stories about the shrine of the Sun. It is told that in this fabled chamber was suspended a brilliant huge disc of finest gold. The whereabouts of this great disc is unknown, and has intrigued treasure hunters for centuries. Some experts suspect that the Sun disc fell into the hands of the conquistadores. Others claim that it was successfully hidden from the invaders and remains still concealed somewhere, lost to memory, waiting for someone to uncover its magnificence.

It was here, in this shrine of the Sun, its walls covered with gold and gems, that the Incas kept the mummies of their royal dynasty. This chamber, buried somewhere beneath the broken structure of the Church of Santo Domingo, was the holy of holies of the Inca world. One day we may yet discover its location.

Finally, past the sacristy, we arrive at last at the most celebrated aspect of the construction of Coricancha — the famous semiparabolic wall. Prior to the earthquake of 1950, this wall could be viewed only from the exterior of the church. It served as apsidal base for Santo Domingo. On it rested structures of the Colonial period: three small arches, supported by twisted columns and surmounted by a latticed balcony. The earthquake of 1950 freed the Incaic wall from its Colonial burden, and now we may truly marvel at its engineering and artistic achievements. Its original use is unknown. Excavation eventually revealed a thick fill of rubble and earth between the wall and the apse. The fill has been removed, and as a result, it is now possible to examine the inside of the curved wall, with its remarkably surfaced and fitted stones.

Each day some new aspect of Coricancha becomes visible. What this progressive restoration of the holy site of the Inca affirms is the brilliance of the workmanship of its architects and masons. The care with which the stones were shaped and placed provides a glimpse into the legacy of the Incas, which has outlasted time, conquest, earthquakes, and the domination of the culture which unsuccessfully attempted to annihilate the pre-Columbian vision of the Incas, here in their capital city at the top of the world — in Cuzco.

THE INCAS WERE THE ROMANS of pre-Columbian America. Cuzco was their Rome. From this wondrous city, they planned and achieved the domination of an empire larger than anything that had come before it in South America — stretching from the modern Ecuador-Colombia frontier to the Rio Maule in southern Chile; bounded on the east by the Amazon jungles, and on the west by the Pacific Ocean. But, like the Romans, the Incas created almost nothing that was truly new. "Both these warrior tribes excelled as soldiers, as engineers, and as administrators, and both are known more for practical achievement than artistic expression. The Romans derived much of their cultural life from Greek and even Egyptian antecedents, and the Incas likewise borrowed many of the refinements of their society from earlier civilizations." (Hemming) Even their language, which

Inca wall construction: Cuzco, fourteenth to fifteenth centuries A.D.

they imposed upon every tribe they conquered as a means of unifying their domain, seems to have been appropriated from another, more ancient culture that originated in the district of Ancash in northern Peru. In fact, it has been said that the only true invention of the Incas was the trapezoidal doorway, which dominates their excellent architecture. Yet the Incas possessed great genius — the same genius which formed and maintained the Roman world — a capacity for organization and administration in war and in peace.

It is generally agreed that the empire began as a loose federation of city-states, such as Machu Picchu, Chinchero, Pisac, and Ollantaytambo. Gradually, it seems, Cuzco gained ascendancy, first by demanding tribute from its neighbors, and ultimately by absorbing them. As military expansion relentlessly took the Incas into regions occupied by other tribes, they imposed their language, their social structures, their religion, and their authority. Like the Romans, they built extensive roads; they constructed armories which constantly stood as symbols of conquest. They built depots for food and supplies. They devised methods of rapid communication over their vast domain. And gradually they evolved a social system so complex and encompassing upon groups and individuals that it has often been described as the nearest things to true communism and absolute totalitarianism in world history.

At the height of the Inca Empire, Cuzco was the heart of Tahuantinsuyo — the Four Quarters of the Earth; with its center located in the main plaza of the city. To the north lay the Chinchasuyo (northern Peru and Ecuador), west lay the Condesuyo (south-central coastal regions), south lay the Collasuyo (the altiplano of southern Peru and Bolivia), and east lay the Antisuyo (the unconquered Amazon basin). It was from the name of the inhabitants of this tropical region — "Antis" — that we derive the Spanish word *Andes.*

The geography of the Andean nations is unlike any other place in the world. On the Pacific coast is a vast desert almost without rainfall. Today, as in ancient times, the only inhabitants of this arid region are clustered around scattered oases nourished by feeble rivers that trickle down from the Andes. Beyond the coastal desert is a succession of barren hills that gradually rise higher and higher, until they become snowbound peaks, often twenty thousand feet high. Hidden among the mountain ranges are many fertile valleys, tropical and abundant in rain and foliage.

Sacsahuamán, the Inca fortress of Cuzco.

By contrast, on the eastern slopes of the Andes, the land descends steeply into the immense rain forests of the Amazon basin. Rivers are choked with the runoff of melting snow from the peaks. The cascades plunge in torrents of white water through rapids and waterfalls, eventually settling into wide, brown, sluggish rivers that wind through the jungle on their course to the Atlantic Ocean, some two thousand miles distant. Many scholars believe that the great succession of Andean civilizations, culminating with the Inca Empire, began here, in the inhospitable tropics. Such a notion seemed utterly unlikely until archaeologist Donald W. Lathrap placed the origin of refined Indian cultures in the Amazon basin rather than the Andean highlands. Now we may have to jettison the prejudice of earlier scholars, who stated as recently as 1965 that "little of artistic importance is known from the vast territory of Brazil; much of the area consists of lowland tropical forest which proved unsuitable for the development of high aboriginal civilizations, and those parts of the east which might be expected to be more favorable were remote and difficult of access from the main centers." In striking disagreement, Lathrap wrote in 1975: "All available evidence clearly indicates that [the origin of pottery] was initially a lowland Tropical Forest development spreading from the west Amazon Basin up the eastern slope of the Andes." It is noteworthy that the great majority of Latin American archaeologists are in agreement with Lathrap: the founders of South American civilization were people of the tropics (much like their Olmec and Maya counterparts in Mesoamerica), who evolved pottery, textiles, metallurgy, and architecture in the jungles, and only gradually carried their remarkable achievements up the eastern slopes and created their triumphant cities in the high Andes.

When Francisco Pizarro invaded Peru in 1532, he and his band of conquistadores encountered the remarkable culmination of Andean civilization: the intricately organized Inca Empire, extending twenty-five hundred miles from Colombia to Chile. These Spanish militarists were deeply impressed by the splendor of the Incaic world. They were also confounded by the numerous ruins they found. The hills were often crested with the rubble of ancient battlements, and in the dry ravines were the remains of villages — roofless adobe and stone dwellings unoccupied for a thousand years. In the intense atmosphere and thin air of the Bolivian highlands the Spaniards discovered great stone sanctuaries and fortifications built by unknown hands, enigmas even to the keepers of history among the educated Inca. "All they could say was that these structures had been created by ancient people or perhaps by giants or gods." (Leonard) The Inca had no written language, and their history was kept orally. They were newcomers to the Andes, for their civilization had achieved real importance and domination only a century before the arrival of the Spanish conquistadores. The Inca oral traditions recounted nothing about the ancient history of the lands they occupied. The folk history of older peoples had been altered, lost, or appropriated by the Incas as part of their political efforts to unify their domain in language and tradition, eradicate all memory of history or achievements but their own.

Only slowly, and essentially during the last century, have specialists begun to piece together the long saga of the pre-Inca world. Apparently the first people to inhabit the Andes were Paleo-Indians ... hunting-foraging peoples who had migrated across the Isthmus of Panama from North America at least fifteen thousand years ago. Their arrival in South America predated the invention of agriculture as well as every other form of post-Paleolithic technology. They were a people almost indistinct from the nomads of the dawn, the Asian hunters who were the first humans to enter the Americas by way of the Bering Strait perhaps some forty-five thousand years ago. These earliest of Andean settlers have left only the most subtle traces of their lives, and we still have no understanding of the arduous process by which their descendants eventually produced some of the most complex societies of the world.

"Fortunately, Peru is rich in archaeological treasures, and there is plenty of material from which to draw conclusions," John Hemming has noted. The aridity of the Peruvian coastal desert has made it an ideal environment for the preservation of objects and materials that could not have survived in the tropics. There are, however, rivers and some fertile oases on the coastal desert. And the sea provides an abundance of fish. The climate is hospitable and warm. "In short, a perfect place for [primal] human beings — and a perfect place for preserving the archaeological artifacts they left behind."

What they left is a trove of crude implements like flake choppers, often found in caves alongside the skeletal remains of an extinct species of sloth and deer. "Archaeological excavations in this century have revealed how early humans progressed in Peru. The most ancient sites, along the coast, are often mere shell middens — great mounds of shells from the mussels and crustaceans eaten by [early] communities. These middens sometimes contained sharpened stone tools and hunting weapons as well. From about 5000 B.C. there is clear evidence of the cultivation of gourds, beans, and cotton, and mortars can be found in village refuse sites — mortars being sure archaeological evidence of food preparation. In succeeding millennia we see the introduction of fishing nets, fish hooks made of shell, bone scrapers, beads, and organized burial sites with cloth mats and shrouds." (Hemming)

Three major developments become evident in the second millennium B.C. — major advances that were either invented locally or were introduced to the desert coastal region by other Andean peoples. For the first time we find the production of pottery in Peru (though Lathrap has established that pottery was invented in the Ecuadorian Amazon and subsequently diffused over a wide region). Maize was cultivated, and rudimentary architecture was practiced in scattered communities, where most of the people now lived in shelters. Then about 900 B.C. a most remarkable leap in culture occurred in an obscure mountain valley in the high Cordillera Blanca, north of present-day Lima. Some unknown Peruvian tribe constructed a temple and a ceremonial center of astounding complexity. The artistic style and the cult that produced it are known today as *Chavin* after the modern name of the place where the temple is located: Chavin de Huantar. "None of the region's preceding cultures had given any indication that early Peruvians were capable of building, designing, and decorating with the advanced skills demonstrated at Chavin: yet, this great temple, far from any town, modern or ancient, was clearly created by a well-organized society with elaborate religious and social structures." (Hemming)

It has been realized for several decades that the Chavin style was the result of a religious cult, and that the diffusion of the style was directly related to the spread of the cult, which apparently displaced older local religions. "We cannot yet identify the exact place of origin of the Chavin cult. . . . The principal problem is to locate the precise place where these various patterns were fused together into the Chavin style, and this we cannot yet do." (Lanning)

Chavin iconography and style can be found all along the northern Peruvian coastal desert and as far inland as the remote highlands of the Andes. Clearly the Chavin cult was inordinately influential during its brief period of domination. It was the first great civilization of the region. The Native Peruvian archaeologist Julio Tello, like Lathrap after him, believed that the Chavin cult — with its characteristic imagery of tropical flora and fauna — originated in the Amazon basin, and then spread up the slopes of the Andes, westward from the jungle to the Pacific Ocean. Recently, a group of Mexican scholars have countered that view by suggesting that the Chavin cult might have some relationship to the early Olmec culture of Veracruz, pointing out that the cultivation of maize reached the Andes from Mexico, via Central America, at about the same time that the Chavin cult was beginning to develop in Peru.

John Hemming's summation puts the debate in focus: "Whatever their origin, the builders of Chavin can fairly be said to have made a dramatic cultural advance. They progressed far beyond the tribal societies of their South American contemporaries, and in so doing they laid the foundation for the succession of advanced civilizations that inhabited [pre-Columbian] Peru."

Though the Chavin culture is no longer thought to have been insular or singular, it is still regarded as a seminal and unifying force in Andean cultural history. At Chavin de Huantar, in a valley 10,200 feet above the sea, located on the high eastern slopes of the Andes, stands the immense stone structure called the *Castillo:* a three-story-high network of small chambers and corridors, connected by stairways and ramps. In one of the galleries a stone figure still stands: a man-jaguar with fangs and downturned lips. Its image is curiously familiar, for a similar countenance is found among the deities of the Olmec people, of the Gulf of Mexico. The Chavin, however, have left a more elaborate profile of their achievements than the equally mysterious Olmec. Carved stone and shell objects, pottery of high quality, masonry architecture, and highly refined goldwork attest to a center of magnificent advancement at the height of Chavin culture. Peru's period of Chavin unification ended for unknown reasons about 500 B.C. But this decline did not signal the onset of a Dark Age. On the contrary, there now evolved numerous separate cultures that flourished immediately after the fall of the Chavin centers. Archaeological evidence indicates that these "new" cultures did not suddenly spring from the ruins of the Chavin cult. Apparently many societies had thrived under Chavin domination, but only began to emerge as distinctive social entities with the demise of the remarkably strong and widespread influence of the Chavin overlords.

"Silk" of the Andes: the remarkable textile of the Paracas culture.

For example, burial grounds dating from two thousand years ago have been discovered in an area of the coastal desert which has acquired a great deal of archaeological preeminence: the arid Paracas Peninsula in southern Peru. We call the people of this society *Paracans*, though — as is the case with all the tribes of pre-Incaic history — we do not know what they called themselves. This we do know: they were among the most aesthetically refined people of South America. They produced textiles of brilliant skill. Numerous examples of their mortuary weavings have survived in excellent condition because of the extremely arid condition of the region. The funeral rites of the Paracas culture were elaborate, suggesting the existence of a complex social hierarchy, insofar as grave offerings varied greatly in quality, apparently in relation to the social position of the deceased. The iconography of textiles and pottery draws from Chavin sources, but is also uniquely inventive. Zoomorphic figures (part animal, part human) are prevalent; and the Paracans also achieve a highly elaborate scheme of abstract designs. What these images mean, what language the people spoke, what gods they believed in . . . every aspect of their life and times is lost to us. They came into history and then, mysteriously, they began to slip out of sight.

Over the centuries the Paracas culture either merged with or was superseded by another culture: the Nazca, centered in the Ica and Nazca valleys about one hundred miles south of the Paracas Peninsula.

Again, we know almost nothing about the people we call Nazca. An outstanding feature of their culture is the so-called Lines, which are so massive that they are visible only from the air. These Nazca Lines are situated on the desert plain between the modern cities of Palpa and Nazca. The designs are astonishingly varied. There are at least eighteen kinds of birds alone, and about twelve other animal forms: monkey, spider, whale, dog, and others. There are, however, no human or humanoid forms on the plain itself. The only human figures were produced on the slopes of the surrounding hills. In addition, there are more than one hundred complex geometric designs, consisting of straight lines, parallels, triangles, trapezoids — all executed with the utmost precision. The dimensions of these designs are highly varied: the straight lines, for instance, measure from about a mile to as much as three miles in length. The monkey figure is about twenty-five feet long, while the spider is about ten feet long. There is one bird with extended wings measuring about forty feet across!

The desert plain of Nazca is not sandy, for the surface is composed of iron oxide of a light brown color. If this topsoil is removed, we discover a contrasting, yellowish subsoil. It is this contrast between the color of the surface and that of the subsoil that enables the designs to be seen. The survival of the Nazca Lines some thousand years after they were made has been made

A painted vessel of clay from the Nazca culture.

possible not only by the solidity of the terrain, but also by the fact that rain is exceptionally rare in the vicinity and has discouraged the encroachment of both farms and towns. The designs were apparently made by the Paracas/Nazca peoples who inhabited the valley between 300 B.C. and A.D. 900. No specific purpose has been attributed to the Lines, though they appear to be based on astronomical calculations.

The Nazca perpetuated the textile tradition of the Paracas culture without ever superseding its achievements. Where the Nazca did rise above their Paracan predecessors was in the production of ceramics: exquisite, polished pottery with as many as ten or eleven colors decorating a single vessel. A common and

The Moche culture of the Andes produced some of the most vivid naturalistic clay figurines.

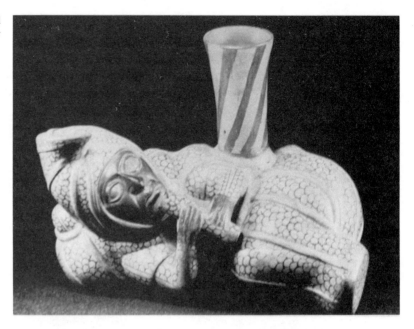

curious Nazca motif is a cat face, often depicted with flared whiskers. An elaborate succession of plumelike tongues normally extend from the mouth; the meaning of this is unknown to us. Also prevalent in Nazca pottery painting are trophy heads, apparently taken in battle, though there is no evidence that the Nazca were a particularly warlike or bloodthirsty people. The nagging truth is that we know almost nothing about them.

A central thrust of both the Paracas and Nazca cultures was a clear and pervasive influence from the Chavin cult. That same impact may also be seen in the material culture of yet another important Peruvian people, the Moche — also called *Mochica*. Living about five hundred miles north of the Nazca centers and contemporaneous with them, the Moche (whose name is derived from the Moche River near the present-day city of Trujillo) were an aggressive and pragmatic people. They produced a grand but also a commonsensical form of genre art unparalleled in the Americas. Between 250 B.C. and A.D. 750, they elaborated upon a naturalistic pottery style that produced some of the best sculptural forms in the history of world ceramics. Admired, perhaps excessively, for its naturalism and humanism (as if these Western qualities were universally admirable characteristics to be achieved by all cultures), the pottery of the Moche is our major source of history and ethnographic data about their lives:

detailed and exceptionally frank in its depiction of human relations (sexual and familial), dwellings, animals and husbandry, farming and vegetables, and even a wide variety of pathological deformities which abound in the sculptural art.

The Moche were accomplished architects. Near the Moche River are two vast ceremonial pyramids, now called, for no apparent reason, the Temple of the Sun and the Temple of the Moon. Constructed of adobe bricks, they tower sixty feet into the air.

Both the Moche and their distant neighbors, the Nazca, flourished on their arid coastline until about A.D. 600, when developments in the high Andes heralded a drastic change in the ethnography of Peru. At Tiahuanaco, twelve miles south of Lake Titicaca on the borders of modern Peru and Bolivia, a vast ceremonial center was gradually taking form, and its dominancy and power were awesome. Its importance is presumably based upon the rise of a new deity. The impact of this new religious cult was the first reoccurrence of a unifying sect since the demise of the jaguar god of Chavin times. The name of this new deity will never be known, but his image is familiar, carved upon a monolithic temple gateway at Tiahuanaco. His prevalent attributes are the head of a puma with tears streaming from his eyes. This new god and the rigid Tiahuanaco sculptural style are the images and symbols of a new religious imperialism, found as far north as Ecuador and deep within Bolivia and Chile to the south. The main centers of Tiahuanaco were built as early as A.D. 300, and by A.D. 600 the culture had expanded widely to the north, where a colony was established at the site of Wari (Huari). Despite many similarities, the Wari and Tiahuanaco were originally distinct and different cultures. It is probable that the Tiahuanacans themselves were not a single people, but a diverse group of Aymara Indians who enlarged upon a vital new cosmology, and then built the structures near Lake Titicaca, which are now enormous ruins, long abandoned and plundered for building materials for hundreds of years by successive inhabitants of the region.

At Wari, near present-day Ayacucho in Peru, a larger and entirely self-sufficient population grew into a vast city-center, which extended its domination northward. But eventually, between A.D. 600 and 1000, a convergence of Wari and Tiahuanaco styles occurred, and became so widespread that the Wari-Tiahuanaco amalgam assumed a pan-Peruvian character, temporarily eclipsing the impressive influences of all other local peoples. There is in this Wari-Tiahuanaco style a strong geometric, rigid influence from the Chavin prototype, though we do not understand the exact relationship between these two cultures.

Eventually the Nazca culture was obliterated by the Wari-Tiahuanaco dominancy. The warlike Moche in the north sank under the impact of the new Tiahuanacan "weeping god," and, after a period of utter silence and apparent transformation, the Moche reemerged as a new culture: the Chimu Kingdom. These restyled and resurrected Moche/Chimu people established one of the vast urban centers of ancient Peru at their splendid capital, Chan Chan, from A.D. 1000 to 1500. According to Chimu folk history, the lands of the Moche were invaded by strangers who came from the sea on large balsa rafts, sailing in from the north. These invaders were the followers of Taycanamo, the cultural hero of the Chimu people. With the help of Taycanamo, the Chimu assimilated the Moche and prevailed over the land. They built an enormous terraced fortress in the Fortaleza Valley as well as the capital city of Chan Chan — a remarkable group of structures, built of adobe brick or cast in great slabs of adobe molded with patterns of birds and mythic creatures, deities, and rainbows — very much in the manner of the iconography of Chimu textiles. All the walls were plastered and painted with bright friezes, which must have made these cities exceptionally dazzling at the height of their power.

Eventually, like all previous cultures of South America, the Chimu Kingdom vanished, but unlike the mysterious demise of its predecessors, we know what brought about the fall of the Chimu Kingdom: it was overwhelmed by the militaristic expansion of the Inca Empire. The Chimu king — called Chimu Capac by the Inca — was taken to the Navel of the World, the holy city of Cuzco, where he retained full honors in exchange for the capitulation of his kingdom.

But the entry into history of the Inca Empire does not signal the end of the remarkable civilizations that predated the Incaic ascendency. There is one more society that is important to our story.

The Ica civilization, A.D. 1000–1500, appears to have been the result of Nazca influences. The Ica were probably a smaller society than their Nazca forebears, for they did not have the population or the material means to support a wide-ranging socioeconomic domain. Although the Ica Valley was an important source of cultural influences, especially in ceramics, most of the population was distributed in small villages scattered throughout the valley. The best-known site, Ica Vieja, in the Tacaraca region and about three miles south of the modern city of Ica, consists of a complex of structures built on mounds. This site was occupied until the Incaic conquest, when it probably served as a regional administrative center for the new Inca overlords.

If the Ica lived to witness the invasion of the warriors of the Inca Empire, the people of Tiahuanaco did not survive long enough to see that devastating event. No one knows for certain when Tiahuanaco declined or why, but it is estimated that the culture vanished about A.D. 1000, though the religious cult at the center of Tiahuanacan culture may have survived in isolated communities until a far later date.

Whatever the fate of Tiahuanaco, its history as an expansionist and religio-political power in the Andes had no precedent. The domain of the Tiahuanacans was the first to include nearly all of geographical Peru, and the influence of this vast religious realm was not surpassed until a new tribe of militarists extended their influences far beyond the borders of Tiahuanaco. That culminating highland empire of South America was, of course, the Inca. Its power, however, was far more extensive geographically than historically, for it prevailed for even a shorter period than the Aztec domain to the north. At the very height of their powers, the worlds of both the Inca and the Aztec ended catastrophically with the invasion of the Spaniards.

AND SO WE FIND OURSELVES once again in the holy city of Cuzco, where Inca historians have told us the vast empire began, in a mythic time when their ancient forebears followed the commandments of the Great Sun god and built a temple called Coricancha at the place which is Navel of the World.

It is often a sense of destiny that compels people to found a city. They "have fallen on their knees when they came to a place where something within them came to rest; they have built a capital in a desert where it is not possible for a city to be; an emperor has *loved* a place of the earth and made it a great city." (Jenison)

Such a city is Cuzco.

It is nestled in a grassy valley about eleven thousand feet above the sea. Smoke from hundreds of fireplaces clouds the sky above the thatched dwellings of commoners. The year is A.D.

1500, a time when the regal heart of the city was still unconquered, glistening on a triangular slope between two small rivers that flow down from the precipitous mountains that
surround Cuzco on three sides. The rivers are canalized with
handsomely worked stone, and fine buildings rise from their
banks. Only five Europeans saw Cuzco before it was decimated,
and one of them, Pedro de Cieza de León, was awed by its beauty: "It was grand and stately and must have been founded by a
people of great intelligence. It has fine streets, except they are
so narrow that only horsemen in single file can pass through
them, and the houses are built of solid stone, beautifully fashioned and joined."

The Peruvian architects conceived Cuzco in the form of a
crouching puma, an American mountain lion whose "head" (according to the architectural plan) is represented by Sacsahuamán — a mighty fortress located on a cliff overlooking the regal
city. The zigzag configuration of the fortress ramparts is the architectonic representation of the puma's teeth: the weapons
which keep enemies at bay. The feline's massive body is envi-
sioned to lie between the two rivers of Cuzco, a place of temples and great palaces. The ceremonial square of Coricancha is
held to be the beating heart of the puma. Where the streams
join in a triangular district is known as *puma-chupan,* or "the
tail of the puma."

In the west is Cusiapata — "the Square of Entertainments,"
the plaza where the common people gather to celebrate their
festivals. In the east is the grander Aucaypata — "the Square of
Joy," the central plaza that is the civic center of Cuzco and from
which spread the twelve wards of the city, divided into four
districts — representing "The Four Quarters [the four cardinal
directions] of the World," which is the empire's proud name:
Tawantinsuyu. Thus Cuzco is a microcosm of the Inca Empire.
At its height, in 1500, it is crowded with people drawn from
every part of the realm, all dressed in their traditional costumes,
proudly individual in their tribal origins, while at the same time
strongly devoted to the realm that unified them. These are the
common people of pre-Columbian Cuzco. For them the day begins when their Father, the Sun, climbs into the sky. Their only
breakfast is a drink of *aka,* a slightly fermented thick beverage.
Then they go to the fields to work, for most of the inhabitants of
the empire are farmers. They are, as Victor von Hagen points
out, members of an earth cell, and each person is thereby a
"symbiont of a soil community" which, together with all the

other soil communities, constitute the essential foundation of the Incaic world.

Working the land is a divine undertaking for the farmers, a form of worship. For the Inca, "work that is not ceremonial lacks sense and meaning." As Harold Osborne observes, "Unlike modern society in which work is regarded as a necessary evil undertaken to secure a leisure which society is untrained to utilize, in Inca society work is regarded as an end in itself."

The midday meal brings together the extended family of children, mother, father, grandparents, and other relatives. The food is boiled or baked in ashes: corn, chili peppers, and herbs — a dish called *mote.* A specialty is *locro,* consisting of boiled llama meat dried in the sun and a powder called *chunu,* made from dehydrated potatoes. Other delicacies are popcorn, although plain corn is more common, and is ground into a paste and baked in hot coals like bread. A major source of meat is the small creatures that freely scamper about in the corners of the houses: guinea pigs, called *cui.*

Time stands still at the Indian market at Cuzco.

The meal is served on a cloth spread upon the ground, with the men crouched around the pots of food. The women sit outside the circle, their backs turned toward the men. All the family members help themselves to the food, using their fingers or drinking broth from ceramic vessels. Conversation is restrained but genial, although there is little exchange between the men and women.

The tropical evening comes quickly, and soon the door-flap is lowered and the people go inside and hover around their fires. Relaxing on animal skins, the young listen intently as the elders recite oft-told tales of gods and battles and ancestors. The women spin or grind corn. The men repair their farming tools.

The education of the young is an imitation of their parents in every act of life. "Parents have no life apart from their children: all acts of their daily life — eating, sleeping, working — the children take part in." Even "sexual acts are witnessed by the children." (Hagen) Thus at an early age the child is already a miniature adult.

At fourteen the boy puts on his breechclout and takes his permanent name, either that of an uncle or of his father, or perhaps, in some cases, that of an animal with which he feels a special kinship.

It is a very different matter for the son of a noble family. For him, reaching maturity involves a pilgrimage to the birthplace of the Inca state at Huanacauri, located far up the Cuzco Valley, and the sacrifice of llamas by priests who smear the beasts' blood upon the young man's face. Then he is adorned in the regalia of a warrior — shield, earplugs, and slingshot — and he makes his public vows of loyalty to his ruler.

Women celebrate the maturity of their daughters with a hair-combing ceremony and the giving of permanent names, derived from the stars and plants. Whereas men remain forever within the social class to which they are born, women, if they possess special talents in weaving or great beauty, can be selected as "Chosen Women" and sent to Acllahuasi — "House of the Chosen Women" — near Coricancha in Cuzco. There they serve the Sun god or become the wife of an official or the concubine of the Lord Inca himself.

Even death separated the rich from the poor. The peasant died as he had lived, communally. It was only the ranking families that were permitted the prestige of a ceremonial burial. "In

death the little man had to be content with the little gods."
(Hagen) He died as he was born, with the simplest of rituals.
The commoners of the Inca Empire believed in immortality; but
it was a physical immortality in which the dead body merely
achieved a different state, becoming "undead" and taking on the
influences of an unseen universal power.

This, then, was the life of the Indian — typical of the countless beings who formed the base of the pyramid which was the
Inca world. At the summit was the Inca himself.

As Wendell Bennett notes, the entire world of the Inca was
built upon a strict architectonic hierarchy: "at the base of the
pyramid was the *puric,* an able-bodied male worker. Ten workers were controlled by a straw boss; ten straw bosses had a
foreman; ten foremen in turn had a supervisor. . . . The hierarchy continued in this fashion to the chief of a tribe, reportedly
composed of ten thousand workers, to the governor of a province, to the ruler of one of the four quarters of the Inca empire,
and finally to the emperor, the Sapa Inca. . . ."

LOUIS XIV, THE SUN KING OF FRANCE, declared the divine
right of kings: *"L'état c'est moi."*

The Sun King of Peru, the Sapa Inca, did not have to make
such a claim. He owned all that existed — "all that lay under the
sun was his." The Sapa Inca was divine, "descended by direct
line from the Sun, the creator-god; and everything — the land,
the earth, the people, gold (the sweat of the Sun), silver (the
tears of the Moon) — belonged to him. He was absolute. He
was God. His empire was no theoretical theocracy, it was an
actual one." (Hagen)

There were no checks and balances, no courts of appeal.
The Lord Inca was a plenary ruler, limited only by ancient custom and a caution of revolt. With a gesture the Sapa Inca could
order the death of a great warrior or even a royal relative.

"I recall," said Pedro Pizarro, the cousin of the conquistador, "the Lord of Huaylas once asked the great Inca if he might
visit his estates. His request was granted, but the Inca gave him a
limited time in which to make the journey and return. The Lord
of Huaylas did not return on time, and when he came back he
brought a gift and arrived in the Inca's presence with great apprehension. The Lord of Huaylas began to tremble before the
Inca to such an extent that he was actually unable to remain
standing. . . ."

The power of the Sapa Inca was unlimited, and yet there is reason to admire the concern that most of the line of rulers felt toward the people. This principle of charity, however, was an essential attribute of the highly communal Inca Empire. "The Inca's position and his wealth and his power came from the people and their well-being. . . . The people and their organization and development within the framework laid down for them were the primary concern of the Inca. . . . The land was owned by the state, i.e., the Inca; the Indian, through his *ayllu,* which was a holding corporation, only had use of the land. Yet he owned his chattels, and while he could, theoretically, pile up personal luxury possessions, actually he did not. An Indian's orbit was restricted; he traveled on the royal roads at the Inca's pleasure; he paid his taxes by labor; even his leisure was ritualistically regimented. Some scholars believe that the Inca, the religion, the state, actually created work artificially as a device of good government to keep the people constantly employed. The Inca, then, demanded *all* from his subjects; in turn he protected them from want, maintained storehouses for prevention of famine, conserved animals and soil. Produce was fairly divided, roads were maintained with superb communications, and the Inca kept the peace within the realm. But it would be a misconception to term this welfare state either socialistic or communistic: the empire was not for the people, and equally was not the ideal; on the contrary, the state existed alone for the Inca." (Hagen)

The palaces built by the Sapa Incas were splendid structures. Amaru-cancha, "Court of the Snake," was built by the last Inca, Huayna Capac, and stood on the south side of the main plaza of Cuzco. Pizarro's secretary was astonished by its elegance: "the most important building in the city, built of ashlars and painted. It has a gateway of red, white and multicolored marble, and has other flat-roofed structures that are also most remarkable."

Opposite Amaru-cancha was Cassana, the palace of the Inca who was the greatest of the conquerors, Pachacuti. His residence had "an ornamental gateway inlaid with silver and flanked by two round towers built of fine masonry and roofed in skillfully laid thatch. The greatest glory of the Cassana palace was its vast baronial hall — a feature typical of Inca palaces. Many had large halls, some of them up to 200 yards long and 50 to 60 yards wide. They were unpartitioned and served as places of assembly for festivals and dances in inclement weather. The largest of these halls was that of Cassana, which could hold three thousand people. Indeed the very name Cassana means 'something to freeze' — because . . . its buildings were so large and splendid that anyone seeing them was 'frozen with wonderment.' " (Hemming)

The emotional impact of the royal sector of Cuzco was essential to the submission required by a totalitarian state, a realm in which the entire life-style of the people, commoner and aristocratic, was controlled by an unshakable authority. State officials even traveled among the villages to arrange marriages, at the same time that they drafted women for service as *mamaconas* or Chosen Women. Such officials also assessed quotas of tribute produce, and assigned military or labor service to adult men. The Inca social system achieved a rare combination of absolute hereditary monarchy with a totalitarian welfare state. "And despite all the controls it seems to have worked rather well." (Hemming)

The success of the Inca Empire was based on its ability to produce not only ample supplies for its religious leaders, armies, and ranking aristocrats at the court, but also vaster stores needed by the peasants. The responsibility of maintaining the welfare of the commoner was appointed to a wide variety of officials, including local chieftains who distributed food and cloth from the state storehouses. Cloth had a particular significance in the Andean world. More valued than gold or silver, cloth was used both as gifts and as objects of economic prestige — a symbol of wealth and a possession of great value, depending upon its quantity and quality.

Though even the peasantry valued cloth as a calibration of its modest social rank, food had a greater political value in a welfare state, and therefore it was a commodity of great concern to the government. The Native Peruvian chronicler Felipe Guaman Poma de Ayala wrote that in the district surrounding Lake Titicaca, the people used the frigid locality to freeze meat and produce for use during the harshest seasons. And even where the climate was tropical, maize, sweet potatoes, chili peppers, coca, and various other essential foods were stockpiled in storehouses called *qollqa*. Such great stocks of materials required a system of meticulous bookkeeping, and although the Incas did not have a written language they did devise a mnemonic system for recording numbers. This device is called a *quipu*, an elaborate arrangement of strings hung in a series upon a master cord. The strings are dyed a multitude of colors, and each string is knotted at points along its length — using knots of different styles and sizes. Together, the colors, the knots, and the location of the knots signified commodities, persons, or accounts, and various numbers and amounts. The secret of reading *quipus* has been entirely lost.

The taxation of the Inca consisted of labor levies as well as materials. The obligation of each agricultural community — each "earth cell" — was to provide not only produce but also a specified number of people to perform imperial service. Despite the fact that the Inca Empire was potentially an uncomfortable amalgam of recently subdued tribal states, officials understood the techniques of imperialism which enabled them to circumvent dissent. As a result, they managed to assume absolute authority without much resistance. This massive subjugation was greatly aided by the inclination of the Incas to use peaceful persuasions: to honor local chiefs and allow them a "panoply of authority" even though the actual power was usurped by Inca overlords. Food was made plentiful to all.

Civil regulations were balanced and remarkably fair, and a state of peace prevailed among tribes that had often fought bitter internal conflicts or struggled persistently to survive the aggression of their neighbors. The sons of subdued chieftains were taken to the court of Cuzco for indoctrination. There they remained as honored guests — though, in truth, they were hostages. The important idols revered by various conquered tribes were "kidnapped" and kept at Cuzco — ostensibly so they could be worshipped alongside Inca deities, but also as hostages, ensuring the good conduct of their communities.

If perchance there were civil disorders within a particular tribe, the Inca authorities had a ploy adopted by many colonialist governments. It was a method the Incas devised at the beginning of the sixteenth century, and involved the movement of loyal persons, called *mitmaes*, into areas of difficulty. When a particular tribe displayed resistance to the Inca rule, the dissidents were exchanged with the best members of another very loyal community.

Sometimes psychology and deviousness were not enough to retain the absolute authority of the empire. And revolts sometimes drew reckless suppression, as when Tupac Inca found it necessary to hurry to the southern territories during his campaign in central Peru in order to put down an uprising among the peoples of Lake Titicaca. The highly independent Cañari of southern Ecuador were subdued by Tupac Inca's successor, Huayna Capac. But they were a restive people, and eventually they rebelled against his famous son Atahualpa, who exterminated all the men of the tribe in a battle at *Yaguarcocha* — "The Lake of Blood."

The success of Inca imperialism was impressive. By the 1520s, Tawantinsuyu, the Inca Four Quarters of the World, was a vast realm, occupying most of the Pacific coast of South America. The Incas were now in total control of Ecuador, and the armies were battling as far north as Colombia, where they were vainly trying to subdue the provinces of Pasto and Popayán. Had they succeeded, they might have eventually overwhelmed the gold-rich tribes beyond the Magdalena and Cauca rivers of northern Colombia, extending their empire to the Caribbean.

The Inca Huayna Capac had a special affection for the northern region of his empire. He loved the graceful valleys of the Ecuadorean Andes, where he built the great cities of Quito and Tumibamba. So ardently did he favor Ecuador that he contemplated dividing his empire, and making Quito into the Cuzco of the north. For ten years Inca Huayna Capac lived in Tumibamba, deeply content in the ideal climate and among the peaceful people. But during these years at Tumibamba, a dreadful event occurred. In the spring of 1528 a messenger stumbled before the Inca with the news that a strange people had appeared upon the sea in ships. These incredible aliens, "as unexpected and unfamiliar as visitors from another planet," were the first Spaniards to be seen by the Incas.

A history later written by Pizarro's missionary, Padre Bernabé Cobo, recounts the events.

One day Huayna Capac was taking his ease at his palace when frightened messengers reported that strange people never before seen had landed on the beach at Tumbes.... They were white, they had beards ... and they traveled by sea in great wooden houses where they slept by night. By day, these monstrosities came ashore and by gestures they asked to see the lord of the land.

Huayna Capac was so stunned by these tales and he fell into such a state of melancholy and apprehension that he went alone into his chambers and did not come out until nearly night. Then other messengers sent by the governors on the coast arrived at court, and told how the strangers had entered royal houses and palaces and carried off all their treasures. These aliens were not even afraid to go into the cages where the Inca kept his collection of wild beasts. Huayna Capac, shaken and pale, called the messengers back to repeat what they had reported, as if he could not comprehend such incredible things. And the messengers whispered, "Lord, ... the lions and the wild beasts you have in your palaces crouched on the earth before the strangers and wagged their tails as if they were tame."

The Inca rose slowly from his stool and, shaking his cloak, said, "Get out! Get out, nobles and soothsayers. Don't disturb and trouble my realm and my authority!" And then, sitting upon another stool, he bade the emissaries to retell their tales once again, not quite believing what he heard.

Eventually the houses of the strangers sailed away, leaving two men at Tumbes. Huayna Capac anxiously ordered them to be brought before him, but apparently he never saw these strangers who wore silver jackets and bore sticks that spoke like thunder, for they disappeared from history.

Shortly after the appearance of the first Spanish galleons came yet another ominous stranger. The Inca tell the story of a black-cloaked figure who brought Huayna Capac a small box. When the Inca opened it, butterflies and moths flew out, spreading a terrible plague. The box was a myth, but the sickness was real, a terrible epidemic of smallpox, which killed thousands of Indians. Huayna Capac himself was stricken in his beloved Quito. Twice he named an heir and twice his priests performed the *calpa* ceremony — a divination ritual carried out by examining llama viscera. All the omens were bad, for crown prince Ninan Cuyuchi soon died of the plague. The second choice as an heir was Huascar, but the soothsayers foretold a dismal reign for him.

Now Huayna Capac lay dying. His priests arrived and prescribed that the great ruler be carried out into the light of his Father, the Sun. The treatment failed. Under the brilliant gaze of his celestial ancestor, Huayna Capac's life slowly ebbed.

Upon the death of Huayna Capac "so great was the weeping that birds fell stupefied from the sky," wrote Cieza de León, recounting the memories of Inca courtiers. The lamenting people lovingly embalmed his body and carried him to Cuzco for burial. In the city, more than four thousand souls were put to death in order that they might have the honor of being buried with the Inca.

Meanwhile the plague ravaged the empire. One chronicler noted that this terrible European disease, previously unknown in the Americas, was so contagious that some two hundred thousand people died of it. Among the dead were not only the

Inca himself and his eldest son and heir, but a large part of the royal court and government officials. The authority of the empire was in a state of chaos. Tawantinsuyu — the Four Quarters of the World — was without a leadership.

Then Huascar was officially enthroned as Sapa Inca.

But the empire's leadership was in dispute. One of Huascar's many half-brothers was Atahualpa, the ruler of Quito. He would not follow his father's mummy to Cuzco, and he would not accept his half-brother's ascendancy. He remained in Quito with a large body of soldiers and three generals renowned for their victories under Atahualpa in his campaigns during the Ecuadorean wars.

The new Inca demanded the presence of Atahualpa in Cuzco. In his place Atahualpa sent messengers with gifts. Enraged, Huascar cut off their noses and sent them back with an insulting present of women's clothes for Atahualpa. At the urging of his loyal generals — Quisquis, Chalcuchima, and Ruminahui — Atahualpa proclaimed himself King of Quito, a kingdom separate from the empire.

Eventually Huascar sent an army to capture Quito and to depose his insurgent brother. But the inexperienced conscripts were annihilated in a battle at Ambato in Ecuador, and Atahualpa had their skeletons piled in the plaza as a memorial of his victory. Cieza de León saw the battlefield about twenty years later, writing: "... from the amount of bones, even more must have died than the official count of fifteen to sixteen thousand men."

The victory at Ambato gave Atahualpa great confidence. Instead of remaining within his protected kingdom of Quito, he sent generals Quisquis and Chalcuchima to assault Cuzco and to capture Huascar. Their crack troops managed to fight their way south toward the throne of the Inca Empire, destroying army after army that Huascar sent against them. Tens of thousands of farmers who had somehow escaped the smallpox plague and who were conscripted as soldiers in this desperate struggle now died in battle.

Atahualpa waited for his brother to show himself, but at first Huascar would not personally lead his armies into battle. Then, when Atahualpa's forces finally reached the great gorge of Apurímac, Huascar was so indignant at his brother's victories that despite the cautious advice of his advisers, he led his soldiers across Apurímac bridges to the far side of the gorge. A chronicler has left a description of the event: "Huascar climbed the highest Apurímac crest and rejoiced to see men numerous as sand. Mountains, valleys, and plains were covered with gold and silver and plumage of a thousand colors.... The peoples of each province beat drums, played instruments, and sang war songs ... they say it was a thing to cause people to take leave of their senses."

One of the bloodiest conflicts in Inca history took place — a battle in which more than one hundred fifty thousand Indians perished. It was the final campaign of the civil War of the Brothers.

The first fighting seemed to favor Huascar's troops. By setting the grass ablaze, he burned or stampeded the major part of the forces of generals Quisquis and Chalcuchima. With a more experienced ruler, the War of the Brothers would have ended that day, but Huascar was naïve and vain. He made the fatal mistake of celebrating his victory.

As the victory fires burned and the songs of the drunken victors arose from their encampment, the generals of Quito gathered in the evening and laid plans for an ambush. In the morning, the troops of Huascar marched into the trap. The litter of the Inca toppled to the ground as bolas entangled the legs of the bearers. General Chalcuchima dragged Huascar from his throne. Then the general himself climbed upon the royal litter and had his men carry him into the enemy camp. The sight of their great ruler's throne occupied by an enemy must have utterly destroyed the spirit of the soldiers of Cuzco, for they turned and fled.

In triumph and with all roads to Cuzco undefended, Atahualpa's armies crossed the Apurímac bridges and marched on to the city that was the Navel of the World. In rage, Atahualpa entered Cuzco and confronted the aristocrats who had befriended his rival brother. He sacked the city. He decimated the palace of Tupa Inca and burned his mummy, for his adherents had been allies of Huascar. He ordered that all the *quipus* be burned, and then he executed all those capable of making and deciphering the *quipus*, for he wished to destroy even the history of those who had fought against him.

It is said that Huascar was dressed in the clothes of a woman and fed excrement. Then the dethroned Inca was forced to watch as his many concubines and courtiers were murdered. Of the royal household, only three of Atahualpa's half-brothers (all sons of Huayna Capac) managed to escape.

Now Atahualpa had the blood washed away, and in great splendor he ascended to the throne of the Four Quarters of the World. But his victory was darkened by a memory. On his way from Quito, he had consulted the oracle of Huamachuco, which predicted a bad end for him. Atahualpa was so embittered by this prophecy that he beheaded the oracle's guardian. Shortly thereafter, news came that the bearded strangers in their floating houses had reappeared on the shores of the empire.

When news of these strangers reached Cuzco, the defeated people gloated with vengeance, for they had prayed to their god Viracocha for deliverance from the wrath of Atahualpa. It was told that Viracocha had made the world and then set off across the ocean near Manta in Ecuador, walking across the great water. Now, the people believed that the news of the strangers signaled the return of their great deity in their time of need. The bearded strangers were surely the soldiers of Viracocha, sent to save the Inca Empire!

DURING THE CIVIL WAR, Pizarro's small band had been making its way down the northern coast of Peru. Only now did the Spanish conquistadores learn of the victory of General Quisquis and the battles that had raged among the factionalized Incas. Pizarro was an admirer of Hernán Cortés, and he understood how his fellow conquistador had used the rivalry of the tribes of Mexico to his great advantage. With even fewer troops than Cortés, he urgently needed to duplicate such tactics if he and his pathetically small band were to survive the multitudinous and brilliantly trained troops of the Inca, let alone wrest power from Atahualpa.

Pizarro cautiously advanced across Peru's northern coastal desert, encouraged when reinforcements finally arrived in two ships, one of them under the command of Hernando de Soto, a veteran of many American military expeditions. But Pizarro was still reluctant to face the thousands of warriors surrounding and protecting Cuzco. Finally, in September of 1532, he decided to march upon the heart of the Inca world. The venture was staggeringly immodest: for Pizarro had a total of only 168 men at his command — sixty-two on horseback and the remaining on foot. Pizarro himself was in his fifties, incapable of riding well and illiterate. A fanatically ambitious and determined soldier of fortune, he planned to overthrow an empire with forces smaller than those of Cortés.

The Spanish assault seemed clearly destined for failure. But it did not fail, for Atahualpa was flush with his victory over his rival brother, and he was amused by the little band of intruders who behaved like thieves as they crept around the edges of his great domain. Pizarro learned that the Inca ruler was at Cajamarca, a city close to the Spaniards' camp. On November 8, 1532, Pizarro made a remarkably bold, even foolish, decision. He led his men into the Andes in order to meet the great Atahualpa. This advance was carefully watched by hundreds of Inca sentries, but strangely enough Atahualpa commanded them to give no resistance. It is likely that he was amazed by the audacity of the intruders, and enjoyed delaying their inevitable destruction.

Eventually the Spaniards entered the valley of Cajamarca, where Atahualpa and some thirty thousand soldiers were camped. Pizarro sent an embassy to the Inca, who was taking the waters at the natural hot springs of the town. The vast assembly of troops gazed vacantly as the small party of Spaniards made its way through the encampment, utterly surrounded by Inca soldiers. Finally, Pizarro's messengers were allowed to approach Atahualpa.

The Inca greeted the strangers with reserve and dignity, remaining totally at ease even when one of the horses pranced before the ruler, who had never before seen such a beast, for horses had been long extinct in the Americas. The exchange was translated by an Indian lad captured four years previously and taught Spanish by his captors.

Atahualpa toyed with the emissaries, gazing at their peculiar dress and listening to their alien language with interest. As a result of this meeting the Inca invited the Spaniards to lodge in Cajamarca, with the promise that he would meet Pizarro on the following day. It is entirely unclear why the ruler made such an offer, although it is assumed that he felt no threat from this greedy band of pirates, knowing nothing of their weapons or their determination to rob the Four Quarters of the World of all its riches.

The main plaza of Cajamarca was an ideal military stronghold for the Spaniards. Low buildings surrounded the square, and in these Pizarro concealed his desperate men. Each building contained numerous doors opening onto the plaza, giving the soldiers easy access if Pizarro ordered a surprise attack. The trap was set. The Spaniards' one small cannon was mounted, ready to be fired on Pizarro's command. It was Saturday, November 16,

1532. The Spaniards waited, peering out from their hiding places.

Finally, in the late afternoon, a messenger arrived with the news that the great Inca was approaching upon his splendid litter, accompanied by thousands of his men. The spectacle of Atahualpa's arrival was both wondrous and fearsome to the Spaniards. The entire valley was filled with troops in full parade: gold and silver head discs flashing, brilliant tribal costumes rippling in the breeze, and the sound of songs echoing between the tall mountains. In advance of each squadron were custodians who swept the ground in preparation for the arrival of the king. Then came battalion after battalion of men, swinging their arms in precise unison, chanting, and gazing proudly into the evening sky. Now the sun was gliding into its crimson bed in the west. Atahualpa entered the plaza, surrounded by six thousand unarmed men. Then came the litters of dignitaries. Then legions of attendants clad in glorious headdresses.

Fearing that he was trapped by his own ambush, Pizarro peered out at the great assembly, certain that he would be killed for the outrages he had committed since reaching Peru. Whether he surrendered or attacked, he had nothing to lose. And so he bullishly gave the signal, and the cannon suddenly exploded.

The Inca world persists in the folk festivals of the Andes.

Spaniards in full armor dashed on horseback from their concealment, charging into the mass of unarmed Indians. They had placed rattles on their horses in the hope of terrifying the Inca. With the burst of shots and the call of trumpets, the Spaniards drove into the startled Indians, who were thrown into utter panic.

Now the Spaniards began to kill. In desperation the unarmed Indians tried to flee, trampling one another in their efforts to escape.

Pizarro rushed the litter of Atahualpa with a contingent of foot-soldiers, clutching the ruler's left arm and trying to pull him from his throne. But the litter-bearers raised their ruler high into the air, out of reach, as they fearlessly attempted to carry him to safety. The Spaniards pursued, cutting off the hands of the bearers, who screamed in pain as they continued to support their Inca's litter on their shoulders. As one litter-bearer fell, another took his place and was in turn slaughtered. These valiant efforts were of no avail, for in the end all those who attempted to save their ruler lay in the great pools of blood that flooded the plaza, and Atahualpa was carried away as a captive.

"During all this, no Indian raised a weapon against a Spaniard, even when the cavalry jumped the broken wall and spread the slaughter among those who were fleeing." (Hemming)

With Atahualpa's captivity, the Inca world was frozen with frustration and indecision. The ruler's bodyguard was composed almost entirely of his major counselors, and in killing them Pizarro had destroyed the administrative heart of the entire empire. Without leaders, the Inca were incapable of defensive action. They simply waited for orders that did not arrive.

"How could so powerful a monarch have been captured by a mere handful of adventurers?" John Hemming has asked. "The answer was clear: Atahualpa had totally misjudged these invaders. His agents had reported that the Spaniards were few and disorganized, and the Inca never imagined that foreigners would be first to attack, especially with the odds overwhelmingly against them."

Atahualpa shrewdly noted the obsession of his captors with precious metal. Quietly he approached Pizarro and proposed the arrangement by which many Inca chiefs had gained their freedom from enemy captivity: with the payment of tribute. Thus Atahualpa offered the greatest ransom ever paid, promising to fill an entire room with gold — a room twenty-two feet long by seventeen feet wide. The Inca smiled as he touched a point on the wall roughly eight feet from the floor, indicating that the room would be filled to that point. Atahualpa said he would fill the room with gold jars, pots, tiles, and other precious objects, and then, he said, he would fill it twice more with silver. This he would command his people to do within two months.

Pizarro agreed.

It took six months to fulfill the promise. The most precious objects from the empire were surrendered to the Spaniards. "By this time the chamber in Cajamarca was . . . filled with a priceless hoard of precious metals. Much of it consisted of vases, figures, jewelry, and personal ornaments, the masterpieces of Inca gold- and silver-smiths. Their destruction in the conquistadores' smelters was an irreparable artistic loss, although such a consideration apparently did not trouble the conquerors. On May 3, Francisco Pizarro had ordered his men to begin the enormous task of melting down more than eleven tons of gold objects and 26,000 pounds of silver." (Hemming)

One day a Spanish soldier dragged an Indian into Pizarro's chamber, declaring that his captive confessed that a great Inca army was approaching Cajamarca from the north, intent upon liberating their ruler and destroying the invaders. Upon this evidence alone, Pizarro declared that Atahualpa had committed treason and sentenced him to death by burning — unless he should elect to become a Christian, and thus would be strangled instead of burned.

The imagined Inca army and counterattack did not exist, but the Spaniards insisted upon carrying out the death sentence.

Atahualpa denied the rumors of an attack and declared that he had kept his word and paid the gigantic ransom he had promised. His eloquence and protests were of no avail. "The Spaniards acted with chilly speed, as if fearful that a delay would produce evidence of the Inca's innocence." (Hemming) On Saturday, July 26, 1533, Atahualpa was taken to the same plaza where he had been ambushed. He was tied to the stake and told that he was to be burned alive.

The Inca feared burning, because it deprived him of royal mummification and the adoration of his people after his death. Therefore he agreed to baptism.

An eyewitness later recalled: "When he was taken out to be killed, all the native populace who were in the plaza, of whom there were very many, prostrated themselves upon the ground, letting themselves fall to the earth like drunken men."

Atahualpa was betrayed even in death, for the Spaniards did not leave his body unmolested. As the eyewitness recounted, "after he had been strangled ... fire was thrown onto him to burn part of his clothing and flesh."

But the death of Atahualpa did not bring the Inca Empire to an end.

Two brothers of Huascar's branch of the royal family had survived Atahualpa's massacre after the civil war. One of these brothers, a prince called Manco, had been a fugitive since the War of the Brothers, and it was only now, with the death of Atahualpa, that he came forward in the disguise of a peasant and disclosed his true identity. Pizarro was delighted. Manco would be an ideal puppet ruler for the disenchanted Inca Empire. But the choice proved to be a poor one, for Manco Inca inherited the pride of his people. As far as he was concerned, he was the descendant of a line of deities, whose ancestor was the Sun. And though he accepted the throne, he was horrified as he watched the Spaniards impose themselves upon the Inca Empire. After much abuse, he finally escaped into the hills beyond the Yucay Valley, where he rallied a vast Indian army. On Saturday, May 6, 1536, Manco's troops surrounded and attacked Cuzco, where only 190 Spaniards were garrisoned. They set fire to the thatched buildings, and in the great wind that swept the city, a vast wall of flame towered skyward. Cuzco was literally burned

Sanctuary of the Inca: Machu Picchu in the high Andes of Peru.

to the ground in one day. After a six-day siege, the Indians re-captured almost the entire city; with the Spaniards desperately holding only the main plaza. But their victory was short-lived. So great was the will of the conquistadores that they managed against insurmountable odds to slip out of their predicament, escaping to the walled fortress of Sacsahuaman, from which they mounted an attack. Gradually they gained the advantage. "As Inca resistance crumbled the gallant [Indian] nobleman who led the defense . . . hurtled weapons down on the attackers in a frenzy of despair. He grabbed handfuls of earth and scoured his face in anguish, covered his head in his cloak, and then leaped to his death from the top of the temple-fortress. The remaining Indians soon gave way, and Pizarro and his men were able to enter — whereupon they put all 1,500 of those inside to the sword." (Hemming)

Manco Inca escaped to the one remaining stronghold of the Indians: Vilcabamba. An attack by the Spaniards upon this jungle-surrounded city failed. And for six years Manco Inca be-came "a true guerrilla leader," harassing communications along the Lima-Cuzco road and ambushing isolated Spanish soldiers. Eventually Manco Inca was assassinated by five Spanish fugitives whom he befriended. Manco had three sons who succeeded him as rulers of Vilcabamba. But their aggression against the Spanish overlords dissipated, and the tiny state of Vilcabamba only wanted to be left in peace. In those few valleys and forest-ed hills lingered a last reminder of the lost grandeur of the Inca Empire. Eventually even Vilcabamba was overwhelmed by a massive Spanish force. But the victors won nothing, for when they entered the city they found that it had been destroyed by its own inhabitants. All the Indians had fled. And Vilcabamba was nothing but smoldering ashes.

The city was abandoned. Within a century it simply disap-peared from history. It was not until the late nineteenth century that a new breed of romantic explorers became intrigued by this last refuge of the Incas.

In 1911, an American explorer named Hiram Bingham made the arduous journey into the valley where Vilcabamba was once located. Traveling down the Urubamba River, Bingham made a sensational discovery: an Incaic sanctuary perched on a ridge high above the gorge: Machu Picchu. "Hiram Bingham insisted that Machu Picchu was in fact the lost city of Vilcabamba, the refuge of Manco Inca and his sons. . . . It was not until 1964 that Bingham's identification of Machu Picchu as

Machu Picchu.

Vilcabamba was seriously contested.... The controversy that surrounds Bingham's claims on behalf of Machu Picchu cannot diminish the splendor of the site itself.... It is, quite simply, magnificent ... a remarkable natural fortress when the Incas occupied it five centuries ago.... Whatever its history and whatever purpose it may have served, Machu Picchu is indisputably the most spectacular of Inca sites, perched as it is some 2,000 feet above the roaring waters of the Urubamba River on a knife-sharp ridge of exposed rock, a single vertebra in the spine of the Vilcabamba cordillera." (Hemming)

The actual city of Vilcabamba was eventually located — one of several Inca sites that have been rediscovered in recent years. Ironically, its ruins are so deeply buried by jungle and its location is so remote that it will probably never be fully excavated. Thus, in the imagination of most people, Machu Picchu — balanced at the summit of the Four Quarters of the World like a crown — remains the symbol of Indian resistance to the Spaniards, a monument to the greatness of the Incas, rulers of the Andes.

Giants of Mexico

FROM THE AIR, the massive brown structures of Teotihuacán merge into the arid plateau that surrounds them. As Karl Meyer notes, "their vast bulk seems deceptively diminished" by the boundless vacancy of the earth. But this airborne impression of the great city of the Valley of Mexico changes abruptly as we begin our descent and catch sight of the tiny human figures that climb the steep steps of the Pyramid of the Sun. Only now do we grasp the remarkable scale of Teotihuacán: a monumentality that inspired reverence and obedience among its now-vanished population, which probably exceeded 150,000 people, making it "more populous than the Athens of Pericles," covering a larger area "than the Rome of the Caesars."

Funeral mask from Teotihuacán, A.D. 400–600.

Teotihuacán florished for over four hundred years. Then, about A.D. 700, the great city was deliberately defaced and burned by unknown invaders. "A nation has passed away," William Prescott lamented in his renowned study of Mexico. "Powerful, populous, and well advanced in refinement, as attested by their monuments . . . it perished without a name."

The history and even the name of Teotihuacán is a legacy of Aztec legend. In Nahautl, the language of the Aztecs, Teotihuacán means "City of the Gods."

IT WAS HERE in the great city of the Valley of Mexico, at the hearth of the heavens, that the gods gathered to warm themselves against the boundless cold and darkness that surrounded them, for all the fires of the cosmos had gone out. They looked around, but there was nothing but themselves to see. For the world was empty — every tree and animal had been destroyed by a terrible flood. Even the Sun itself had been lost, and so there was no light in the sky.

It was during those dark days that the gods gathered in Teotihuacán and decided that one among them must be sacrificed in the divine hearth. Only then would a new Sun rise from the fire.

> Although it was night,
> Although the day had vanished,
> Although the heavens were dark
> They came together
> Here in Teotihuacán.

"But who shall be sacrificed so there will be light in the heavens as it was before the Sun was extinguished?" the gods asked one another.

The most wretched among them, Nanautzin, stood up timidly and offered himself to the flames.

Outraged that such a grotesque should become the Sun, a rich and powerful god named Teciztecatl insisted that he too be sacrificed so he might bring his beautiful light to the world.

For four days Nanautzin and Teciztecatl fasted in preparation for the ceremony. Then, on the fifth day, the gods came together around the divine hearth and instructed the volunteers to throw themselves into the flames, promising that they would reemerge as a glowing Sun.

The rich god and the poor god prepared for the ordeal — one with lavish gifts to the fire and a great show of bravery, while the other made the simplest of offerings. Finally the moment had come, and it was decided that the rich god Teciztecatl should be the first to be sacrificed. Three times he summoned his courage and three times he ran toward the great fire, only to fall back in fear as the flames lashed out at him.

Now it was Nanautzin's turn. The wretched god stood stood with a sad expression on his disfigured face. He closed his eyes in fear. Then he took a great breath and raced forward, leaping high into the air and plummeting into the flames that quickly consumed him.

So ashamed was the rich god Teciztecatl, when he saw the courage of Nanautzin, that he quickly hurled himself into the fire, and he too vanished.

Now the gods searched the sky expectantly, looking for the new Sun. Finally the poor god Nanautzin appeared — a bright orange ball glowing high above them, lighting the world with his radiance. Then, almost at once, the rich god Teciztecatl also burst into the heavens as the Moon, trying to outshine the Sun. So angry were the gods by the audacity of the Moon that they struck it in the face with a rabbit, leaving the scars that it still carries today.

The gods were contented, for now the sky was filled with sunlight. But the Sun would not move. It clung fearfully to the horizon and would not make its long journey across the heavens. In desperation, all the gods threw themselves into the smoldering ashes of the divine fire, and when they ascended into the sky, the Sun moved, and they became the many stars of the night.

THUS THE AZTECS EXPRESSED their utter reverence for Teotihuacán, claiming for it the birthplace of the Sun which lights the Fifth World in which they lived. So profound was their regard for Teotihuacán that they said its enormous structures had been built by giants, an assumption they felt justified by the huge mammoth bones they unearthed at the site.

The Teotihuacán Valley is not a particularly hospitable area, and for many years archaeologists wondered why the architects of a grand civilization would have selected such an undistinguished site for their incomparable city. Then in 1971, a cave beneath the Pyramid of the Sun was accidentally discovered. A survey of this cave offers some reasons why Teotihuacán was constructed on its particular site. "The ancient use of the cave predates the pyramid, and it remained as a cult center after its construction.... In [pre-Columbian] Mexico such caverns were symbolic wombs from which gods like the Sun and the Moon, and the ancestors of mankind, emerged in the mythological past. And as it will be recalled the Aztec tradition placed the creation of the Sun and Moon, and even the present universe at Teotihuacán." (Coe)

Teotihuacán was already a dusty ruin when Lord Montezuma, ruler of the powerful Aztec domain, made religious pilgrimages to the deserted city. Sixteenth-century European invaders, like Cortés, and nineteenth-century historians, like Prescott, knew little more about the city than about the Aztecs. Only recently have archaeologists finally begun to understand the rich saga of Teotihuacán and the triumph of the human imagination that suddenly brought the greatest American city into existence.

Teotihuacán, Valley of Mexico: the city where the gods were born.

As Karl Meyer points out, "We can now say with some confidence that the urban revolution in the Western hemisphere had its beginning here, some thirty miles northeast of Mexico City, in a tableland where today one finds more lizards and clumps of cacti than people." To this statement, Michael Coe adds: "Perhaps the strangest fact regarding this great city plan is that there is absolutely no precedent for it anywhere in the New World." It literally arose out of nothing.

Even the wreckage of Teotihuacán is awesome for its epic scope and sophistication. Yet the city was not the result of countless generations of formative efforts in architecture. It sprang up suddenly about 50 B.C., rising above a small and rustic pyramid that the local people apparently had used for the worship of their deities since the second century B.C. Over this trivial earth mound, the Pyramid of the Sun was produced in one continuous effort — an almost unbelievable achievement given the fact that it was constructed by workers who did not have the use of wheeled vehicles or beasts of burden . . . and considering that it is as broad at the base as the greatest pyramid of Egypt and is two hundred feet in height (about half as high as its Egyptian counterpart). The core of the pyramid is composed of more than 1,175,000 cubic meters of sun-dried brick and rubble. In its days of glory, a stone stairway led to a thatched temple at the summit.

Scholars feel certain that Teotihuacán was built by highly sophisticated architects who devised a complex master plan for their city. In front of the great pyramid they constructed a ceremonial causeway, now called the Avenue of the Dead. Along the full length of this "processional way" were the various temples to the gods, whose original names were lost in prehistory. At what is now the end of the Avenue of the Dead (in ancient times it extended into a vast quarter of residences) is the smaller Pyramid of the Moon. Surrounding this sacred precinct are more than twenty-six hundred structures spread over eight square miles, consisting of apartment houses, marketplaces, civic buildings, and minor temples, laid out like a modern American city "in quadrants on a precise gridwork pattern . . . its ceremonial, official, and private buildings linked by ruler-straight streets." (Meyer) By A.D. 600 there were perhaps as many as two hundred thousand people living in Teotihuacán, making it the sixth largest city in the world of its day. "The city was cosmopolitan: in its western part there was an Oaxaca ward, in

The Pyramid of Quetzalcoatl, decorated with carved images of the Plumed Serpent and the Rain god (Tlaloc), with seashells connecting the images of the two deities. Teotihuacán, A.D. 140–450.

which Zapotecs carried on their own customs and worshipped their own gods, while on the east there was apparently one made up of merchants from the lowland Veracruz and Maya areas." (Coe)

The rise of Teotihuacán marked the Golden Age of Mexico both in terms of its practical life as a political and cultural domain and also in terms of its interior life as a spiritual center with immensely widespread influence — exceeding by far the prior world of Olmec dominancy and outdistancing all future aboriginal civilizations with the single exception of the Aztec Empire. We have abundant reason to believe that Teotihuacán devised, in one strikingly creative moment of history, everything that is most essential to Mesoamerican culture: its cosmology and deities, its religious philosophy and social customs, its urban and ceremonial architectural tradition, as well as its intellectual values and ethical principles! For instance, "in Teotihuacán for the first time we find an architectural style which continues almost without change until the end of the Indian period. It consists of a talus and vertical wall adorned with a panel: the steps always have flanking balustrades. The walls are covered with a coat of very fine white stucco, frequently painted with frescoes. . . . In Teotihuacán we do not find [any of the hallmarks of Maya civilization]: no steles, nor corbeled vaults, nor the zero of Maya mathematics. Curiously, a ball court has never been found there either. Here everything was done to elevate the soul of the onlooker. It was not a matter of pleasing but of exalting." (Bernal) All successive societies of Mexico would have distinctive artistic styles, but fundamentally all such styles were variants of the forms created by the mysterious people we now call Teotihuacanos.

The power of Teotihuacán was enormous, but it was not the kind of militaristic power that we understand in the twentieth century. In fact, the city had very few defensive structures. "Soldiers and weapons are not prominent in its art. . . . The bloodthirsty gods that rose to power in later times are notably absent, [although] this does not mean that human sacrifice was unknown." (Leonard)

Teotihuacán was apparently a vital center of religious ideology — a cultural situation not unlike the world of the earlier Olmecs, whose feline deity and unique iconography infiltrated a vast geographical region. Art historian Laurette Sejourne has shown that the gods of Teotihuacán were adapted by later Mexican societies. Apparently Tlaloc (the rain deity) was the major god of the Teotihuacanos' pantheon, but there were many other supernatural powers whose attributes also resemble the gods worshiped throughout Mexican history: the Feathered Serpent, the Sun God, the Moon Goddess, and Lords of the Winds, and a god of annual renewal of the earth, later named Xipe Totec and much revered by the Aztecs.

Teotihuacán also had wide intellectual influence. We have no evidence of the language spoken in the great city, but some examples of calendric symbols have survived, and most scholars believe that the Teotihuacanos possessed a written language and books, probably produced on perishable materials like leather and fiber. "Although none have survived, books must have been in both ritual and administrative use, for these people had writing. From the few isolated glyphs that have been identified on the pottery and in the frescoes, it is known that they had bar-and-dot numeration [like the Olmec and Maya] and used the 260-day count.... By any criteria, the period from about A.D. 150 to 900 was the most remarkable in the whole development of Mesoamerica ... and it is at this time that the peoples of Mexico built civilizations that can bear comparison with those of other parts of the globe." (Coe)

Teotihuacán directly influenced, "though probably did not dominate," many of the people of Mexico. At the same time, Teotihuacán artifacts found their way into virtually every part of Mesoamerica, from the highlands of Guatemala to the Pánuco River and the Pacific coast. As C. A. Burland notes, "The great city was the symbol of power for the period. Its riches and glory were stupendous in that world, and its warriors and tradesmen travelled far, bringing in tribute for the glory of Tlaloc and the fertility deities. Even the rituals of sacrifice seem to have been established. One cannot estimate the antiquity of heart sacrifice in Mexico; it may have occurred in Olmec times [although] no overt representation is known. However, it was a great force in Teotihuacán life and is represented in the religious art quite strongly. But also there was another spirit, the Morning Star which prefigured the later Quetzalcoatl and presumably represented the idea of a god opposed to blood sacrifice.... This is not a confusion but an expression of the importance of opposites in religious mythology. Such a duality becomes clear for the first time at Teotihuacán. It is clear that the entity which we call Mexican culture had come into being and flowered strongly in this mighty imperial city."

Who were the founders of Teotihuacán? According to Michael Coe, "In view of the strong continuities between Teotihuacán on the one hand and the [later] Toltecs and Aztecs on the other, in both sacred and secular features, the Nahua affinities of this civilization would appear to be the most probable." Nahua is a major language group — a vast array of peoples in northwestern Mexico (including parts of what is now Arizona and Southern California) and central and southeastern Mexico. The most significant form of Nahua is Nahuatl, the language of the Aztecs, still spoken today by hundreds of thousands of peasants in the central highlands and in the state of Guerrero. The traditions and the language are all that is left of ancient Teotihuacán.

Incensario from Classic Teotihuacán, circa A.D. 250.

About A.D. 700 the great city was utterly devastated. The torch was put to the grandest of its palaces and temples along the Avenue of the Dead. "Some internal crisis or long-term political and economic *malaise*, perhaps the disruption of its trade and tribute routes by a new polity such as the rising Xochicalco state, may have resulted in the downfall, and it may be significant that by A.D. 600 almost all Teotihuacán influence over the rest of Mesoamerica ceased. No more do the nobility of other states stock their tombs with the refined products of the great city. The luxurious palaces of Teotihuacán were now in ruin, and squatters were living within jerry-built walls thrown across the floors, sometimes placing their dead beneath the old rooms like the former inhabitants. This barbaric occupation persisted for about two hundred years after the fall of the city. . . . A mighty crisis overtook all the Classic civilizations of Mesoamerica during the ninth century A.D., the most drastic convulsion being reserved for the Classic Maya, who were forced [two centuries later] to abandon most of their centers." (Coe)

The Pyramid of Quetzalcoatl — the Plumed Serpent — at Teotihuacán.

What does Mexico owe to the Golden Age of Teotihuacán? C. A. Burland suggests several major debts: the concept of a dominant religio-political society that unifies and subjugates numerous tribes; a complex cosmology that envisions a three- or four-layered cosmos in which the powers of nature are the subject of adoration; the staggering conception of a vast urban complex in which sacred and secular precincts were organized into a cosmopolitan and authentic city built on a plan rather than haphazardly. "In all these fields Teotihuacán succeeds Olmec ideas to such a degree that the face of civilization was totally changed. A great and truly Mexican Indian civilization was established which would endure for all future generations."

Ignacio Bernal notes that "although Teotihuacán left embers whose flames would rise again, with time the identity of the early inhabitants was obscured. Their history was transformed into myth." The myths of Mexico confirm the demise of wondrous civilizations, for time is not a continuous evolutionary process as it is for the Christian West. The Fifth Sun that was born at Teotihuacán when Nanautzin threw himself into the divine hearth perished in the process of time — a concept of time familiar to Mexican Indians: a series of closed circles, "each one, independent of the other, disappears with a tremendous cataclysm in such a way that at the end of each era the gods are

obliged to create everything anew, including the sun and men."
(Bernal)

In reality, however, the cataclysm did not destroy everything nor did it decimate the population. Some isolated societies of Mexico continued to flourish. And where cultural
desolation did occur in the Valley of Mexico, the defenseless-
ness of the region permitted the once-civilized land to be overrun by nomadic tribes from the northern frontier.

El Tajín, on the Gulf of Mexico, is an example of a culture
that did not vanish with the decline of Teotihuacán. It persisted
as an important link between the vanished Golden Age and the
world of the Toltecs — the next society to achieve greatness in
the Valley of Mexico. Tajín culture evolved in the middle of
Veracruz. There, in the deep, inhospitable jungle, a mysterious
people built a vast and astounding city. Their culture has strong
resemblances to both the Teotihuacanos and the Olmecs, but
Tajín was clearly an independent society; and very little is
known of its history. A unique art style ultimately developed at
Tajín out of various influences. Characteristic of its architecture
is the niche — a square alcove decorating the vertical walls of
each level of the major pyramid at El Tajín . . . a building which
many experts regard as "one of the most impressive buildings of
pre-Columbian art." (Bernal) The niches appear to have had a

The Pyramid of the Niches at El Tajín, on
the Gulf Coast of Mexico.

Classic Olmec head from San Lorenzo, Mexico, circa 800 – 200 B.C.

Machu Picchu.

The gold of the Andes: Chimu culture of Colombia.

A herd of llama outside Cuzco.

Teotihuacán: the city where the gods were born.

Model and panoramic restoration of the capital city of the Aztecs, Tenochtitlán (in the Museum of Anthropology, Mexico City).

Kingdom of the Natchez and their ruler, the Great Sun. A tinted engraving made from the

Art of the Adena culture: a two-thousand-year-old ceremonial pipe found in 1901 in Ohio. The figure is a dwarf, with a thickening of the neck probably caused by a goiter. In his ears he wears large spools.

The mysterious Cliff Dwellers of Mesa Verde built this remarkable village in a sandstone cliff in southwestern Colorado.

Warriors of the Plains — a Bison Dance of the Mandan Indians, 1833, by Karl Bodmer.

Bear's Heart: "The Troops at Fort Marion."

R. Lee White: A modern Indian painter employs the technique of ledger art to reenvision Custer's Last Stand, 1982.

calendric significance insofar as the number of niches (365) corresponds to the days of the solar year. The population that produced Tajín culture has been identified with the historic people called the Pipiles. Eventually they moved outward from their geographical home on the Gulf Coast. Curiously, many Tajín artifacts have been found at the Palace of Palenque in Chiapas. These objects were deposited toward the end of the Classical period, a fact that has caused scholars to speculate that marauders from Tajín may have been the invaders and destroyers of that magnificent ceremonial center of the Maya.

Tajín has been the subject of only the slightest excavation, and despite our high regard for its main pyramid, we know exceptionally little about the Tajín people themselves. Prominent in its iconography are winged dancers, Eagle Knights, scenes of human sacrifice, as well as possible proof of literacy: bar-and-dot numerals along with various day glyphs. From archaeological evidence, Michael Coe has determined that "the inhabitants of El Tajín were obsessed with the ball game, human sacrifice, and death: three concepts closely interwoven in the Mexican mind." Among the most important Tajín relics are reliefs that magnificently depict the ritual drama of the sacred ball game: scenes of the players in elaborate courts, dressed in the complex regalia associated with the sport. One set of stone panels depicts a ritual panorama presided over by a death god. The captain of the losing team is apparently being sacrificed by one of the winners, who holds a flint knife over the victim's chest. For Tajín, the ball game was a ceremony of immense significance: probably a divining ordeal which helped to determine tribal decisions and calendrical events.

The oracle of the game, however, did not protect El Tajín from extinction. After surviving the upheaval of the dark age between the end of the classical domination of Teotihuacán and the onset of the militaristic Post-Classic period, Tajín was destroyed by fire at the beginning of the thirteenth century A.D. Folk history recounts that the city of the Pyramid of the Niches was overrun by the so-called Chichimecs, a group of nomads from the north whose reckless descent into civilized Mexico is often compared to the assault of European "barbarians" upon the crumbling Roman Empire. Much as Europe was born out of the Romanized barbarian tribes, so the final stages of Indian Mexico evolved out of these lawless Chichimecs, whom the Toltecs, Mixtecs, and Aztecs claimed as ancestors.

A funeral urn depicting a human figure from the Zapotec culture.

Like the settlements of the Olmecs and many other tropical centers of the Gulf of Mexico, El Tajín sank into the jungle, vanishing so utterly that at the time of the Spanish invasion no one was aware that it had ever existed. Not until the end of the eighteenth century, when Padre Alzate stumbled upon the gigantic ruin, did Tajín emerge from its leafy obscurity.

"The ancient cultures of the Valley of Mexico had frequent contacts and were still strongly influenced by the established peoples on the Atlantic coast, the [feline] worshipers. But the new groups which we shall study are a typical product of the plateau and their distinctive animal is the eagle. From this moment on, the eagle of the high valleys vanquishes the tiger of the tropical coasts." (Bernal)

TEOTIHUACAN WAS ROME, and with its decline and fall in the seventh century A.D., the mentality that had unified civilized Mexico vanished. Tribes that had once lived in the relative security provided by the balance of power under the religious rule of Teotihuacán were now torn by factionalism, each striving for domination, each promoting its own culture, each petty kingdom attempting to acquire more power than its neighbors, while living in almost total isolation from one another. By A.D. 900 even the elegant world of the Maya in the south had collapsed. What direct relationship, if any, exists between the fall of the Maya and the decline of Teotihuacán is purely speculative. But there is no doubt that the momentum of civilized Mexico had dissipated. Mesoamerica was disunified, structureless, and defenseless. We do not know for how many decades the barbarians of the north had chipped away at Mexico, but the helpless confusion of the Post-Classic dark ages provided an ideal opportunity for them to overrun and conquer all that remained of the glories of a vanquished Golden Era. The beginning of the tenth century saw a deluge of outsiders, whose place of origin is highly controversial. Some experts insist that these barbarous hordes came from either the Jalisco region or southern Zacatecas. Other scholars believe that the barbarians came from the area that now constitutes Southern California and Arizona. There are also archaeologists who locate the original homeland of the nomads who descended upon Mexico in the south, as far south as Central America. Whatever their origin may have been, their eventual domination of Mexico transformed most of Mesoamerica. Militarism becomes the major theme of the new age. The art style perfectly reflects this Spartan mentality: hard-edge figuration, geometric style almost to the exclusion of curvilinear forms, abstraction that curtails all vestiges of exuberance and sentience. What emerges is the kind of static art that we usually associate with totalitarian regimes: a doctrinaire aesthetic with politically committed monumentality.

The Aztecs would eventually give a name to the invading barbarians who reshaped Mexico, calling them Chichimecas, meaning "people of the dog." It was not a derogatory term, for several generations of rulers in the Valley of Mexico prided themselves upon their Chichimec ancestry. Padre Bernardino de Sahagún, the sixteenth-century priest who was the major chronicler of Aztec culture and history, claimed that his Indian informants told him that the barbarians were nomads who knew nothing about farming. They had bows and arrows and dressed in animal skins and yucca-fiber sandals. Their diet consisted entirely of wild fruits, tubers, and seeds, as well as the meat of the small animals they hunted. It is possible that the Chichimecas were driven into Mexico by a succession of droughts that decimated their homeland.

Out of the upheaval and disorder of this dark age came the Toltecs, who forged a new culture out of both the remnants of the classical world and alien traditions brought into Mexico by so-called barbarians. It was a historical process not unlike the founding of Europe out of the ashes of Rome.

Myth and history intermingle in the story of the Toltecs. Folk history recounts that the Toltecs were led into the Valley of Mexico by a great chief called Mixcoatl. He was a warrior who coaxed his followers into an exhaustive invasion of the Valley. By A.D. 908, the great lord was victorious and proud, and he wished to build a city to celebrate his triumphs. His capital was founded at the foot of the hill Cerro de la Estrella in Culhuacán. Despite his victories and the prestige of his city, Mixcoatl was restless and sought additional conquests, and so he invaded parts of Morelos, Toluca, and Teotlalpan.

While he waged war in Morelos it is said that he encountered an exceptional woman who is known in history as Chimalman. She came out to meet him as if she were a warrior. But she did not attack him. She placed her shield upon the ground and then she took off her clothes and stood naked before Mixcoatl. In a rage he shot four arrows at her: the first flew above her head; the second grazed past her ribs but did not wound her; the third she seized in her bare hands; and the fourth she

The Main Pyramid at Tula.

caught between her legs. After this happened, Mixcoatl surrendered to the woman; and they lay with one another, and she was then with child. In this way, the first dynasty of the Toltecs began.

Before Chimalman gave birth to the son she carried, Mixcoatl was assassinated by one of his captains. This usurper claimed the throne of Culhuacán, and the pregnant Chimalman fled to the village of her mother, where she died in childbirth. Her son, born in either A.D. 935 or 947 and called Ce Acatl Topilzin, later assumed the name of an important god of the Toltec pantheon: Quetzalcoatl, "the feathered serpent." And it is by this name that he emerges as the most fascinating personage of Mexican history ... a mysterious king, hero, and god whose very appearance added to his legend, for he has been described as having fair skin, long hair, and a black beard.

In one of his appellations, Quetzalcoatl also represents Venus — which appears at times as a morning star and at other times as an evening star, and is therefore a celestial twin. Quet-zalcoatl "therefore appears not only under the form of two animals joined in one, the bird and the serpent, but also as two in one, since Venus is only one 'star' which appears to be two . . . a duality that deeply disturbed the mystical spirit of ancient Mexicans." (Bernal)

The child was instructed in the religion of the old god of Teotihuacán — the Feathered Serpent — although it was the faith of his mother and not his barbarous father, Mixcoatl. Under the tutelage of the few remaining teachers of the old faith of Teotihuacán, the royal son became a brilliant student, and eventually, when he grew into manhood, he was appointed the high priest of the god Quetzalcoatl, taking the name of the deity as was the native custom among holy men. (Ce Acatl Topilzin's assumed name — Quetzalcoatl — has caused many historical problems, insofar as the actual person and his god namesake have often been confused.)

Secure in his cloistered life as a priest, Quetzalcoatl apparently wanted no part of the barbarous world in which his father had been slain. But one day a group of emissaries came to his temple and begged him to reclaim his father's throne. Touched by the misery of his people, he returned to Culhuacán, where he confronted and killed the usurper. Now Quetzalcoatl became the indisputable lord of all the Toltecs. But unlike his father, he was not a militarist and he did not worship the bloody god of the Chichimecs. Instead, he wanted to bestow upon his Spartan people the high ideals of his mother's ancient religion of which Quetzalcoatl was the primary deity.

It is possible that part of his planned reformation motivated him to move the Toltec capital that had been founded by his father. Thus, in about A.D. 980, he built the fabled city of Tula (Tollan — "Place of the Reeds") in Hidalgo. His plan was grandiose, for he wish to eclipse all memory of the old capital. And so he commissioned artisans from many parts of Mexico, the descendants of the greatest craftspeople of the Golden Age.

Quetzalcoatl ruled his realm for only nineteen years, but so great were his achievements and so important his renaissance of devotion to the ideals of the old civilization that eventually all the greatness of the past was attributed to him. According to legend he was the giver of culture and the father of agriculture. Among the most precious gifts that he gave his people was maize, which he had stolen from the terrible place of the dead. The horoscope, the measure of time, the ritual calendar, writing

Detail from the Pyramid of Quetzalcoatl, Teotihuacán.

and books, and medicine were among his many inventions. Every positive aspect of the vanished worlds of the Olmecs and Teotihuacanos was attributed to the god-king Quetzalcoatl.

The native informants of Padre Sahagún offered boundless praise for the Toltec king: "And they say that he was very rich and that he had many good things to eat and to drink, and that corn was abundant during his reign, and the squash was stout and an arm's length around, and the ears of corn were so long that the farmers had to carry them in both arms; and they also sowed and reaped cotton in many colors, red and yellow and green and blue and gray and orange . . . for in all these hues the cotton grew naturally. And Quetzalcoatl was rich beyond measure, having all the wealth of the land as did his vassals."

In legend and in history the reign of Quetzalcoatl was prosperous. He was a ruler who provided great abundance for his people. But he wanted to give his subjects more than practical comfort. He wished to impart a faith in the god Quetzalcoatl in whose temple he had served as high priest. He wanted to bring down the barbarous tribal god, Tezcatlipoca, whom the Chichimecs had brought with them from their northern wilderness, and to replace him with the benevolent deity of his mother — the Feathered Serpent — who opposed human sacrifice. But the great ruler's ideals resulted in intertribal conflict. "Quetzalcoatl, like [most] great religious reformers, had to end up as a victim of his faith." (Bernal)

The enemies of the god-king Quetzalcoatl were fanatic followers of the fierce deity Tezcatlipoca ("Smoking Mirror"), the

The heart of the Toltec world: fifty miles from Mexico City at Tula stand huge carved monoliths, which once supported the roof of a Toltec temple.

giver and taker of life, lord of sorcerers, and the chief patron of warriors who took captives for heart sacrifice. The priests of Tezcatlipoca constantly plotted against their king, fearing that the Feathered Serpent to whom he was dedicated might succeed in destroying the power of their own deity. The stories of their treachery are recounted in Toltec folk history. It is said that they used sorcery and magic against their king. It is told how they used curses and evil spells in the hope of bringing about his downfall. One day they sent their god Tezcatlipoca in the disguise of an old man to the palace of King Quetzalcoatl. He asked the king's attendants to take him to their lord, but they refused. When Tezcatlipoca insisted that he be allowed to see the king, the guards reluctantly took his message to Quetzalcoatl. But the king said, "I do not want to see this old man. Send him away!"

Undaunted, the disguised Tezcatlipoca sent another message: "Tell your king that I wish to give him something that he has never seen before. Tell him that I wish to give him his body."

When the message was given to Quetzalcoatl, he said: "What thing is this? What is this *body* he wishes to give to me?"

"Tell the king that I will not explain unless he allows me to see him," retorted Tezcatlipoca.

Base of the Temple of Quetzalcoatl, Teotihuacán.

At last the king gave orders to bring the old man to him.

When Tezcatlipoca came before King Quetzalcoatl, he carefully drew a mirror from under his cloak, and he held it before the lord and said: "I give you your body!"

The sight was so new and strange that Quetzalcoatl instantly fell ill. The treacherous old man persuaded the king to drink a "medicine." But the drink did not cure him. It made him drunk. For Tezcatlipoca had tricked Quetzalcoatl into drinking the inebriating potion called *pulque.*

Filled with drink and the ardent desire of his newly discovered body, Quetzalcoatl summoned the high priestess of his temple and slept with her. And so he lost the purity required by his religious office. Soon he also lost the dignity required by his throne. Tezcatlipoca threw off his disguise as an old man and appeared without his loincloth in the marketplace, where the king's daughter was so aroused by his naked beauty that she persuaded her father to let her marry the wicked magician.

"This legend, and many other similar ones, shows us how his enemies tried to topple Quetzalcoatl, not so much in his capacity as king as in his position as a religious representative. Indeed, what we sense in this episode of the last phase of Quetzalcoatl is the struggle between two religious groups, or more probably between a priestly group and a military group which wore the mask of the Tezcatlipoca priests. At the moment that Quetzalcoatl lost his prestige as a representative of his god, he found himself obliged to abdicate as king." (Bernal)

In the year 987, after burning his treasures, Quetzalcoatl left Tula forever. The tragedy of his departure is preserved in Toltec poetry:

> As he gazed upon Tula
> He wept
> And his tears came down upon his cheeks
> And fell to the ground
> Where, drop by drop,
> They broke the rocky earth.

Now Quetzalcoatl — like Oedipus — became a vagabond, making his way through Mexico, followed by a small band of the faithful: acrobats, dwarfs, jugglers, and the pages of his palace. For a time he dwelled in the city of Cholula. Then he continued on his way. When he reached the pass between the volcanoes Popocatepétl and Iztaccíhuatl, many of his loyal followers froze to death in a storm. Finally he reached the Gulf Coast. Some say that he built a pyre and set himself afire, rising into the sky as Venus, the Morning Star. Others tell of his departure for Yucatán, the land of black and red. Together with a group of dwarfs and other deformed people, Quetzalcoatl set sail upon a raft formed of entwined serpents, promising those he left upon the shore that one day — in the year One Reed — he would return to reclaim his throne.

Five hundred years later (precisely in the Aztec year One Reed), when the bearded and pale Hernán Cortés made his landfall at Veracruz, Montezuma II was easily convinced that the Spaniard was truly Quetzalcoatl, come to make his claim upon his rightful throne.

If this curious coincidence were not enough, there is also the fact that Maya history recounts the arrival from the west, in the year A.D. 987, of a Mexican conqueror whose name in their language was Kukulcan ("Feathered Serpent").

There is abundant archaeological evidence of a seaborne Toltec invasion of Yucatán in the late tenth century. The Tolteca built their capital at Chichén Itzá, a place demonstrating an extraordinary amalgam of Maya and Toltec influences.

Chacmool: a Toltec deity at the summit of the Temple of the Warriors at Chichén Itzá, Yucatán, showing strong Toltec influences upon the famous city of the Post-Classic Maya.

Legend and history overlap at Chichén Itzá. The exiled king of Tula became the overlord of the Maya of Yucatán. "The god of this new Maya-Toltec Chichén Itzá is the same Quetzalcoatl, but his name was translated into Maya as Kukulcan, which means exactly the same thing, that is, 'the plumed serpent.'" (Bernal)

Once Quetzalcoatl was exiled from the Valley of Mexico, the militant faction representing Tezcatlipoca took power in Tula, and the Toltec Empire ascended to its period of greatest power and dominancy, asserting control over most of central Mexico from the Pacific to the Atlantic.

Tula is much celebrated in folktales: a city of miracles where there was great prosperity, where artists and scholars invented all the knowledge and culture of Mexico. It was said, for instance, that the potters were so brilliant that they "taught the clay to lie."

But the Toltec reputation as great givers of culture has proven to be a grandiose fiction of the later Aztecs. In actuality, the Toltecs were rather simple artisans despite the fact that their name means "master builders."

Finally, during the reign of King Huemac, Tula was subdued by a succession of terrible droughts. Intertribal conflict began to undermine the power of the Toltecs. The great city

The Castillo in the Central Plaza of Chichén Itzá, Yucatán — center of the Post-Classic Maya world, showing strong influences of a Toltec invasion from Central Mexico.

faltered and began to collapse. Eventually it would be utterly destroyed by a reckless invasion.

King Huemac lost control of his great city, and so he moved his capital from Tula to the summit of the hill called Chapultepec, in present-day Mexico City. There Huemac, the last of the great Toltec kings, committed suicide. During the years between 1156 and 1168, the militant followers of the brutal god Tezcatlipoca lapsed into silence. A few Tolteca and Chichimeca stubbornly remained in the desolate city for more than a decade, but eventually even they deserted Tula to the wind and feeble memory of time.

The end of Toltec rule over Mexico was a horrendous event. Tales survive of arson and murder, of drought and plague caused by the countless rotting bodies of warriors. Oral histories recall that only seven royal families survived. For generations the rulers of other regions of Mexico would marry the heirs of these Toltec families in order to claim the Toltec "divine right to rule." There is irony in the fact that an entirely militaristic society was destroyed by unrestrained and furious invasion, its capital decimated almost beyond recognition. And yet, by associating their rulers with divinity and thus providing them with the divine right to rule the land, the Toltecs invented a new form of theocratic government — a form so successful that in all subsequent eras Mexican chieftains were given the right to rule only if they could demonstrate some trace of Toltec descent among their ancestors.

"All evidence points to the death of the city through sudden and overwhelming cataclysm. . . . The fury of the destruction visited on Tula makes one wonder about the hand that performed the act . . . the finger of accusation points most logically once more to the Chichimeca, for Tula was perilously close to their frontiers. It was just at this time that the barbarians were again pushing south into cultivated lands." (Coe)

The Valley of Mexico would not rise again to such imperialistic power until the flowering of the empire of the Aztecs in 1244. Eventually these brutal and clever warriors would lay claim to all the legendary achievements of the Toltecs, rewriting history so they were identified with the Toltec lords as direct forebears. Archaeological evidence denies this claim of the Aztecs. Their descent from the Toltecs is also challenged by a series of pre-Columbian books — or codices — created by a Chichimec people known as the Mixteca. The first of these codices dates from about A.D. 850 — and is therefore the earliest chronicle produced by any tribe of the Valley of Mexico.

The codices were painted on deerskin, and then fanfolded so they could be read in *boustrophedon* fashion — zigzag from top to bottom. The writing in the codices is not a true hieroglyphic form, but an amalgam of rebus principles, pictographs, and dates based on the fifty-two-year Calendar Round. Though the exquisiteness of the eight surviving books suggests that the Mixtec were probably the inventors of the codex, the origin of these books is uncertain. Their invention was also claimed by the Nahua tribes of the Valley of Mexico, including the Aztecs. Many of the Mixtec codices were apparently taken as tribute by the Aztecs, for they were in their possession at the time of the Spanish invasion.

The *Vienna Codex* (so named because it is deposited in Vienna) provides a comprehensive picture of the era after the collapse of Tula in the eleventh century A.D. The fall of the empire occurred at the same time as a devastating drought in the American Southwest (Arizona and New Mexico). Legend claims that in this terrible period the Mississippi River dried up and the people of the desert abandoned their lands and migrated southward, forcing their way into the region once dominated by the mighty Tolteca. There are also tales of a great Chichimec chieftain named Xolotl who led his people out of a rainless wilderness and into Mexico, where he founded many great cities. It is also told that Xolotl came upon the gutted ruins of Tula one day, and he wept for its terrible destruction by prior bands of Chichimecs, who had not left a single building standing in the once-imperial city.

The land of the Mixtec people is located in the mountainous region in western and northern Oaxaca. Their highland home lent significance to their name — Mixteca, meaning "cloud people." They were one of the most important and powerful tribes during the period of transition after the decline of the Toltecs. Their book of history, *Codex Zouche-Nuttall* (in the British Museum), recounts their emergence in the sixth century A.D. from a sacred tree at Apoala. Thereafter an alliance was made between the Mixteca and the Tolteca, when a chief, Lord Smoking Eyes, married Lady Three-Stone-Knife in the capital city of Tula. Eventually the Mixteca gained control over a vast territory, mainly through the familiar European form of statecraft based upon marriage between various royal lines. "Extensive intermarriage eventually resulted in the Mixtec aristocracy being one family, under a single dynastic house ... claiming descent from [Quetzalcoatl] the Feathered Serpent." (Coe)

During the Second Dynasty of Tilantongo, we come across a flamboyant person named Eight-Deer, whose history is elaborately depicted in the *Codex Zouche-Nuttall.* Born into an era when the Toltecs were still in power, in A.D. 1011, Eight-Deer lived until 1063. He became chief of his people at the age of nineteen. Through shrewd conquest, strategic marriages, and the sacrifice to the gods of his rivals, Eight-Deer slowly extended his sphere of power. Year after year, Eight-Deer was victorious in his campaigns against his neighbors. After a successful battle he would kill the males of the royal family he had overthrown, and then he and his many sons would marry the widows and princesses, forging ever wider alliances. Eventually Eight-Deer extended his empire from the Mixtec highland south to the Pacific Ocean, and perhaps as far north as the city of Cholula. War and intrigue were constant preoccupations of Eight-Deer. Intrigue within his own family was treated with the same ruthlessness as his dealings with foes, and the sacrifice of brothers, uncles, and nephews played a central part in his rise to power.

One of his most important campaigns was fought against the town of Xipe-Bundle. Eight-Deer long wanted to rule Xipe-

Bundle, but his chance did not come until the town's chief, a Mixtec named Eleven-Wind, died in 1047. The complexity of Mixtec royal families can be seen in the problem of succession created by the death of the chief of Xipe-Bundle. Eleven-Wind had three children by one of his several wives, who was Eight-Deer's half-sister and the full sister of Eight-Deer's half-brother, Twelve-Earthquake. To prevent either his half-nephews or his half-brother from succeeding to the throne of Xipe-Bundle, Eight-Deer allied himself with a Toltec chief named Four-Tiger. Then, with the assistance of several other allies, they set out by water and by land. On the way to Xipe-Bundle, Eight-Deer captured his half-brother, Twelve-Earthquake, and sacrificed him. In 1049, Eight-Deer succeeded in occupying Xipe-Bundle, where he captured another of the heirs, Four-Wind, whom he

A page from the Mixtec *Codex Nuttall,* a pictorial representation of a voyage across a lake and the siege of a city.

spared and who eventually became an important figure in Mix-tec history. Then Eight-Deer captured the other two heirs, Six-House and Ten-Dog. Six-House was sacrificed, and Ten-Dog was killed in gladiatorial combat. Now there was no claim to the throne but his own, and so Eight-Deer married the sister of one of his victims, Thirteen-Serpent, and became ruler of Xipe-Bundle.

Eventually Eight-Deer lost a major battle, and in 1063, at the age of fifty-two, he himself was sacrificed, just as he had often sacrificed his own vanquished enemies.

"The most mysterious event in his life is the record of his visit to the king of a place called Hill of the Sun, believed by some to be in southern Puebla near Teotitlán del Camino; not only Eight-Deer, but the lord of Tula paid homage to this man. Who was he? Was there some empire more powerful than the Toltec about which we know nothing? This is one of the great unsolved puzzles of Mexican archaeology." (Coe)

The Mixtec survived the fall of Tula and the decline of their great Toltec allies. They persisted as a singular force of continuity during the Dark Age that followed the Toltec collapse, extending their realm until they produced the hybrid Mixteca-Puebla culture that created some of the most refined artifacts and manuscripts of Post-Classic Mexico. They retained a sphere of prominence even while the Aztecs ascended to an extent of political power long missing from Central Mexico. The Mixtecs were not friendly toward the new rulers; in fact, they persistently resisted the efforts of the Aztecs to conquer them. They successfully united with the Zapotecs and were able to remain independent of the Aztec Empire until the invasion of Hernán Cortés. Their freedom, however, was marginal after A.D. 1244, for it was in that year that the Aztecs rose out of humble obscurity to become the most powerful rulers of Mexico.

THE HISTORY OF THE AZTECS is in almost every respect a factual tale that strains the imagination. From their abrupt rise out of barbarism to their bloody political triumphs and their tragic and brutal destruction, there is in the Aztec chronicles something of the impossible, magic realism that now characterizes the literature of Latin America. "The beginnings of the Aztec nation were so humble and obscure that their rise to supremacy over most of Mexico in the space of a few hundred years seems almost miraculous. It is somehow inconceivable that the magnificent civilization witnessed and destroyed by the

Spaniards could have been created by a people who were not many generations removed from the most abject barbarism, but such was the case. It is only through an understanding of this fact, namely the tribal roots of the Aztec state, that these extraordinary people can really be comprehended." (Coe)

The origin of the Aztecs is recounted in legends. Accordingly, the tribe was born in a cave on an island called Aztlán, located somewhere in western Mexico. They were a most humble tribe, led by four priestly warriors. The power of these chieftains was symbolized by a bundle in which a statue of their god was carefully wrapped. His name was Huitzilopochtli ("Hummingbird-on-the-left") — fearsome deity of war and human sacrifice. According to folk history, it was in Tula that Huitzilopochtli was born to an old widow. One day she was sweeping the temple when she noticed a tiny ball of feathers. Fascinated, she placed it between her breasts. Soon she became pregnant, and her daughter and four hundred sons were so outraged by their mother's impiety that they decided to kill her. And so her sons took up arms against her and went in search of their helpless mother. When she saw her innumerable children approaching her home, she became frightened and started to flee. But then she heard the voice of her unborn child, saying: "Mother, do not flee and do not be afraid, for I will protect you!"

Almost at once, a strong and fully mature son sprang from the womb of the old woman. He was armed with a sword and a spear-thrower and a bolt of lightning, and he slew his many brothers and threw their bodies into the sky, where they became the Stars; and he dismembered his sister, the Moon, and tossed her disfigured corpse high above the clouds.

Triumphantly, Huitzilopochtli left his loving mother, the Earth, and ascended into the sky as the Sun, vanquishing the Stars and the Moon whenever he presided over the heavens. It fell to the children of the Sun — the Aztecs — to venerate Huitzilopochtli and to assist him in his endless battle against the night by feeding him with the only food that could keep him strong: human hearts and blood. But even with so great a god as Huitzilopochtli, the Aztecs remained a forlorn and poor people, despised as bloodthirsty intruders by the numerous civilized tribes that had built splendid chiefdoms in the Valley of Mexico. They were rebuffed everywhere they wandered, allowed to settle temporarily on the land of other tribes and then turned away because their neighbors found them to be "quarrelsome, cruel, unfaithful to their word, and women-stealers." Even their enemies, however, admired them for their prowess as warriors and their exceptional bravery.

King Achitometl of Culhuacán took pity on the bedraggled Aztec nomads and allowed them to live a degraded existence on the most undesirable of land in Tizapán, a place of countless snakes, which the great monarch secretly hoped would destroy his barbarous guests. Legend tells us that, ironically, the Aztecs "rejoiced when they saw the serpents, and soon captured, roasted, and ate every last one of them!"

The king of Culhuacán was utterly repulsed when his emissaries told him what the Aztecs had done. "Do you see what terrible rascals and savages they are!" he exclaimed. "Let us talk of them no more."

The king's disdain for the Aztecs, however, was not so great that he did not recognize their strength as allies. He therefore gave one of his daughters — a princess of Culhuacán — in marriage to one of the barbarous Aztec chiefs. This benevolence was not appreciated by the Aztecs, for in 1323, they sacrificed the young woman with the hope that she might become the consort of Huitzilopochtli. Then they flayed the princess and a priest dressed in her skin. The unsuspecting king of Culhuacán was invited to witness this "great god" of the Aztecs, and he came with incense and tobacco and food as offerings to the deity. He was taken into a dark room where the "god" was kept, and he placed his gifts at its feet. When the king lighted the incense, a small flame leaped up and illuminated the room. He cried out as he realized to his horror that the god was a priest dressed in the skin of his own daughter. Enraged, the king of Culhuacán drove the Aztecs from his land, and they became homeless wanderers once again.

It was in this forlorn state that Huitzilopochtli appeared to the Aztecs as a small bird. And as previously recounted, the bird spoke to the people, saying: "Listen to what I say to you. We will remain here no longer, but we must seek a land where we may be the kings of many men and the husbands of many wives. Follow where I lead, and we shall find a land of our own! Within the marshes and the fields of tall reeds I will watch over you. Hear me! Go into the water until you find an island of rock where an eagle rests!"

Dutifully the people wandered among the marshes that were so dreadful that no one could live among the bogs. On

A page from the *Florentine Codex,* depicting the long migration of the Aztecs in search of their promised land. When they finally found a place where an eagle with a serpent in its beak was perched upon a cactus, they built the first temple of the city that would eventually be their capital: Tenochtitlán.

they wandered, despised by everyone, until they reached a group of water-logged islands near the western shore of the Lake of the Moon. There the chiefs rejoiced, for they encountered an eagle perched upon a cactus, holding a snake in its beak.

It was the sign that Huitzilopochtli had promised his chosen people. And therefore the priests raised a humble temple on the site, where they enshrined the statue of their god. From that temple, which would eventually become one of the grand monuments of the Aztec capital city of Tenochtitlán, "Huitzilo-pochtli spoke indefatigably on all important occasions as the cruelest yet most agile politician. He never wearied, never halted; nothing satisfied him. For fifteen generations, his dreadful voice bore down on the people with tragic advice for violent action, without a minute of respite." (Bernal)

Huitzilopochtli then said: "Listen, O people, here must be your task and your holy office, and here must you be sentinels and wait, and the four quarters of the world you must conquer, subjugate, and rule. You must have command of body, breast, head, arms, and strength. And your victories and rule shall cost you sweat, work, and pure blood, if you wish to obtain the emeralds, the gold and the silver, the precious feathers, the cocoa from afar, the cotton of many colors, the many fragrant flowers of the field, and the many other good things that give contentment and pleasure."

Reconstruction of the Main Temple of Te-nochtitlán, circa A.D. 1519 — the year of the Spanish invasion.

The uninhabitable marshland was gradually transformed by the Aztecs, for whom agriculture was a relatively new skill. On earth-covered rafts, they planted their famous floating gardens, whose roots worked into the bottom-soil after several generations, becoming stable and forming a network of connected islands, intercut by narrow canals. By approximately 1345, the Aztecs had formed two adjoining chiefdoms, each with its own capital and chief. One group had its capital in Tenochtitlán while the other was centered immediately to the north, in Tlatelolco. As the swamps were drained and cultivated, the separated capitals became part of one continuous land mass, and their governments merged, becoming two districts of a single, monumental city.

Despite the founding of a homeland and the acquisition of much technical ability, the Aztecs of the mid-fourteenth century were still a humble people. Taking full advantage of their characteristic military abilities and shrewdness, they began to insinuate themselves upon the tribes that surrounded them, becoming mercenaries of the powerful Tepanecs, ruled by a chief called Tezozomac. As the various city-states of the Valley of Mexico fell to Tezozomoc and his allies, the Aztecs not only shared in the booty, but were also taken under the protection of the Tepanecs. Then, in 1367 the Aztecs were finally strong enough to reap a terrible vengeance upon an old enemy. They methodically destroyed Culhuacán, the city that had vanquished them after they sacrificed and flayed its princess. Significantly, Culhuacán had been the last of the "fabled cities," whose rulers claimed Toltec descent. The Aztecs saw their opportunity to ally themselves with the prestige of Toltec ancestry, and so they elected as their first king a man named Acamapichtli, a relative of the family of the deposed king of Culhuacán.

During all of these formative years, the Aztecs were assimilating much of the Toltec heritage that was fundamental to all the civilized peoples of the Valley of Mexico. They learned much from their powerful allies, the Tepanecs — particularly the arts of military expansion, statecraft, and empire. After generations of humiliation, the Aztecs were ready to become a singular and dominant force in Mexico. Their opportunity came in 1426, when the Tepanec king Tezozomoc was succeeded by his son Maxtlatzin, who wished to dispense of the Aztecs because of their ever-growing power. This plan to subdue the Aztecs came precisely when a new and remarkable king was elected to

the Aztec throne. His name was Itzcoatl, and he was a determined and ruthless militant, who decided to fight the Tepanecs
rather than be crushed by their young king.

Within two years the Aztec lord Itzcoatl and his brilliant
adviser, the great Tlacaelel, had crushed the Tepanecs and destroyed their city. This victory left the Aztecs the greatest power in Mexico. It was Tlacaelel who most gloried in this triumph,
becoming the grand vizier to the Aztec throne through three
successive reigns, and exerting a tremendous influence on the
most important period of government policy. According to Michael Coe, "Tlacaelel conceived of and implemented a series of
reforms that completely altered Mexican life. The basic reform
related to the Aztec conception of themselves and their destiny;
for this, it was necessary to rewrite history, and so Tlacaelel did,
by having all the books of conquered peoples burned since
these would have failed to mention Aztec glories. Under his ae-
gis, the Aztecs acquired a mystic-visionary view of themselves
as the chosen people, the true heirs of the Toltec tradition, who
would fight wars and gain captives so as to keep the fiery Sun
moving across the sky."

The Sun, as we know, was represented by the god Huitzilopochtli, and that cruel god required human hearts for his survival. To keep the peace but also to make captives available for
sacrifice, the Aztecs devised the so-called Flowery Wars, a series
of battles between allies with a long history of animosity toward
each other. The sole purpose of these wars was to secure captives for sacrifice. But, as Ignacio Bernal insists, "it is obviously
absurd to suppose, as many historians have stated, that the motives behind their wars were simply religious. War held out the
promise of material advantages, conquests, booty, tributes, and
a constant expansion of territorial boundaries. But the Mexicans
were not the initiators nor the ones responsible for the 'almost
permanent state of war' in which they lived. We have seen how
war had become an ever-present cultural trait from the very
early times of Mixcoatl, and I believe since Olmec times. What
the Mexicans seem to have carried further than others is a religious sense of war." This would have been particularly true of
the Flowery Wars.

The greatest empire-builder and perhaps the bloodiest of
all the Aztec rulers was Ahuitzotl (1486–1502), who subjugated the peoples as far from his capital as those on the Guatema-
lan borders and who brought almost all of central Mexico under

The Aztec Calendar was found buried in the Main Plaza of Mexico City in December 1790. It weighs about twenty-five tons and is about twelve feet in diameter. It was carved and dedicated to the Aztec Sun god, Huitzilopochtli, during the reign of the sixth Aztec emperor, Axayacatl.

Aztec control. A man of immense ambition and energy, Ahuitzotl had the Great Temple of Tenochtitlán completed during his
reign. For its dedication in 1487, some twenty thousand persons were sacrificed.

The most tragic and illustrious of the Aztec lords was Montezuma Xocoyotzin. He was a remarkably philosophical king,
unlike his ardently militaristic predecessors, and it was his
meditative nature and his profound interest in the intellectual
and spiritual heritage of the Toltecs that destroyed him and ultimately brought down the entire Aztec world. On the fateful day
in 1519 when Cortés arrived on the shore of Mexico, Montezuma was certain that the bearded alien was Quetzalcoatl, come
back with his Toltec retinue from the east as the old books had
prophesied, to reclaim his throne and to punish the Mexican
people who had exiled him. Every decision Montezuma made,
even his terrible inability to defend himself and his empire
against the Spanish invaders was the result of his belief in Toltec
legend. "It was his destiny, foretold by a series of magical por-
tents, to preside over the total destruction of Mexican civilization." (Coe)

MONTEZUMA'S CAPITAL was one of the great cosmopolitan
centers of the sixteenth-century world. We enter it by water,
for it was virtually a floating metropolis. The distant city spar-
kles in the sun. Tenochtitlán is the glorious stronghold of the
Valley of Mexico from whose gates stretch forests of oak and
sycamore and tall cedars. And beyond the forests are wide valleys of maize and maguey. At the center of the vast valley are
many lakes, their shores studded with handsome towns and villages. And in the midst of this lovely valley is the great city itself,
with its towers and pyramids and awesome temples that are the
eyes of the gods.

We come to Tenochtitlán from a great distance, walking for
several days until we hear a faint hum of life in the distance. The
clay landscape ends at the water's edge, where we lower ourselves into a grass boat and cast off into the brown stream. The
wide waterway that leads into Tenochtitlán becomes narrow as
little islands of floating vegetation appear one at a time — drift-
ing gardens made of mud dredged from the shallow lake and
suspended on the water's surface on wickerwork rafts. These
random gardens gradually entangle, becoming large stationary
plots of rich land, with narrow canals separating them. The canals are the causeways of the city, through which white-clad

farmers swiftly pole their dugouts as they cultivate their gardens. Along the banks and among the flowers and trees are the thatched huts of farmers. Then, as the boats loaded with city-bound produce become numerous, the adobe walls of richer homes appear among the foliage — at first made simply of naked clay and then plastered more elegantly and colored muted shades of red. Narrow roads appear beside the canals where merchants with armed guards and trotting carriers bring their goods to markets. Soon people of rank are seen along the banks of the canal. Clan leaders wear the rich mantles of their office; and they alone are permitted to carry an aristocratic bouquet of flowers, which they sniff lavishly. They meander among the black-garbed priests, whose faces are painted black, whose ears are scarred by self-inflicted penance, and whose long black hair is matted with blood.

It is market day, and the crowds are large and noisy. Humble and great men hurry in every direction, the rich carrying flowers and the poor carrying burdens. In a small ball court, with its sloping masonry sides and narrow playing field, a few men are practicing the game called *pot-a-tok,* and we momentarily watch the skill of the players of this difficult game. The expressions of the young athletes are grim as they race after the hard rubber ball and, using their heads, their thighs, and their feet, try to keep it from striking the floor of the court. It is a sport of great daring and deep significance. And as we watch the ball fly through the air, again and again, the players on the two teams try to score a point. They thrust and leap and sing as they play, trying to put the ball through the rings set at intervals in the walls of the court.

Now we hurry away and push through the Great Plaza. We can see nothing but human bodies and human baggage as we press forward. Then suddenly we step out of the tangle of the crowd into a vast open space at the entrance of the palace. Only men of power and rank may walk here. One by one they come to the Council Chamber of Montezuma to plead for favors or to beg for his forgiveness. He is a sublime ruler — so great and holy that we may not look upon his face. He was elected from the most royal of the Aztec lineage by a council of nobles, warriors, and priests. But once he ascended to his throne he has been utterly out of the reach of even those who elected him, so vast is his power. Even great lords are required to wear the plainest of garments in his presence. One speaks to him only through an "interpreter" and may not address him directly.

The fearsome Aztec deity Xipe Totec — "Our Lord of the Flayed Skin" — depicting the god dressed in the flayed skin of a sacrificial victim.

Wherever Lord Montezuma goes he is carried in a litter on the shoulders of nobles, and when he walks the ground is swept and covered with precious textiles so his feet do not touch the ground. Even when he dines, Montezuma is concealed behind a handsome screen. In all the world there is no king greater than the lord of the Aztecs.

YET MONTEZUMA WAS a complex and troubled man. Aztec history reveals that even before the coming of the Spanish invaders he agonized over his fate and that of his people. But the mentality of Montezuma is no more remarkable than that of the Europeans who destroyed his realm. Laurette Sejourne has written a highly perceptive study of the Aztec world, in which she states: "From the point of view of what we know today, it seems impossible that Europe could have remained completely ignorant until the sixteenth century of a civilization which by that time had existed in Mexico for over fifteen hundred years. Equally surprising is the indifference shown by the conquerors toward the universe it was their fate to stumble upon. Nothing shows Cortes's inner attitude, maintained up to the end of the conquest, better than his gift of glass beads to the Aztec leaders: in spite of his surprise at finding signs of great cultural refinement, he never for a moment doubted that he was in the presence of a barbarous people interesting only because they were fabulously wealthy. Nowhere in his writing does he show the least desire to understand them; in fact, he condemned them out of hand before he had made more than the most superficial acquaintance with them."

Tenochtitlán and its neighboring city Tlatelolco consisted of more than sixty thousand houses and a population in excess of three hundred thousand — five times the size of Henry VIII's London. In little more than five years after the arrival of the Spaniards the exquisite city and its massive population had been destroyed. And this stunning destruction was somehow achieved by a force of not more than six hundred Spaniards and their numerous Indian allies.

Hernán Cortés was born in 1485 in Medellin, a provincial Spanish town. His first biographer, Francisco Lopes de Gomara, depicts him as "restless, haughty, mischievous and given to quarrelling." Broad-shouldered, medium in height, and pale-complected Cortés developed a social air of affability but was still haughty and aggressive when his authority was challenged. His lofty ambitions were perfectly suited to the imperialistic

mood of Spain in the fifteenth and sixteenth centuries. After
Ferdinand and Isabella united Aragon and Castile in 1479, Spain
became the most formidable military power of Europe. The
non-Christian Moors who had long been the loathed enemies of
Spain were driven from their last Spanish foothold in Granada in
1492. It was the year that the resolutely Catholic and expansionist Spanish nation looked with unbridled greed at the lands
stumbled upon by Columbus. In 1511 the Spaniards invaded
and subjugated Cuba. Cortés was among the conquerors. Here
he married and resettled. When Ferdinand and Isabella died, the
Spanish throne passed to Charles V, who eventually also reigned
as emperor of Austria, Germany, Luxembourg, the Low Coun-
tries, and part of Burgundy. An extravagant Hapsburg, Charles
was always looking for new sources of funds to lavish on his
munificent tastes, and the Western Hemisphere and its legends
of immense riches fascinated him.

Cortés saw his moment and promptly volunteered to lead
an expedition in search of riches. He was appointed commander of such an expedition by the governor of Cuba, Diego Velásquez, who was as ambitious as Cortés and did not trust the
independent young commander. He therefore cautiously autho-
rized Cortés only to explore, not to conquer. One clause in the
governor's instructions, however, indicated that Cortés, in the
event of emergencies, could take whatever measures would
conform with "the services of God and their Highnesses." The
cunning Cortés interpreted these words to suit his purposes,
gaining from them a very doubtful legality to what became his
brazen and brilliant act of insubordination to the authority of
Governor Diego Velásquez.

When Cortés landed on the coast of Mexico in February
1519, his flotilla consisted of eleven ships, about five hundred
soldiers, one hundred sailors, numerous servants, and sixteen
horses. Eight months later he had already reached the heart of
the Aztec world, the great city of Tenochtitlán, and had been
received there as an honored guest. Absolutely nothing of a
militaristic sort was done to prevent Cortés from entering
Mexico, despite the fact that the Aztecs and their allies consti-
tuted an awesomely large and fierce military force. The march
of Cortés through the Mexican countryside can be explained
mainly, as Sejourne has pointed out, by the undoubted talents of
Cortés for intrigue and betrayal, which enabled him to orient
himself very quickly in the maze of Mexican politics. "Soon after
his arrival, he discovered resentment and rebellion simmering

among Montezuma's subject tribes, and at once formed the military alliances that made his dazzling victories possible. An indomitable will, not shrinking from assassination or wholesale massacre, accomplished the rest."

In his first landfall, at Cozumel, an island off the coast of Yucatán, Cortés had encountered a shipwrecked countryman named Jeronimo de Aguilar, who had lived among the Indians for about eight years and had therefore learned their language. While among the people of Tabasco, Cortés also acquired a second interpreter as well as a cohort with as much cunning as Cortés himself. Her name was Ce Malinalli or Malinche (or Doña Marina, after her baptism), a young native woman who spoke Nahuatl as well as the languages of the Yucatán that Aguilar understood. Ce Malinalli quickly learned Spanish from Aguilar and became the consort of Hernán Cortés.

Using Ce Malinalli's exceptional abilities to turn her own people's religious faith and political dissatisfaction to the advantage of Cortés, the Spanish commander was able to impose the despotism of Spain on the vast Mexican territory by posing as a liberator of tribes oppressed by the Aztec overlords. Cortés also possessed the advantage of his missionary zeal as a justification of his exploitation of the Mexicans. He made a good case against the Aztecs by pointing out their use of human sacrifice and cannibalism. Those accusations still shock the twentieth-century sensibility, but they have a somewhat different impact upon us when viewed against the gross inhumanities practiced in Europe in the time of Cortés. The Inquisition, which flourished in southern Europe from 1237 to 1834, is famous for its wholesale use of torture and the horrendous violations of human decency in the name of the faith. Spain was a stronghold of the most unconscionable acts in the name of God. The expulsion of the Jews from Spain and the defeat of the Moors were two long-term struggles involving staggering cruelties and inhumanities. Though Cortés and his soldiers made the most of their shock and consternation over human sacrifice, it must be remembered that in the Mexican city of Cholula, the Spanish commander ordered the slaughter of hundreds of unarmed religious celebrants. As Sejourne notes, a man capable of ordering six thousand throats to be cut in less than two hours must certainly earn a reputation for bloodletting no less shocking than that of the Aztec sacrificial priests.

Extravagant actions and reactions were typical of Cortés. From the outset of his Mexican exploits he took fantastic risks.

For instance, soon after landing at Veracruz he ordered his most curiously daring stroke: the destruction of his own ships, which would prevent any conspiracies within the ranks led by those loyal to Governor Velásquez of Cuba. Then the army of Cortés marched inland, watched but unmolested by thousands upon thousands of Aztec warriors who were restrained by Montezuma's belief that Cortés was Quetzalcoatl. On August 31, 1519, it entered the lands of the Tlaxcalans, an Indian people who loathed the Aztecs and had long fought against them. Cortés easily won the alliance of Tlaxcala against Montezuma, and thus secured the massive forces required to subjugate all of Mexico. Horses, cannons, muskets, and European battle techniques were doubtless of great assistance to the Spaniards in defeating Mexico, but without the fierce dedication of Montezuma's Indian enemies it is extremely doubtful that Cortés could have survived his unbelievable ambition to subdue the vast and powerful realm of Montezuma.

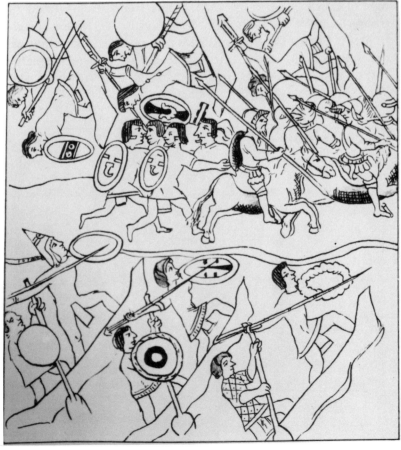

The Spanish invasion of Tenochtitlán (Mexico City) in 1520 (*Florentine Codex*).

No one will ever really know all the motives that prompted Montezuma to allow the Spaniards to march across Mexico, to enter the capital and then wander freely in the great city without the least resistance. All we know is that the great Lord of Tenochtitlán, who was absolutely unyielding in his political aggressions against native cities, somehow offered the strangers scarcely any opposition. He even surrendered to house-arrest and permitted the plundering of his treasury. Once he was held captive by the Spaniards, his people were helpless to defend themselves for fear that the invaders would retaliate by assassinating their Great Lord. Eventually, however, the massacre of unarmed warriors at their sacred feast so infuriated the Aztecs that they drove the Spaniards out of Tenochtitlán, where they had been encamped peacefully for about five months. This counterattack was known to the Spanish as the "Night of Sorrow."

During this time, Cortés had left Tenochtitlán in order to fight a battle against his own countrymen. He ordered his troops to attack the forces sent by Governor Velásquez of Cuba to arrest Cortés for insubordination — in short, for acting like the monarch of Mexico. Cortés defeated these Spanish soldiers and then, with promises of gold, managed to win over most of Velásquez's troops to his own cause.

Aztec Emperor Montezuma II is captured by the Spaniards (*Florentine Codex*).

Upon his return to Tenochtitlán, Cortés found his men surrounded by hostile Mexicans, virtually held prisoner in their own fortress. Angered by the insurrection, Cortés forced Montezuma to confront his people and demand their withdrawal. The angry crowd fell utterly silent when they saw their lord high above them on a terrace, but they refused to yield to his commandments. Then something remarkable happened: a stone was thrown at Montezuma by one of his own subjects, and then another and another. Voices cried out against his weakness and folly. A stone struck the Great Lord and he fell back and was taken to safety inside the building. There, apparently, he was murdered by the Spaniards.

The long-repressed fury of the Aztecs was so great that they again drove the Spaniards out of their city. But Cortés refused to be beaten. He built several boats and transported them in sections overland to the lake where the "floating" capital of Mexico was located. Nearly a year passed while the Spaniards prepared for their terrible siege of Tenochtitlán. The rigid war ethics of the Aztecs assured their war chiefs that, once formally defeated, the humiliated white strangers would depart for their own land and never return to Mexico. But Cortés did not know the Aztec rules of war and he certainly did not accept the defeat of being driven from the capital city on two different occasions.

With the boats he needed to attack the city from the water, Cortés marched upon Tenochtitlán. The terrible siege lasted seventy-five days (the native accounts claim it was eighty days). And by the time the city surrendered, it no longer existed. Its temples and houses were rubble. Its magnificent works of religious art were destroyed. Its treasures were stolen and melted into ingots, and the population had been decimated. In 1525, the Aztec civilization ended.

The great metropolis vanished — battered, broken, and dismembered during the siege. All the great buildings were deliberately and painstakingly demolished in order to fill in the many canals which once ribboned the city. In accordance with the evangelical stance of the Spanish conquistadores, Cortés insisted that the artifacts, the houses, and, especially, the temples of the Aztec world had to be razed in order to stamp out a satanic religion and make room for the introduction of Christianity.

Before the Spanish debacle the vast Aztec capital had possessed two major religious and civic centers: Tlatilco, which

The capital of the Aztec Empire, Tenochtitlán is plundered and burned by the Spanish invaders (*Florentine Codex*).

was the older of the two and lay in the northern quarter of present-day Mexico City, and the great plaza of the Main Temple, located in the heart of the city. But tragically, these remarkable architectural districts were dismembered — lying like corpses where once they had glistened in the sun. The very stones of the ancient monuments were used by the architects of Spain to build the palace and the great cathedral of Mexico City. Thus the glorious capital of the Aztec world was buried alive under the new stronghold of its merciless invaders.

Since the beginning of the sixteenth century there has been considerable debate and a good deal of confusion about the exact location and the precise design of the Main Temple of Tenochtitlán. It was speculated, upon the basis of a map attributed to Cortés himself, that the vast temple court lay at the intersection of the ancient Aztec causeways known as Iztapalapa and the Tacuba; which would roughly conform today to a zone bordered by Calle de San Ildefonso on the north, by the Calle de la Moneda on the south, by the Calle de Carmen on the east, and by the National Pawnshop on the west.

According to an early authority on the Aztec civilization, Padre Sahagún, there were over seventy-two different temples within the great court, the most important of which was the Great Pyramid dedicated to the gods Tlaloc and Huitzilopochtli. Marvelous descriptions of this majestic and remarkable structure have survived, but it has always been very difficult to spec-

The rediscovery of the Main Temple of Tenochtitlán: excavation at the base of the pyramid, showing the carved serpent heads.

ulate about the exact character and details of buildings destroyed over four hundred years ago. Thus, the intriguing culture of the capital city of the Aztecs was forever vanquished and lost beneath the reckless traffic and commotion of Mexico City. For years the only memorial to its grandeur remained within the extraordinary National Museum of Anthropology — one of the most dramatic and luminous of world museums.

Some small inkling of the magnitude and marvels of the Main Temple of Tenochtitlán was accidentally discovered when, in 1900, a sewer line cut through the inner structures of the monument, suggesting for the first time that the Great Pyramid is not one building, but at least four complete temples stacked like nested Russian folk dolls one within another. The existence of these successive layers as well as several additional façades was further verified in 1913 when the southwest corner of the temple was uncovered. But the true splendor of the Main Temple remained a legend hidden under centuries of rubble and construction.

Then suddenly, on February 23, 1977, a staggering discovery was made. At nine o'clock in the morning a woman, who refused to identify herself, called the Departamento de Salvamento Arqueologico in Mexico City. She claimed that the nonstop work on a new segment of the subway system had kept her up all night. Irritated and determined to register her complaint, the woman explained that she had gotten out of bed, dressed, and went down into the street, where she approached the workers digging a deep trench for the installation of electrical transformers. Air hammers and other equipment set up such a commotion when she confronted the laborers that she could not possibly make herself heard. She was about to shout into a foreman's ear when abruptly all the equipment fell silent and the men whispered excitedly among one another. A laborer with the brown skin and strong facial features of his Aztec forebears came stumbling from the trench, a look so intense in his eyes that the woman feared he had been mortally wounded. When he finally composed himself, he murmured to the foreman that he had just unearthed "the arm of a goddess."

The man's claim was not exaggerated. He had stumbled upon one of the most important archaeological finds of the century. Within hours, three scientists were dispatched to the site. After a quick survey they cautiously reported that the workmen had accidentally unearthed a series of hand-carved steps and precious sculptures some fifteen feet below the intersection of Argentina and Guatemala streets — immediately next to the Cathedral and just a street away from the National Palace and the Plaza de la Constitución.

The news of the discovery swept Mexico — a nation where a persistent and strong pride in Indian heritage animates the entire population. President José Lopez Portillo visited the archaeological site only five days after the Departamento de Salvamento Arqueologico received the excited phone call from the anonymous woman who announced the discovery. The world press swarmed over the closely guarded dig; and those of us lucky enough to be admitted viewed for the first time in four hundred years the remains of one of the most dramatic and glorious capitals of ancient civilization.

What we saw when we crept along the network of catwalks quickly constructed to transverse the rugged subway excavation was the corner of the enormous Main Pyramid of Tenochtitlán, dedicated to the gods Tlaloc and Huitzilopochtli. This was not actually the final and probably fourth temple structure, but the façade and structural walls of the earlier third temple. It had been part of a succession of expanded and enlarged buildings, and had always been the principal sanctuary of the great plaza. It once towered above all the other buildings of the immense Aztec city. For centuries it was thought that this pyramid lay directly under the cathedral, but discoveries in 1913 and 1977 made it clear that the great double stairway of the pyramid and the temple substructures are located at some distance southwest of the cathedral. The gigantic Main Temple of Tenochtitlán at the time of the invasion by the Spaniards was the last of a series of splendid renovations which had been carried out by three Aztec lords: Itzcoatl (1427–1440), Montezuma Ilhuicamina, the Elder (1440–1468), and Ahuitzotl (1486–1502), the uncle and immediate royal predecessor of Montezuma Xocoyotzin, the Younger (1502–1520), who reigned over Mexico when the Spaniards arrived.

The pyramid rose over a rectangular area measuring approximately one hundred by ninety meters. The front of the structure, facing west, consisted of a grand stairway flanked by ramps — one on each side and another running down the center of the stairway itself. This appears to have been the floorplan of all the successive renovations. The ramps were decorated at the base with the heads of serpents, several of which may now be seen along the base of the third temple at the excavation.

The rediscovery of the disk dedicated to the Moon goddess.

The magnificent stairway served the two temple-shrines at the top of the truncated pyramid and had, in its final form, 114 steps leading to the awesome pinnacle of the structure, where ceremonies and human sacrifices took place one hundred feet above the surrounding city.

After several years of meticulous excavation, the entire substructure of the Main Pyramid has now been uncovered, with its huge ramp that divides the main stairway. What remains of the original structure is a segment of the vast platform surrounded by serpents' heads which once served as the foundation for the whole mighty third temple. Also visible are the large square chambers on the platform; two rows of pillars upholding the roof and flanking the central court where long stone benches were once used by high priests and officials during sacrificial rites and other ceremonial meetings.

By far the most artistically and historically exciting find has been a colossal carved disc at the base of the third pyramid stairway. It depicts the goddess of the Moon, Coyolxauhqui, whose graceful arm the workman had first uncovered. Carved in a handsome buff-colored stone, the relief depicts the dismembered body of Coyolxauhqui that resulted when she was attacked by her rival brother Huitzilopochtli. As we have seen, the myth of this confrontation is a major feature of the Aztec genesis. And the Aztec people commemorated the victory of their tribal god Huitzilopochtli with the immense disc depicting the broken body of the Moon, which they carved and placed at the foot of the stairway of the Great Pyramid dedicated to the Sun god Huitzilopochtli and the associated Rain god Tlaloc. The disc was a symbol of profound significance to the ancient Mexicans, for it offered assistance to the Sun, who daily raged against the cunning darkness and fought his way back into the night sky. This everlasting battle wearied the Sun and threatened his precious life. Only human blood could renew the sunlight in which the Aztecs prospered. And so, for generations, the Aztecs took thousands of captives in battle and, after honoring and handsomely costuming them, led them up the 114 steps of the Main Pyramid to the sacrificial stone in front of the temple to Huitzilopochtli. There the priests threw the victims upon their backs, cut open their chests with one terrific thrust of an obsidian knife, tore out their beating hearts, and offered them to the sky. Then the bodies were tossed down the long stairway. They tumbled downward, leaving a wide trail of blood, until they landed in a heap upon the disc of the Moon goddess, Coyolxauhqui, strategically placed at the bottom of the stairs. Thus, the ritual of sacrifice and renewal was completed; the Sun, Huitzilopochtli, rose rejuvenated and victorious against the night into the morning sky.

The splendid and the macabre live together in the remarkable excavations of Mexico City. Even today, emerging from beneath the congested traffic of the crowded and noisy city are the shadow and the reality of the ancient landscape of an undying Aztec Mexico.

A page from the *Florentine Codex* depicting a human sacrificial ceremony. The victim was stretched over the altar at the summit of the pyramid; his chest was cut open and his heart torn out; and then the body was thrown down the steps.

People of the Four Directions

THERE WAS ONCE A MAN who had a very loyal Dog, and they lived comfortably in a good land. One day Dog whined loudly with fear, and he warned his master to make a raft as quickly as he could, for soon a great flood would overtake this world, destroying everything. Man trusted the good sense of Dog, and so he hurried to cut trees in order to make a large, strong raft.

"You must pack much food for us," exclaimed Dog.

Man nodded and hurried to collect provisions.

"You must make a small fire in the middle of the raft, and gather dry sticks with which to feed it," said Dog.

Man quickly built a fire on the raft and collected dry wood.

No sooner had Man completed all these tasks than the water began to rise. Dog and Man saw the great mountains burst open, and in a torrent of white water many hideous monsters emerged, consuming all the people and all the animals. Nothing seemed to remain of the good land except Dog and Man, who clung to their raft as the water rose higher and higher, carrying them far above the mountains and above the clouds. When they could rise no higher, the water withdrew silently, leaving the raft gently floating in the air. It was very cold high in the sky, but Man and Dog were able to warm themselves in the little campfire that Dog had insisted be taken on the journey. In the early morning Man peered cautiously over the edge of the raft and, far below, he could see a beautiful land of trees and flowers. Man reached for the pole with which to steer his craft down through the clouds to the beautiful land, but Dog told Man that he would surely perish if he tried to land in that strange place. "You must return to the place from which we came," Dog warned. "But in order to do so, you will have to sacrifice me."

"Oh no!" exclaimed Man, for he did not want to harm his loyal Dog.

Dog, however, insisted that Man throw him into the terrible flood that still covered the land from which they had come. Unwillingly Man threw Dog into the waters. Then almost at once the flood began to subside.

From afar Man could still hear the voice of Dog, telling him not to land his raft until the mud had dried for seven days. Man poled his raft back into the sky and watched as the brown water rolled back and left a vast sea of deep mud. Then gradually all the puddles disappeared from the land from which Man had come.

When seven days passed, the ground had turned hard. Almost at once grass and trees sprang up. Cautiously Man steered his raft toward the land from which he had come, floating down into a familiar valley. As soon as he stepped from the raft, Man saw strange people coming in his direction. And some were naked and deformed. Some wore terrible rags. Some had very handsome regalia. Each group had a leader and each leader approached Man and begged him to share his fire with them. Man consented at once, for he pitied these strange people. The three groups divided the fire between them. They lived in peace in the land where the flood had washed away the world. Man, having known the place where the Great Sun dwells, became the ruler of the people, and those with handsome clothing became his Nobles, while those in rags toiled and served, and those who were naked became slaves.

So it was long ago in the days of the flood.

THIS TALE OF A GREAT FLOOD is a rare clue to the mentality and cosmology of some of the most bizarre and mysterious of American civilizations, those created by various ancient peoples whom we now call Mound Builders. We know nothing about the languages nor the philosophies of these people. We can only make some educated guesses that mythic elements discovered by early European missionaries among the Creek and Natchez Indians of the Mississippi Delta might contain shadows of the folk history of these forgotten ancestors. In the tale of the flood,

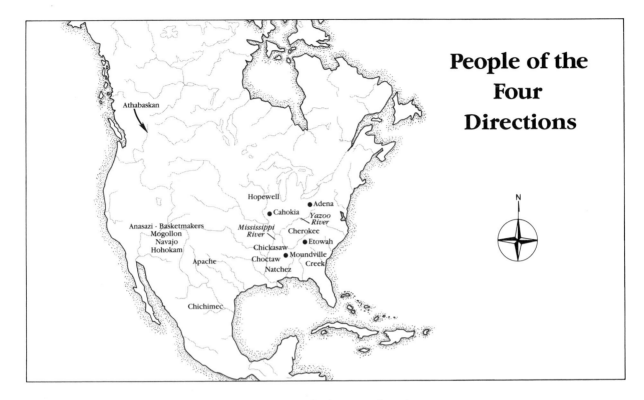

People of the
Four
Directions

we may have a glimpse of the mythical origin of the social rank that was an obsession of the Mound Builders.

It was only gradually that we have come to recognize how truly extraordinary were these architects of massive earthworks along the Mississippi River. The first European to visit Native North Americans in recorded history was Hernando de Soto. When he traveled across the southeastern United States with his conquistadores in the sixteenth century, he was disappointed by the relative poverty of the tribes he encountered. By comparison to the rich Aztecs, the native people of the north seemed rustic and plain to the gold-seeking Spaniards. The explorers were impressed, however, by the large communities of Indians living along the Mississippi in complex hierarchical societies under the control of powerful chiefs.

Wild accounts of these Mississippian tribes greatly roused the curiosity of Europeans, but before a complete study could be made of their cultures, they vanished: the victims of smallpox, measles, tuberculosis, influenza, and assimilation. These vanquished Indians were probably the last of the "Mound Builders" — a remarkable series of independent cultures that had existed along the Ohio and Mississippi rivers since 2000 B.C. Exceptionally little is known about the people who built "uncounted thousands of mounds" in a vast eastern territory reaching from Florida to Canada. In fact, what we do know of them is the result of research in just the last few decades. That scant knowledge has helped us recognize the complexity and sophistication of these tribes of master builders, who constructed massive earthworks, evolved classic social organizations, produced masterful works of art, and then vanished.

Archaeologists are in great disagreement about the history of the Mound Builders. Dr. Antonio J. Waring, Jr. has suggested that "at one happy time, the coast between Port Royal and the Altamaha [River] was presumably the most civilized spot in the Eastern United States." Some experts see in the artifacts and architectonic forms a degree of ceremonial refinement unparalleled in eastern North America's archaic history (circa 2000 B.C.). "To some archaeologists, the presence of fiber-tempered pottery and Southeast shell rings suggests an intriguing possibility: remarkably long coastal voyages from South America to Georgia and South Carolina about 2400 B.C. For the combination of shell rings and similar pottery is known from only one other area of the Western hemisphere — on Colombia's Caribbean coast. It is a striking coincidence, but archaeologists so far have been unable to corroborate the theory." (Stuart)

By the early eighteenth century, when French explorers arrived at Louisiana, pathetically little remained of the glorious achievements of the Mississippians. A century earlier, settlers had frantically battled the so-called Creek Confederacy — a powerful alliance of about fifty large settlements of Indians in the southeast. In reality, the "Confederacy" was not composed of a single people, but was made up of several different tribes speaking their own distinctive languages: the Creeks themselves, the Chickasaws, the Choctaws, and the Cherokees — all of them long-standing enemies of each other who were forced to unify in order to combat the assault of white invaders.

"The European colonists found the lower Mississippi from the Yazoo River to the delta ruled by a series of small, riverside states. Some of these states, notably that of the Natchez, perpetuated [ancient] Mississippian culture, including the tradition of mound building, into the eighteenth century." (Fagan) The Natchez were studied with considerable interest by various Frenchmen, who have left us elaborate memoirs and narratives. According to these early observations, the Indian villages were scattered along St. Catherines Creek and around the complex of mounds located to the east of the present-day city of Natchez. Reportedly there were still four thousand Indians in the region in the late seventeenth century.

These reports have proved to be of great importance both for their depiction of eighteenth-century Indian life and also as a reasonable profile of the early societies of the Mississippi, for it is generally agreed that the Natchez, more than any other North American tribe of the period of European contact, provide a valid picture of the social and religious values of the ancient Mississippian civilizations. In other words, we may assume that the surviving accounts of life among the Natchez provide a rare glimpse into the world of the vanished Mound Builders.

The French chronicler Le Page du Pratz wrote: "The Natchez nation was one of the most estimable.... Their manners were besides gentler, their way of thinking truer and fuller of feeling, their customs more rational, and their ceremonies more natural and more serious, which made this nation more brilliant and distinguished it from all others. It was indeed easy to recognize that it was much more civilized."

The Natchez were ruled by a despotic chief, the Great Sun, whose power was virtually unlimited. He owned all the land and all the personal property, and the lives of his subjects were totally in his control. His house, constructed of timber, was on the top of a truncated mound. A second mound was the location of a wooden temple in which the bones of deceased Great Suns were kept. An early-eighteenth-century eyewitness description of the rule of the Natchez chiefs and the social organization is found in the anonymous "Luxembourg Memoir" (*Memoire sur La Louisiane en Le Mississipi*, written prior to 1718): "The chief of the entire nation is the Great Sun and his relatives are called Little Suns, who are more or less respected according to their degree of proximity to the Great Sun. The veneration which these savages have for the Great Chief and for his family goes so far that whether he speaks good or evil, they thank him by genuflections and reverence marked by howls. All these Suns have many savages who have become their slaves voluntarily, and who hunt and work for them. They were formerly obliged to kill themselves when their masters died. As the relatives of the Great Sun regard the other members of their tribe as scum."

Below the Great Sun and his immediate family, the Little Suns, was a rigidly graded aristocracy, consisting of Nobles and then War Chiefs, High Priests, and, finally, the lowest-ranking of the aristocrats, the Honored Men or Honored Women, including master artisans, rich merchants, and important soldiers.

The commoners, consisting of farmers, workers, warriors, and slaves, were all referred to as Stinkards or Stinkers — a sadly mistreated and massive population of serfs without any input into the running of their world or their own lives. They were apparently killed at whim, should their actions or comments displease the Great Sun and his coterie. Their situation might have been utterly hopeless were it not for one exceptionally curious rule of Natchez life: all the aristocrats, including the Great Sun himself, were required to marry Stinkers. This marital arrangement did not relieve commoners of their wretched situation, but, on the other hand, the children of such a union were permitted to rise in rank, depending on the station of the mother. Thus the offspring of a Noble mother and her Stinker husband became a Noble; while the child of a Noble father and a Stinker mother assumed the next rank below that of the higher-ranking parent, becoming an Honored Man or Honored Woman. The son of the Great Sun could not inherit his father's supreme rank; instead, the Great Sun was succeeded when he died by the son of his highest-ranking female relative.

"Marriage was not the only way to advance in social class. An Honored Man or even a Stinker might be promoted one level for bravery in war. And special sacrifices in honor of the gods or of a notable chief also brought advancement. But the cost was high, for such sacrifices were human; the ambitious social climber had to participate in the ritual murder of a member of his own family. One of these bloody ceremonies, which were part of funeral rites, was witnessed by French explorers during the interment of a chief of the Natchez." (Claiborne)

The Penicaut Narrative (Margry; 1614–1654) offers some observations about the European view of Natchez nobility: "Their nobility is very different from that of our Europeans, for in France the more ancient it is the more it is esteemed. Their extraction, on the contrary, is no more esteemed noble at the seventh generation; moreover, they draw their nobility from the woman and not from the man. I have asked them the reason for this, and they have replied to me that nobility can come only from the woman, because the woman to whom children belong is more certain than the man."

The Natchez had a remarkably liberal view of women. Chastity in unmarried women was not valued. "Those [women] who are not married have great liberty in their pleasures; no one can disturb them. Some are found whose chastity can not be shaken; there are some also who desire neither lovers nor husbands, although chastity among the Indians is one of the least virtues. The greater number take good advantage of the liberty which custom gives them." ("Luxembourg Memoir")

Only the Stinker wife of the Great Sun had the right to sleep with him. Only she ate at his table. The other members of his family, the so-called Little Suns, were given the leftovers from the Great Sun's table, which he offered to them by pushing the food toward them with his foot. The daughters of Noble families had to marry Stinkers, but they had the right to turn them away when they pleased, and to take another husband. If their Stinker husbands were unfaithful to them, they could order them to be killed by being knocked on the head, although they themselves were not subject to the same rule. They could have as many lovers as they wished, and their husbands could not object. The Stinker husband of a Noble woman had to stand in her presence; he could not eat with her; and he had to salute her in the same abject manner used by slaves. The only privilege of the Stinker husband was his exemption from labor.

Male concubines existed openly among the Natchez. Dumont de Montigny (*Memoires Historiques sur La Louisiane,* 1753) stated that a male concubine "among the Natchez, and perhaps also among many other Indian nations, is called 'the chief of the women.' It is certain that although he is really a man he has the same dress and the same occupations as a woman. Like them he wears his hair long and braided. He has, like them, a petticoat or alconand instead of a breechcloth. Like them he labors in the cultivation of the fields and in all the other labors which are proper to [women] .... When a party of warriors or of Honored Men leaves the village to go either to war or to the chase, if they do not make their wives follow them, they always carry with them this man dressed as a woman, who serves to keep their camp, to cook their hominy, and to provide, in short, for all the needs of the household as well as a woman might do."

Except for its class orientation, marriage was not a very serious part of Natchez life. When boys and girls arrived at the age of puberty they freely associated with each other, socially and sexually. The Stinker girls were taught that they would have to be constant after marriage and would not be able to give their favors as they wished. They knew, however, "how to dispose of them to their advantage in forming their wardrobe as the price of their pleasures, for in that country, as elsewhere, the rule is nothing for nothing." (Du Pratz) In short, much of the dowry of a woman was obtained by her as gifts from lovers in exchange for sexual favors. "And a woman for being common is not the less esteemed."

If marriage did not have the importance among the Natchez that it does in the European world, death and mortuary rites were regarded with far greater seriousness than almost any tradition found in the West. The rites surrounding death were, by our standards, both grotesque and barbarous. It is possible that such macabre aspects of Natchez ceremonialism accurately reflect upon the obsession with mortuary rites that was central to the lives of the Mound Builders.

In a letter of 1730, the Jesuit missionary Father le Petit provided a remarkable account of the death of a Great Sun of the Natchez. From his narrative we can reconstruct one of the most astounding of Indian rites.

The Great Sun lies cold and pale upon his bed. His servants bring food and his wife offers it to the dead man. "Do you not wish to enjoy the food we bring to you?" she asks. "You make no answer. Therefore you must surely be dead, and have left us to go to the land of the spirits!"

Now the wife weeps in agony, throwing back her head and howling her death cry. The sound is taken up by all the attendants and relatives of the great ruler. The cry echoes from house to house until the entire village resounds with the lamentation.

For two days elaborate preparations for the funeral are undertaken by the people. The Great Sun lies in state, adorned in his finest regalia, his face painted red. By his side are the emblems of his power: a war club, numerous stone pipes handsomely carved to commemorate his victories, his bow and arrow, and a chain of cane woven with a succession of links, each representing an enemy he killed in battle. Surrounding his bed are his retainers and his wife, silently awaiting the gruesome rite which is their customary role in the burial of a great person.

Now whispers arise as the High Priest makes his splendid entrance, elaborately tattooed and dressed in feathers and shell beads. At a signal from the priest, the attendants lift the litter of the dead king. Now the solemn procession begins. It winds down the stately mound on which the Great Sun's house is perched, slowly making its way into the plaza. The ruler is carried in a wide circle among the silent people who fill the plaza, and each of the dead man's retainers is joined by eight relatives, their arms and hands painted red. Eventually, these relatives will be the executioners of their own kin — a ritual that is central to the funeral of the Great Sun.

Now the litter bearing the dead man is carried toward the temple mound that flanks the plaza. A group of women raise their voices in the doleful chant of death, as the procession starts the climb to the temple. Suddenly there is a great outcry and the strangled corpses of infants are cast under the feet of the litterbearers. The children are sacrifices, killed by their own parents, whose social rank is increased by their terrible offering to the dead king.

The cortege ascends to the summit of the truncated mound, where the retainers and the wife of the Great Sun dutifully take their places on mats which have been spread on each side of the dead man's litter. Now the funeral ceremony begins. The High Priest asks the Great Sun's wife: "Is it your wish to live forever with your great husband and to go with him to the land of the spirits?"

"Yes!" she exclaims, "for in that land we have never to die again. The days are beautiful and there is abundant food, and people are peaceful and do not make war upon one another for they are all of one family!"

The priest then asks the same question of the fifty retainers, and they cry: "Yes! We wish to accompany our king to the land of the spirits!"

The death chant rises abruptly and a dance begins, figures weaving in and out among the sacrificial victims, who sit upon the mats and move solemnly to the rhythm of the singing.

As the music swells and the voices rise to a shrill pitch, each victim is given a ball of narcotic herbs, which is quickly swallowed. Soon they become drowsy and begin to slip into unconsciousness. They smile peacefully as a cord is placed around their necks and relatives assemble beside each victim, four on each side, grasping the cord tightly in their hands.

The High Priest stands before the eternal flame that burns in the temple. He lifts his ceremonial staff and brings it to the earth with an elegant gesture. The cords are drawn tight, and the fifty retainers struggle momentarily and then slump to the ground. The dead king is now surrounded by a large ensemble of corpses who will accompany him into the land of spirits.

The howls rise louder than ever, and to the accompaniment of this immense lamentation the bodies are carried to the summit of the burial mound and placed in graves along with offerings of fine ornaments, weapons, and pottery. Slowly the graves are filled, while on the mound across the village where the Great Sun once lived a cloud of smoke rises as the royal house is burned to the ground.

THE NATCHEZ GREAT SUN was still the supreme ruler of his people when Europeans arrived in North America. That aristocracy and the society it dominated soon came to a terrible end. "Exactly thirty years after the first missionary visited them in 1699, the Natchez made their final desperate attempt to fight back against the encroaching French. They attacked a trading post and massacred about two hundred whites. Retaliation was brutal; within two years the French and their Choctaw allies had utterly crushed the Natchez. Most of the Natchez were slaughtered, and about four hundred survivors (including the Great Sun) were sold into slavery in the West Indies. A few managed to escape and take refuge with the Chickasaw, Creek, and Cherokee. The sacred fire that had been intended to burn as long as the sun shone was forever extinguished." (Farb)

The fragile tradition that had linked the Natchez to the great and ancient societies that had built the mounds was broken. The vast earthworks of the Ohio and Mississippi valleys became monuments without architects, and the time and cir-

A painting on muslin by John J. Egan, 1850, depicting "Dr. Dickeson Excavating a Mound" in the Mississippi Valley.

cumstances of their origin became the subject of wild specula-
tion. Scholars and amateurs constructed elaborate tales of a
great race that had lived in the land long before the Indians and
had produced the mounds before vanishing mysteriously.
"What all these theorists agreed upon was that the mounds had
been built by 'a superior race, or more probably a people of
foreign and higher civilization' who had occupied America long
before the North American Indians." (Fagan)

The many myths of the Mound Builders were forged into
literary fantasies by the renowned New England poet William
Cullen Bryant. When he visited the mounds in Illinois in 1832,
he was deeply touched by a sense of history. He believed that
he could feel the spirit of countless dead warriors beneath his
feet, and so in "The Prairies" he wrote:

> And are they here —
> The dead of other days — and did the dust
> Of these fair solitudes once stir with life
> And burn with passion? Let the mighty mounds
> That overlook the rivers, or that rise
> In the dim forest crowded with old oaks,
> Answer, A race, that long has passed away,
> Built them; — a disciplined and populous race
> Heaped, with long toil, the earth, while yet the Greek
> Was hewing the Pentelicus to forms
> of symmetry, and rearing on its rock
> The glittering Parthenon. . . .
> Then enter the villains:
> The red men came —
> The roaming hunting tribes, warlike and fierce,
> And the mound-builders vanished from the earth.

The facts were considerably different from but no less fascinating than those of Bryant's romantic poem. We now know
with certainty that it was Bryant's "red men" who actually created the famous mounds — and not a vanished race of white
strangers. Prose writers like the American statesman Thomas
Jefferson — who had previously undertaken excavations of a
mound in Virginia — long felt that the enormous earthworks
had been made by Indians. At the Jefferson dig, a series of
trenches were dug with care. As Jefferson later wrote, the
mound contained "collections of human bones, at different

depths, from six inches to three feet below the surface." Eventually, Jefferson discovered that there were about three layers of human skeletons, so meticulously arranged that Jefferson decided his mound must have been a traditional burial site in which as many as a thousand bodies had been interred over a great period of time. He also discovered that the mound was much celebrated by local Indians. Only thirty years earlier a party of Indians had been seen worshipping on the summit of the mound, and Jefferson concluded that it was almost certain that their ancestors had built it.

Jefferson's intuition helped solve the mystery of the Mound Builders, though it would be fifty years before support of Jefferson's position would become available from scientists. In the meantime, during much of the late eighteenth and early nineteenth centuries, the mounds were the target of what has been called "the worst archaeological disaster in American history." Treasure hunters decimated the mounds, carelessly digging for artifacts or virtually blowing them up with dynamite. Farmers plowed through the earthworks to prepare their fields for crops. Artifacts were casually collected by amateurs and hobbyists or shattered and discarded by people too naïve to recognize their historical significance and artistic worth. The geographical possibilities for this archaeological disaster were unlimited, for "nearly every major waterway of the Midwest was rimmed by clusters of mounds." (Silverberg) In the north there were mounds in western New York, extending along the southern shore of Lake Erie into Michigan and Wisconsin, and down to Iowa and Nebraska. In the south, mounds lined the Gulf of Mexico from Florida to eastern Texas, and reached as far north as the Carolinas and Oklahoma. By far the greatest concentration of earthworks was located in the middle of the continent: Ohio, Indiana, Illinois, and Missouri.

The serious studies of the mounds by people like Jefferson were hampered by a popular and scholarly inclination to fantasize about their relationship to the classical cultures of Greece and Egypt or to Atlantis and other legendary cradles of civilization. Even organized explorations, such as the elaborate program undertaken in the mid-nineteenth century by the American Ethnological Society, came to dubious results. According to the two Ohio men commissioned to make the survey — Ephraim George Squier, a journalist, and E. H. Davies, a physician — the great mounds were part of a defense system erected by the Mound Builders (whoever they may have been) to protect themselves against "wild" Indian invaders from the northeast. The Indians, according to the report by Squier, "were hunters averse to labor, and not known to have constructed any works approaching in skillfulness of design or in magnitude these under notice." In short, Indians could not have built the mounds.

Despite many shortcomings, the efforts of the American Ethnological Society were nonetheless significant, if only because they provided a vast corpus of data obtained from the excavation of over two hundred mounds, the exploration of countless earthen enclosures, and the collection of a vast trove of artifacts from the digs. But the report made no headway in identifying the creators of the mounds. It did point out some important, if obvious, information. For instance, it was now evident to even the casual observer that the mounds had specific regional styles. In the North were effigy mounds. In the Midwest were conical mounds and geometrical enclosures. The South was dominated by Mexican-like mounds with truncated summits.

It was not until 1887 that the confusion and fictions about the Mound Builders were finally replaced by credible scientific information. Cyrus Thomas of the Smithsonian's Bureau of Ethnology, summarizing a survey of more than two thousand sites, was able to provide a sound and precise overview of the Mound Builders. "The links discovered directly connecting the Indians and Mound Builders are so numerous and well established that there should no longer be any hesitancy in accepting the theory that the two are one and the same people. A study of the works in Ohio and their contents should convince the archaeologist that they were built by several different tribes and pertain to widely different eras."

It was Cyrus Thomas who established beyond all reasonable doubt that American Indians had, in fact, built the mounds. He also insisted that the popular view of the Mound Builders as a single and persistent race or tribe was an error. There was no such thing as a civilization of Mound Builders, but rather a number of different and various peoples, living in different regions over a long period of time, who had built the mounds.

As Robert Claiborne has pointed out, "reality, once it started to emerge, turned out to be as remarkable as the Mound Builders myth itself. Some of the settlements were large, sophisticated cities inhabited by traders and manufacturers who carried on a thriving commerce over much of North America. They

Art of the Mound Builders: a pipe in the form of a diabolical figure made five hundred years ago, plundered by treasure hunters who blew up that mound in Oklahoma in 1933.

Strong Mesoamerican influence is seen in this seashell gorget, depicting a bear and an eagle. Unearthed in Texas, the gorget was incised more than five hundred years ago and was probably worn as an amulet by a member of the Mississippian culture.

produced a culture — urbane, rich and complex, though also cruel, bigoted, and caste-ridden — that was the most highly developed Indian society in North America."

Almost a century has passed since Cyrus Thomas completed his landmark report. The field of archaeology has been revolutionized by new dating techniques, new instruments, and new methods. The mounds of North America have not yielded all their secrets by any means, but we now know a great deal more than we did in 1887. For instance, it has been established that most of the earthworks were constructed within the last three thousand years. Several distinctive peoples, with no apparent cultural or historical connections, built the mounds, and their incentive for building them and their use of them were often strikingly different from culture to culture. Some of the mounds have a clear connection to Mesoamerican prototypes, though we still do not know much about the process by which influences flowed northward into the midwestern United States from Mexico. On the other hand, we do know as a fact that the enormous mounds of North America were temporally (if not culturally) part of the same vast impetus which saw the development of massive architectural works throughout the Americas. "North American Indians were building mounds while the Olmec and later the Maya were rising to prominence in Mexico. They were still building them at the threshold of recent historical times. But, by the time the first white settlers crossed the

Alleghenies, no trace of the Mound Builders remained but their silent earthworks." (Fagan)

WE ARE NOW ABLE to reconstruct the history of the Mound Builders with a good deal of valid detail. It begins about three thousand years ago, shortly after the introduction of agriculture in the eastern region of the United States. At about this time the hunter-foragers of the area gradually settled in large villages where they began to produce crude clay vessels, often decorated with fabric or cord impressions — pressed into the clay while it was still soft. One of these settlements, called the Baumer site, is located on a levee of the Ohio River in southern Illinois. This large village covered more than ten acres and was composed of houses about sixteen feet square. It is unknown if the people of the Baumer site were farmers, but we do know that they made pottery and dug large pits for the storage of food. The people of Baumer were also hunters, and their major food supply may have been provided by hunting rather than farming.

The first signs of cultivated crops — corn, squash, and beans — appear in the Midwest about 1550 B.C. Then, about 1000 B.C., the first mounds were being constructed. Excavations have proved that the earthworks were well planned and were not simply haphazard constructions. Some mounds were used as burial sites, while others were apparently designed as ramparts; still others, like the immense effigies of birds and serpents, had ceremonial functions. The existence of postholes at the summit of the mounds strongly supports the theory that wooden temples and official buildings and noble residences were constructed on at least some of the mounds.

An unbelievable amount of effort and dedication was needed to build the mounds. For instance, the huge mound near St. Louis, covering fifteen acres and one hundred feet high, is estimated to contain more than twenty-two million cubic feet of earth. All of that dirt was carried by hand, one basketful at a time, by a large population of dedicated or driven people who did their work entirely without the assistance of beasts of burden or wheeled vehicles.

We do not know the location of the first mounds to be built, although the most complex early structures are located in the Ohio Valley, where people began, in about 1000 B.C., to conduct somewhat elaborate funeral rites, burying their dead under low earth mounds. It was a new custom in North America, and it diffused throughout the Midwest in a few centuries. At about the same time, the same people began to construct narrow ridges that enclosed large tracts of land. The significance of these typical earthen enclosures is unknown. Sometimes mounds devoted to burials are found within such enclosures, while other mounds were constructed in groups without evidence of enclosures.

After a formative period in which certain architectonic styles were established in the construction of the mounds, a distinctive culture arose. This earliest Mound Building culture is called Adena, after an estate near Chillicothe, Ohio. It came into existence about 1000 B.C. and endured until about A.D. 200. The Adena mounds were conical in form and were used for burials. A major aspect of the Adena ceremonial life seems to have been focused upon a sacred bird, for its image has been found repeatedly in Adena graves: a hawk, eagle, or vulture. Some experts suggest that the "Adena Bird" might well have been a sacred vulture insofar as the skeletal remains seem to have been interred after all flesh had been removed, presumably by scavenging birds.

At one point it was thought that the Adena people were invaders of the Ohio Valley, militant immigrants from Mexico. This theory was based, in part, on the fact that the Adena skeletons have round heads, whereas the earlier peoples of the region were typically long-headed. Subsequently this notion was abandoned, largely because it was established that the Adena culture did not have a thriving agricultural life: and, of course, the cultivation of corn was a foundation of Mesoamerican civilization. As a consequence of these views, it is now assumed that the Adena culture originated and evolved independently among the native people of the Ohio Valley.

Examination of burial offerings has suggested several predominant cultural traits of the Adena. Kinship groups were apparently strong elements of social organization. "By descent from a common ancestor the lineages of one village might be further linked with lineages of another village in larger relationships, or clans. The leaders of such clans and lineages would probably have enjoyed a special social and economic status in Adena society." (Fagan)

The Adena religious traditions were much preoccupied with death. The extraordinary effort to construct a burial mound and the complex paraphernalia associated with interment attest the importance of death as a rite of passage. Grave offerings were exceptionally well wrought objects of clay and stone. Some of these objects, like the famous carved ceremonial pipe of a dwarf, suggest that the Adena — like some of the peoples of Mexico and Peru — may have honored persons who were deformed.

Whatever the shape and substance of Adena culture, we know that its influence was exceptionally widespread. We discover elements of Adena burial customs, artistic traditions, and religious practices over a wide region, "perhaps as far afield as Chesapeake Bay and New York State." (Fagan)

The Adena culture began to collapse after about a thousand years. Many aspects of the life-style faded away, while others seem to have been perpetuated in drastically different forms. What is suggested is a continuity of cultural forms that were invented by the Adena people, but we cannot say with any certainty if Adena elements were continued forward by new carriers of culture or if such elements were largely reinvented by subsequent peoples. In any event, the Adena culture vanished as mysteriously as it had been born.

The Adena people may have been destroyed by the invasion of a new and stronger people. But no one knows exactly what became of the Adena world. It may have been displaced, destroyed, or simply absorbed by a superseding culture made up of many diversified groups of Mound Builders. These new people are regarded collectively as members of the so-called Hopewell culture, a term derived from the name of a farmer in Illinois whose land was covered with mounds.

It is unknown if the Hopewell people originated in the southern Ohio Valley or migrated there from elsewhere. Wherever their origin, they were physically distinct from the prior Adena people. The Hopewell had long skulls, unlike the round ones of the Adena. They also produced a ceramic and figurine tradition that, though similar in style to the Adena materials, was noticeably superior in detail and manner. In many ways, the Hopewell demonstrated a greater degree of sophistication than their Adena predecessors. They were much wealthier. Their mounds were grander in scope and design, and the burials contain exceptionally rich offerings.

The geographical range of Hopewell influence was immense. Hopewell influences are seen over much of the eastern United States, extending from Ohio and down the Mississippi River to the Gulf Coast and as far east as Florida. We know little

Adena effigy pipe, circa 1000 B.C., Ohio.

about Hopewell social and political forms, but we do know that they had an elaborate agricultural life centered upon loosely allied permanent villages. There is reason to believe that the Hopewell were master traders — the first in the East and perhaps the first north of Mexico. They had highly developed and wide-ranging trade routes. Their characteristically carved stone pipes have been discovered as far east as New York, and the unique kind of flint that was available in their region has turned up as finished artifacts on the Eastern Seaboard. The Hopewell also obtained the raw materials for their crafts from an even wider geographical range. Surface copper ore came from Lake Superior. Obsidian for knives and arrowheads was obtained from the Yellowstone area of Wyoming; while other stone came from as far away as Montana and North Dakota.

Whereas the Adena were apparently very much concerned with social rank, "the Hopewell seem to have been a society without social class, but clan or lineage leaders enjoyed a special prestige that is reflected in the great wealth of their burials." (Fagan) In one matter, however, the Hopewell and the Adena had much in common: both cultures were religiously obsessed with death and mortuary rituals. Hopewell burials were markedly similar to the graves of the Adena but on a much grander scale. For instance, "the builders of Crook's Mound in Louisiana began by raising an earthen platform in which 168 bodies were buried; then 214 more were placed on top of the

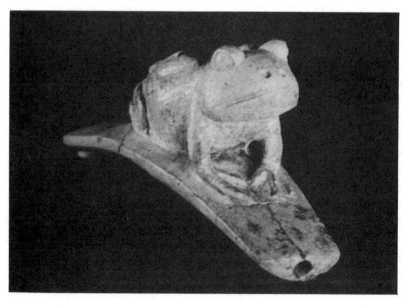

Hopewell effigy pipe, circa 300 B.C., Ohio.

platform before the mound was completed above the burials. On some mounds [basket upon basket] of soil was piled forty feet high. Important individuals were buried with lavish arrays of ceremonial vessels and other valuable objects." (Fagan)

Burial offerings rarely show signs of use, presumably because they were especially created for interment. These grave goods provide an excellent succession of Hopewellian style. The finest pottery displays modeled birds of prey or ducks, usually in combination with various geometric, grooved, and zigzag motifs. Some vessels have ears that apparently served as handles. The modeled figurines are sculptural portraits of both men and women with braided, knotted coiffures and robes. Women are often depicted seated, with an infant held at their breast.

The Hopewell heartland was rather limited (Ohio and Illinois), and the villages were both few in number and small in size. The power of the Hopewell culture may have been based upon immense religious influence (in the manner of the Mexican Olmecs), remarkable ability in trade, and an absolutely unified, monolithic social attitude that is reflected in the "rigid conformity to certain religious and artistic conventions. . . . The complicated overlay of ritual and artistic tradition that forms the most distinctive feature of the Hopewell is so exotic and polished that many Hopewell art objects seem at first glance to be almost alien to a simple agricultural society." (Fagan)

The golden age of the Hopewell occurred between 200 B.C. and A.D. 550. During this period there was truly remarkable invention and refinement in artistic and religious ideals. The reason for this cultural efflorescence is unknown, but it may have been connected with the great prosperity that accompanied the introduction among Hopewell farmers of the cultivation of corn, possibly from Mesoamerica. But whatever the basis of the triumph of Hopewell culture, its golden days were numbered, for after about seven hundred years it began to decline rapidly. The trade routes broke down and the range of Hopewell influence greatly diminished. Yet, even during this dark period, there remained some important but isolated Hopewell outposts, such as the renowned "Effigy Mound" culture, located on the upper Mississippi Valley, that produced numerous mounds in the form of lizards, panthers, birds, bears, deer, and other animals. Most of these mounds contained burials at critical anatomical points in the bodies of the depicted animals: heart, hip, head, knee. The meaning of both the mounds themselves and their specifically located graves is unknown.

THE MOST FAMOUS of these effigy mounds is the Great Serpent Mound in Adams County near Chillicothe, Ohio — a structure that may rank as the most remarkable nonmasonry monument of North America. No one is certain just what culture was responsible for this extraordinary earthwork. "This is only conjecturally an Adena mound, for no human artifacts have ever been found in it; but excavation of a conical burial mound about 400 feet away has yielded characteristic Adena objects." (Silverberg) The exact date of construction of Serpent Mound is also unknown, though it has been suggested that the work probably began about 1000 B.C. (Stuart) As Brian Fagan notes, "this huge earthwork uncoils along an Ohio ridge for 1,254 feet. The jaws of the serpent are open, clasping a low conical mound in the shape of an egg. The body of the snake twines along the hilltop, its tail tightly coiled in a spiral. . . . The Serpent Mound is not a burial mound, nor does it appear to have any connection with the effigy mounds of the upper Mississippi Valley. [Though] most archaeologists believe that the serpent may have had a special Mound Builder symbolism . . . few share the belief of a well-known nineteenth-century Baptist minister, who argued that the great serpent was built by the Creator Himself to commemorate the site of the Fall. In that interpretation, the serpent is about to swallow the forbidden fruit, represented by the small mound between the jaws. In support of his claim, the minister cited Job 26:13: 'His hand hath formed the crooked serpent.'"

THE DEVOURING SYMBOLISM of the Serpent Mound may also be viewed as a monument connoting the endless feast of time, which saw first the Adena culture and then the Hopewell culture swallowed up by oblivion. For reasons we do not know, the golden age of the Hopewell had ended by about A.D. 600, and the cultural supremacy of North America passed from the Hopewell area in the north to the lower Mississippi Valley. The wide flood plain between St. Louis and New Orleans saw the rise of the greatest of all North American Indian states, the "Mississippian."

By the early eighteenth century, when European explorers encountered the last tribes of this Mississippian culture — like those remarkable Natchez people whose world we have already discussed — most of its vigor had dissipated. For about eight centuries, beginning in A.D. 600, the influences of that civilization reached an immense geographical region in the central and

eastern areas of what is now the United States. As Brian Fagan proclaims, "The scale and flamboyance of Mississippian society dwarfed anything known before in North America." Aspects of this new culture clearly perpetuated old traditions of the Mound Builders, though we do not know the exact nature or form of this continuity. At the same time, the Mississippian people created many cultural elements quite different from those of their North American predecessors. Today we realize that many of these Mississippian characteristics were not unique but, as we shall see, were introduced from Mesoamerica.

Serpent Mound, Ohio: an earthwork in the form of a snake with an egg in its mouth.

The city of Cahokia is the most renowned Mississippian center. Here we can reconstruct many aspects of the society of the last of the Mound Builders. Located near present-day East St. Louis, Illinois, it was a vast urban complex that flourished for at least seven hundred years. By the time French explorers encountered the city it was in ruins, but carbon 14 dating indicates that it was occupied until A.D. 1550, although its great days as a center of commerce, farming, and religion were between 900 and 1100. In its prime, the city was an elaborate metropolis dominated by a massive fifteen-acre truncated pyramid, several ceremonial ridges constructed as enclosures, platforms, ter-

Mississippian (Temple Mound) Period, Ohio, circa A.D. 1200–1600: a mask carved of yellow sandstone.

races, dwellings, a market area, and, outside the enclosed city itself, extensive farmlands dotted with four major mounds and plazas and an astronomical structure, often called an "observatory," apparently used to determine the planting and harvesting cycle. The whole city had a curiously Mexican mentality and form. A powerful force in Cahokia was a new religious ideal that suggests an obsession with human sacrifice and a cosmology centered upon elements such as fire and the sun. Beyond the fortified city stretched a massive realm, probably bound together by both the religious and economic domination of Cahokia. Across the broad Mississippi Valley were broad fields of corn, shining green and golden as far as the eye could see. Here and there amidst the sumptuous farmland were villages where prosperous fishermen and farmers lived a good life, working hard and chatting earnestly to one another as they carried their produce along small paths that wound among the simple houses where women ground corn and prepared meals.

Beyond the village the path widened into a lane where many people made their way toward Cahokia, whose impressive pyramids rose into the air above the fields. Entering the city, the farmers made their way to the marketplace, passing the central plaza where the great temple, the warehouses, administrative buildings, and the dwellings of nobles were located. People greeted friends they had not seen in the fields for many weeks, for the farmers were regularly conscripted to spend time in the city, building and repairing civic structures. At the market there was a marvelous array of produce and artifacts: copper, stone, pottery, shell, and wood worked into handsome forms. Upon shells were incised the images of birds, spiders, and the sun. Sheets of fine copper were embossed with human figures. Pottery vessels were sculptured as human portraits. Many objects contain a mysterious icon of the Mississippian religion: faces with distinctive "weeping-eyes," which suggest the importance of rain as a symbol — an inconographic form similar to imagery found in Mexico.

At its apogee, Cahokia was one of several major centers scattered along the Mississippi Valley from the Gulf of Mexico to the Great Lakes. Under the control of these powerful cities and their priestly aristocracy lived a large population of farmers whose fields spread outward from the river valley in every direction. The influence and power of this Mississippian realm were unmatched in North American prehistory. Then, in the late fifteenth century, for reasons still unclear, the Mississippian culture began to dim. The chronicler of the 1539–1542 de Soto expedition, Garcilaso de la Vega, encountered a temple on the Savannah River and left this exasperatingly incomplete description: "The ceiling . . . from the walls upward, was decorated like the roof outside with motifs of shells interspersed with strands of pearls. . . . Among those decorations were great headdresses of different colored feathers . . . it was an agreeable sight to behold."

By this time Cahokia and other Mississippian cities such as Etowah and Moundville were abandoned and in a state of ruin. The massive population which had inhabited the once-rich farmland had dissipated or had been annihilated by disease. The great work force that had farmed the land, created artifacts, and built the cities and their huge mounds was gone. The Mississippi Valley was largely depopulated and "the earthworks at the river's edge merged into the levees and ridges and became virtually indistinguishable from the natural landscape. Complete oblivion had overtaken the last of the Mound Builders." (Fagan) But the story of these remarkable people was not yet finished, for archaeologists are still piecing together their exceptionally complex history. Today it is clear that the Mound Builders did not create a self-contained civilization, but were an integral part of a much larger world. Recent evidence suggests that the Mound Builders, in the east, and the ancient Pueblo people of the American Southwest were part of a vast domain that stretched southward and northward, forming a network of societies linked by a central Mesoamerican cultural impulse.

This greatly revised view of North American prehistory is the result of archaeological research that has redefined territorial concepts. For instance, it is clear that the Valley of Mexico was for many centuries the heartland of American civilization. To the south was the world of the Maya. In the east was El Tajín and the various Gulf Coast cultures. In the west was an equally various center of societies: Jalisco, Nayarit, Colima. In the Valley of Oaxaca was the Zapotec civilization. The major archaeological revision of geopolitics has taken place in the north. For many years this northernmost zone of Mexican influence was designated as the arid "Chichimec land" that extended to the banks of the Rio Grande River, which now marks the boundary between the United States and Mexico. It used to be acceptable to speak of the Mound Builders or the Pueblo Indians of the American Southwest as discrete cultures of the United States. That cultural geography has proved to be completely wrong. It

From the Spiro Mound in Oklahoma, circa A.D. 1200–1500: an effigy pipe depicting a warrior bending over the body of his victim. Mississippian (Temple Mound) Period.

was, as a matter of fact, the Mound Builders in the northeast and the forebears of today's Pima, Papago, Zuni, and Hopi Indians of Arizona and New Mexico who were the most northerly people of Mesoamerica. As the result of recent research and a different and less ethnocentric view of North American geography, we have relocated the northern boundary of Mexican civilization so that it reaches deep into what is now the United States. Richard Woodbury has summarized this revised view of the Americas: "Archaeologists coming to the Southwest from the eastern United States, largely uninformed about Mesoamerican civilizations, and later studying it from local Southwestern museums and universities with relatively parochial attitudes, tended to see the evolution of Southwestern culture as taking place in far greater isolation than is now known to be the case. Although it has a distinctive configuration of culture patterns, the Southwest clearly is peripheral to the centers far to the south from which came its first domestic crops and farming techniques, its pottery making, and later a large number of exotic trade goods.... When the Spaniards conquered and settled the Southwest in the seventeenth century, it had had two or more centuries of relative isolation from Mesoamerica, an ebbing of the long, intermittent contacts that had provided so much of the basic culture that it reworked in its own ways."

The relationship of these Mexicans of the four directions was originally based on commerce, but once contact was established between widely separated regions, elements of religion, social structure, ritualism, and art were also transmitted along a

Mississippian (Temple Mound) art of the so-called Southern Cult: two painted marble figurines (two feet high), one male and one female, from Etowah, Georgia.

"Turquoise Road" which Michael Coe has compared to the famous Silk Road that once linked Asia and Europe. Coe has provided an excellent summary of the cultural movement along
this Turquoise Road. He points out that the southward invasion
of the Chichimecs who overran the Toltec world was only one
aspect of the geopolitics of Mexico. From the Early Classic Period (A.D. 150–650) there had also been a persistent effort of the
civilized peoples of Mesoamerica to push northward along the
eastern flanks of the Sierra Madre into Chichimec country.
These Mexican pioneers lived a frontier life in the desert land,
"sowing their crops in what had once been barren ground . . .
but it is not until the Post Classic [circa A.D. 900] that one can
see any major results, when a series of strongpoints was constructed. The deep interest of the central Mexicans in the Chichimec zone lying between them and the American Southwest
went far beyond the mere search for new lands, however. The
site of Alta Vista, near the town of Chalchihuites, Zacatecas, lies
astride the Tropic of Cancer, about 390 miles northwest of Tula.
It was taken over by Teotihuacán (or Teotihuacán-controlled)
people about A.D. 350, and was exploited all through the Classic
for the richness of its local mines, probably . . . through slave
labor. Alta Vista itself is little more than a ceremonial center
with a colonnaded hall on a defensible hill, but it is possible that
this architectural trait, along with the *tzompantli* or skull rack,
may have provided a Classic prototype for these [same] features
at Tula." Thus the cultural exchange between the "barbarous"
north and the civilized heart of Mexico moved in both directions, with numerous Chichimec influences finding their way
into Mesoamerica at the same time that many elements from
central Mexico were making their imprint upon the far northern regions.

Mississippian (Temple Mound) effigy of a
kneeling man, from temple mound in
Tennessee.

For instance, a surprising connection between Alta Vista
and the Pueblo Indians of New Mexico has been established. As
Coe points out: "At some time in the Classic [A.D. 150–800],
turquoise deposits were discovered in New Mexico, in all likelihood by the Pueblo farming cultures that had old roots there.
Whether it was they or the Alta Vista people who actually
mined the deposits is not known, but turquoise was taken to
Alta Vista and worked there into mosaics and similar objects, for
export into central Mexico."

The power of Alta Vista apparently faded when Teotihuacán collapsed and when the Toltecs became the dominant force

Buried more than five hundred years at Key Marco in Florida, this wooden figure of a cat was carved by the Mississippian people at the height of their power.

of Mexico (circa A.D. 900). It was at about this time that access to the rich New Mexican turquoise deposits was passed along to the Toltec outpost La Quemada, a hilltop fortress in the state of Zacatecas, 106 miles southwest of Alta Vista. "The two-way nature of the Toltec contact with the Pueblo peoples can be seen at the site of Casas Grandes, Chihuahua [in Mexico], not far south of the border with New Mexico. The florescence of Casas Grandes was coeval with the late Tollan phase at Tula, and with early Aztec [A.D.1200]. While the population lived in Southwestern-style apartment houses, the Mesoamerican component can be seen in the presence of platform temple mounds, and I-shaped ball courts, and the cult of the Feathered Serpent. Warehouses filled with rare Southwestern minerals, such as turquoise, were found by Charles DiPeso, the excavator of Casas Grandes. What was traveling north? The Pueblo Indians have a deep ritual need for feathers from tropical birds like parrots and macaws, since these symbolize fertility and the heart of the summer sun. Special pens were discovered at the site in which macaws were kept, apparently brought there by the Toltecs in exchange for the wonderful blue-green turquoise, or perhaps to pay the natives of New Mexico for working the turquoise mines.... It is fairly clear that all these sites were involved in the transmission of Toltec traits into the American Southwest, in particular the colonnaded masonry building and the platform pyramid; the ball court and the game played in it; copper bells; perhaps the idea of masked dancers; and the worship of the Feathered Serpent, which still plays a role in the rituals of people like the Hopi and Zuni. It is also clear that these traits ran along a trading route, a 'Turquoise Road.' A similar movement of Toltec traits took place in the southeastern United States at the same time, probably via the people living on the other side of the central plateau, but little is known of the archaeology of the region. In Alabama, Georgia, Tennessee, and Illinois, sites with huge temple mounds and ceremonial plazas, and their associated pottery and other artifacts, show strong Toltec influence.... Most of the more spectacular aspects of the late farming cultures of the United States have an ultimately Toltec ancestry." (Coe)

For instance, in the Mississippi Valley there are countless examples of influences from Mexico: towns laid out around central squares, rectangular houses of pole and thatch construction, matrilocal residence and descent, various kinds of philosophical and civic dualism, marked class divisions, human

Cliff palace at Mesa Verde, Colorado — the hidden village of the Anasazi.

The White House, cliff dwelling of the Anasazi, Canyon de Chelly, Arizona, circa A.D. 825.

sacrifice, a priest-temple-idol cult, eternal temple fires, rituals in the town square culminating in a Green Corn ceremony, litters for carrying dignitaries, and an emphasis upon incised and sculptural pottery. Yet many aspects of Indian tradition of the midwestern United States from the Great Lakes to the Gulf Coast show unquestionable independence. Clearly, much of the character of both Mound Builder and Southwestern culture was the result of local invention, and it is precisely their rich amalgam of Mexican influences and independent innovations that created the fascinating civilizations of the Mississippi Valley and the American Southwest.

Today this amalgamation of many elements is less visible in the Southeast than it is in the Southwest. Tribes like the Natchez and Creek were decimated, relocated, and acculturated, while the farming peoples of New Mexico and Arizona are still living a quasitraditional life-style on their original lands. But even the vanished Midwestern civilizations were not entirely Mexicanized. Many of the foundations of Mound Builder civilization and the subsequent evolution of tribal cultures in the Southeast were unique. As Bruce G. Trigger points out, on the one hand "nothing like the Adena-Hopewell burial complex is known in Mesoamerica." And on the other hand, "nowhere has it been possible to trace the historic cultures of [the Southeast] irrefutably back to Mississippian antecedents. The Central Algonquian cultures of the Potawatomi, Sauk, Fox, Kickapoo, Mascouten, Shawnee, Miami, and Illinois were variants of a common and very different pattern, which archaeologically seems to have its roots in the local cultures of the upper Mississippi Valley."

In the Southwest there is a clearer, if not indisputable, line of development from prehistoric times. As Alfonso Ortiz has said, "here Indian people remained in their traditional home-lands, and much that is vital in life remains as it was, timeless. Here is the oldest continuous record of human habitation on the continent outside of Mesoamerica, a habitation that has fashioned this region into a humanized landscape suffused with ancient meanings, myths, and mysteries."

The trend toward Mexicanization that we have described in relation to the Mound Builders of the Mississippi Valley is also vividly apparent in the cultures of the American Southwest. And whereas scholars generally see this Mexican presence along the Mississippi as the result of the diffusion of ideas via trade routes, many experts believe that in the case of the Southwest the influence, at least in part, may have been the result of a major immigration of the so-called Hohokam people into Arizona from Mexico in prehistory. "The origin of the Hohokam has long been disputed. The debate centers on whether they represent an indigenous development with strong Mesoamerican relationships or whether the Hohokam were the result of a direct migration of Mesoamerican people from the south. . . . Whether the Hohokam relationship with Mexico after their arrival was one of continual independent trade or the domination of them by Mesoamericans is debatable. Whichever way the data eventually lead, it seems certain now that the Hohokam society strongly reflects Mesoamerican societies with modifications due to their distance from the original homeland and their adaptation to the southern Arizona environment." (Gumerman and Haury)

The effort to pinpoint the origin of the Hohokam (600–1450) is important because much of what is distinctive about Southwest culture evolved out of Hohokam culture. Many of the customs of the ancient Hohokam have been retained among modern Pima and Papago Indians, who are apparently their direct descendants. Another ancient people who lived to the east of the Hohokam and had elaborate cultural connections with them — the Mogollon (900–1200) — were the first potters of the Southwest. The Anasazi (900–1800) of the Colorado Plateau are apparently the immediate forebears of the modern Pueblo Indians. These were the "ancient ones" of the American Southwest, a wide scattering of people in Arizona, New Mexico, and Colorado. Their prehistoric world still remains in the shadows, only slightly understood, and their relationship to the modern Indians of the region is highly debated. Either these "ancient ones" wholly vanished, leaving only their remarkable dwellings and artifacts as evidence of their rich lives, or, perhaps, they were ancestral to the various tribes that now live in the Southwest. Whatever their origin and subsequent history, it is clear that they were the most northwesterly of the people of the four directions. Their exceptional world was seeded by the powerful influences of the Valley of Mexico. That world grew splendidly in its dusty desert, where the Hohokam created distinctive pottery, ritual, architecture, and textiles at the same time that they methodically reproduced the ball courts and the platform mounds of their Toltec neighbors to the south. They celebrated their gods in rituals using icons and images, tropical feathers and masks which probably had their origin in Mexico. Then, when the Toltec world crumbled, the cultural and economic impulse that had allied Mesoamerica and the American Southwest faltered and failed. By the time the Spaniards invaded their great domain, the "ancient ones" had vanished; many of their wondrous buildings — like Mesa Verde — were ruined and utterly forgotten. The precious debris of structures of stone and adobe still stood under the brilliant sun, but they were abandoned, the voices of their inhabitants were silenced by the centuries. It is only in our own era, with the gradual rediscovery of the world of the Southwest, that we have begun to glimpse something of the depth and breadth of the marvelous heritage of today's Pueblo Indians, who till the same soil and sing the same songs as those who have vanished from the cliff dwellings long long ago.

TWO LONE COWBOYS leaned over the frost-covered manes of their exhausted horses as they made their way against a freezing wind one December day in 1888. These rugged cattlemen, Richard Wetherill and Charlie Mason, had started out at sunrise searching for strays that would surely perish if left to wander the canyons and mesas above the Mancos River. Already the sun was low and the temperature was dropping fast as night approached. The cowboys eventually broke out of the underbrush along the rimrock high above the river, where they stopped momentarily to get their bearings and to rest their horses that heaved billowing white breaths into the steel blue Colorado air. All around them was the great escarpment that dominates the southern horizon of the Montezuma Valley between the towns of Cortez and Mancos. So rugged is this vast landscape that explorers and pioneers used to pass through the quiet valley below rather than confront the defiant north edge of the river canyon's massive walls.

Wetherill and Mason peered through the shifting snow that whirled in the wind, trying to catch sight of their lost cattle. As they scanned the broken canyon walls and the valley below, the air suddenly cleared; a rush of frigid air swept the snow away, and in the brilliantly clear atmosphere they momentarily saw what looked like a stone house ... a whole series of stone houses ... floating in midair.

The two cowboys stared incredulously at one another. Without knowing it, they were the first white people to discover some of the most remarkable archaeological ruins north of Mexico. For here, standing silent and protected by a gigantic recess in the face of the cliff across from them, was an awesome sight. Under the roof of a huge cave that ages of seeping water had eroded in the cliff face were some of the best-preserved cliff dwellings in North America, ruins that lay totally undisturbed for centuries after the last survivor of the mysterious people who built them had vanished. The cowboys knew the stories told by Ute Indians about the ancient relics said to exist on the mesa, but they still could not believe what appeared before them in the snow-filled air. Hanging as if in empty space was a network of rooms and towers bound together in a single structure of shaped and fitted sandstone.

The exploration of the ruins found by Wetherill and Mason in 1888 has been beset with many problems. Not until 1962 was a complete survey and archaeological examination of Mesa Verde carried out. This research program, conducted over five years by the National Park Service and the National Geographic Society, gleaned numerous clues from the ruins, but countless questions about them remain unanswered.

About thirteen hundred years ago, a distinctive, though still not satisfactorily identified, group of Indians inhabited the so-called Four Corners region of the American Southwest. This unknown tribe selected the Mesa Verde for its home. They lived and prospered on the top of the mesa, and then, for unknown reasons, they began to build unusually well-fortified houses in the canyon wall itself. Eventually, at the end of the thirteenth century, they suddenly abandoned their cliff homes and simply vanished. The Navajo Indians who now live in the area have long-standing oral traditions about these "ancient ones," or Anasazi.

When the Anasazi abandoned their cliff homes, they left behind their villages and many of their personal possessions. Today these relics are preserved in Mesa Verde National Park. The scholars who have been studying these relics since their discovery have named the earliest inhabitants of Mesa Verde the "Basketmakers," insofar as they possessed very advanced skills in that craft. During the first days of their habitation of the region, these people lived in pit houses, dwellings dug into the ground so that the walls of the pit formed the interior house walls. They clustered their pit houses to form small villages on the top of the mesa. There the Basketmakers lived in relative peace, a fact deduced from the absence of any sort of fortification. Their only domesticated animals were dogs and turkeys; and the turkeys seem to have been raised less for food than for feathers, which were woven into blankets for the cold winter months.

Beginning about the fifth century A.D., the Basketmakers began to cultivate small gardens in their semiarid area. For eight hundred years they lived there, developing farming techniques, building small dams and storage ponds and rather complex irrigation systems. By the middle of the eighth century A.D. the descendants of the Basketmakers, whom we now call Pueblo Indians, began building houses above ground. They set poles upright in the soil to form the outline of the house and then wove sticks among the poles. They constructed their roofs in much the same way, and then added a thick coating of mud to weatherproof both the walls and roof. These first houses of the Southwest were built one against another in a long, curving row. Sometimes they built one or two deep pit houses in front of the crescent-shaped row houses, and it is possible that these pits were the beginnings of the famous underground ceremonial chambers called *kivas* by today's Pueblo Indians.

Gradually a distinctive style of architecture evolved. During approximately the same period that the Anasazi became skilled in the art of basketmaking, they also made great advances in pottery. This Anasazi pottery is unique in both its beauty and style, representing one of the artistic and archaeological treasures of North American prehistory. Stone masonry began to replace the pole-and-mud construction in about the year 1000, when sturdy, compact, apartmentlike buildings were produced with shaped and fitted sandstone blocks. By the twelfth century, the familiar style of Pueblo architecture was fully developed, producing extraordinary buildings two and three stories high, containing as many as fifty rooms.

Near the end of the twelfth century the radical change we have already discussed occurred, causing the people of Mesa Verde to abandon their houses on the mesa tops and to relocate in the caves in the cliff face. There they built the cliff dwellings we find today. We cannot yet determine why this sudden move occurred. The caves may simply have been more "comfortable" places to live in terms of temperature control, yet life there required a difficult climb up and down cliffs to reach the cornfields, and surely such arduous access must have also been hazardous for children and the elderly. So experts are inclined to believe that the relocation was precipitated by the coming of an alien, warlike people — perhaps, as oral tradition indicates, the

Athabaskan bands that migrated into the region from the far north to become today's Apache and Navajo Indians. Whoever these enemies may have been, it is generally agreed that the end of the twelfth century was a time of intense warfare for the Anasazi, and the caves were used as fortification.

The cliff-dwelling period lasted less than one hundred years, and just before the close of the thirteenth century the people of the cliff houses abandoned Mesa Verde forever, leaving their entire world behind them. What caused the Anasazi to abandon their stone village remains a mystery. Perhaps the people were exhausted by warfare and strife. Many experts tend to blame the migration on a long drought that plagued the region and brought major changes to many of its tribes.

We may never know why the Anasazi abandoned their homes, but we do know that the entire population moved away almost six hundred years ago. What we see at Mesa Verde today is evidence of the achievements by a great people in an arid and inhospitable environment over a period of eight centuries. Scholars believe that when the Anasazi left Mesa Verde they migrated to the south and southeast — to the valley of the Rio Grande and its tributaries. Their descendants are thought to be the Pueblo Indians of New Mexico and the Hopi Indians of northern Arizona.

For centuries the ancient cliff dwellings lay silent and abandoned. The Spaniards who came into the area in the mid-eighteenth century did not find the ruins, lost in the remote caves of Colorado. Then, finally, in 1888 one of the finest archaeological treasures of North America was rediscovered by a couple of cowboys. Preserved in the silence of Mesa Verde is the long shadow of the people of the four directions.

The ruins of one of the first apartment-house cities of the Anasazi, circa A.D. 900–1100, in New Mexico.

Warriors of the Plain

SINCE THE DAWN of the Plains Indian world, history was preserved in both images and tales. The enigmatic pictures from prehistory remain on rock face and cliff walls, but their meanings have been lost in the memories of the descendants of those who made them. The tribal stories, however, travel in the minds of people, and they still speak to us through the centuries.

Here is such a story of the Mandan Indians.

Painted shield cover of buckskin, with scalp lock suspended from one side, depicting a guardian vision of its owner, Pretty Bear, a Crow Indian chief, Montana, 1860.

LONE MAN AWOKE and walked upon the great water. Then he began to think, and as he thought he realized that he did not know where he came from or how he had come into existence. This was a puzzlement. So he stopped and looked all around him, but there was nothing but the great water and himself to see. Then he noticed that he had left his tracks upon the surface of the water, and so he followed them in the hope of finding his way back to the place where he had been born. He journeyed very far, until at last he came to a blood-striped flower. There his tracks ended.

Just as he was about to give up his quest for his origin, the red flower began to speak, telling him that she had given birth to him so he might move through the world.

Then the flower fell silent and would not speak again.

Lone Man shook his head in dismay. He was certain that there was something beneath his feet, something far below the surface of the water from which his mother had given him life.

Two ducks settled upon the water. Lone Man spoke to them, asking them to dive under the water and to bring back whatever lay hidden far beneath him. The ducks dived deep into the black water, and when they reappeared they brought four pieces of earth. Lone Man scattered the pieces, which became the four directions that float upon the world and are covered with grass and flowers.

Now Lone Man wandered everywhere upon the water and the land, and wherever he went new things sprang up: fruit trees and butterflies, foxes and deer, and the many other animals and plants of the earth. One day Lone Man came face to face with Coyote, who called himself First Man. No sooner had Lone Man and First Man confronted one another, than they began to quarrel about which of them was the elder. "I was the first being of the world!" insisted Lone Man.

"No!" shouted First Man Coyote, "I was the first!"

Lone Man became so angry that he thrust a spear into the heart of First Man, who fell dead.

For a long time Lone Man sat beside the body of First Man, until at last the body became a skeleton with the spear still piercing its bony chest. "Ha!" cried Lone Man with delight, for now that First Man was truly dead there was no doubt that Lone Man was the oldest being in the world.

No sooner had Lone Man rejoiced than the bones leaped into the air, forming a body upon which flesh quickly grew — and so First Man Coyote stood alive once more.

Lone Man and First Man glared at one another for a long time, but finally they decided not to argue anymore. And so they began to travel together as friends. Wherever they went each of them made a different kind of world, filling it with different kinds of beings.

One day while First Man and Lone Man were busily making their worlds, they came upon the Indians. They were amazed to discover someone that they had not created, and so they secretly watched the Indians for a long time.

They seemed like such good people that Lone Man decided he wanted to be one of them. He searched for a woman who would take him into her body so he could be born to her. When he saw a young woman hungrily eating corn, he ran away from her, fearing that she might chew him up before he could sneak inside of her. Then he saw a very handsome woman who was fishing on the banks of a stream. Shrewdly Lone Man slipped into the current, where he changed himself into a dead

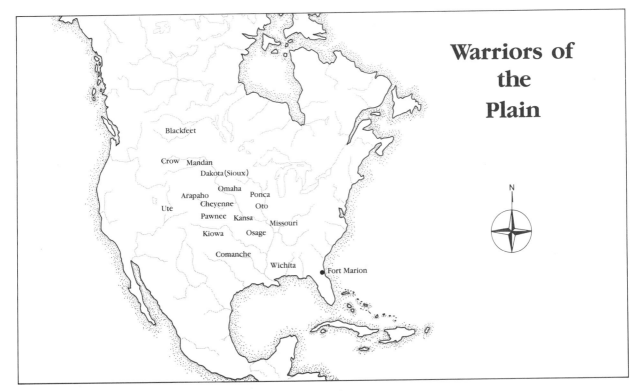

buffalo floating in the water, a delicious bit of fat visible through a wound in his back. The girl laughed with delight when she saw the morsel, and snatching it from the water, she swallowed it. Almost at once she was large with child, and fell to the grass where she gave birth to a wondrous boy.

The child grew at a phenomenal rate, achieving youthful manhood before the summer's sun had faded. No sooner had Lone Man reached maturity in his new body, than a powerful spirit called Hoita became jealous of the many favors the magical Lone Man bestowed upon the people of his village. In an envious rage, Hoita schemed against the Indians, leading all the animals away in a mysterious dance. He confined the beasts in a cave, so now there was no food for Lone Man's village. The magic that had spellbound all the animals of the grassland was cast by Hoita with the use of a magical drum, which he beat with a great thumping sound that made the trees shake and the water of the ponds shudder. Lone Man heard the great pulsing music and realized at once that he would have to find a drum more powerful than the drum of Hoita. The Giant Turtles on whose back the world rests advised Lone Man that if he wished to have a drum more powerful than that of Hoita, he would have to make an instrument in the form of a turtle, for only such a drum could break the spell that Hoita had cast upon the animals.

When the drum was made and Lone Man began to beat upon it, Hoita listened in wonderment. So perplexed was he by the power of the drum of Lone Man that Hoita freed some of the animals and sent them to find out who owned such a great drum. As soon as the animals came into the village, Lone Man trapped them and gave them back to the people. Now Hoita admitted that he was defeated, and so he released the rest of the animals, scattering them across the land so that wherever Indians hunted they would always find good hunting.

Lone Man did many fine things for his people. And after making all the wonderful things that exist in the world, Lone Man departed forever, leaving his sad people with the promise that he would remember them forever.

WITH THIS TALE the Mandan Indians recount the creation of their world — the Great Plains of North America that stretch between the Mississippi River and the Rocky Mountains, from Texas to the windy flatlands of Alberta, Canada. By the time Europeans arrived in America, it was an immense world filled with many different tribes, a world stretching over a million square miles of grassland, bluffs, forested valleys, and wide,

The sacred buffalo of the Great Plains.

stepped terraces. The Plains are truly a sea of grass, for there are virtually no barriers to hold back the wind that perpetually sweeps the landscape. "Grasses sway before the wind and the passage of wind-blown clouds is repeated in the reflection of swiftly flowing shallow rivers; earth, air, and water combine to convey an impression of continual motion. This was formalized by the Plains Indians into a belief that every element of the environment was vital and dynamic but that no part could be considered as separate, or separable, from any other: everything existed, interrelated and harmonized, within a continuous expanse where movement on a massive scale was able to occur. The source of motion, harmony, and unity lay with the Sacred Powers, and the landscape therefore had both physical and metaphysical meaning: man moved, theoretically, from one spiritual state to another in much the same way as he moved physically [across the limitless land]." (Bancroft-Hunt)

Little remains of the ancient history of Plains Indians, for unlike the Mound Builders of the east and the peoples of the south who created masonry architectures, the Plains tribes did not produce a world of temples and villages. Instead, they were nomads and hunters whose most ancient traditions were derived from the years prior to 4000 B.C., when Paleo-Indians hunted the massive animals of Paleolithic North America. With the exception of scattered ceremonial circles, the so-called medicine wheels that are outlined with stones and rocks, very few elements of the material culture have survived to tell the story of the people of the Plains. Their history is not written in stone, and with the exception of their mythology — like the story of Lone Man and the creation of the world — the Plains Indian past resounds with silence. Just as the past is mysterious and empty, so too the vast grassy prairie was a desolate place. The Great Plains was not a densely populated area nor did the vast expanse of grassland possess any of its widely publicized color and character until the eighteenth century, when the nomadic tribes of the region acquired the horse. Only with the mobility provided by horses did these tribes become great hunting and warring peoples, famous for their fanciful porcupine-quill decorations, dramatic buckskin and beadwork costumes, flamboyant feathered headdresses, and elegant painted and quilled buffalo hides. Even the holy of holies among the Plains people, the ritual known as the Sun Dance, is of relatively recent origin, for the nomadic bands were too scattered and

The Bull Society Dance, painted in 1832 by George Catlin at a Mandan village with earthen pit-houses.

poor to sustain an elaborate ceremonial life. The Dog Days were hard times. That was the period when the only beast of burden of the Plains Indian was the dog. People traveled in small enough groups that they were capable of supporting themselves by gathering wild plants and hunting on foot. Theirs was a highly individual world, incapable of sustaining priests or producing civic and sacred architecture. Therefore, the religious life of the Plains was largely in the hands of the individual — with many personally "owned" chants and icons as well as private paraphernalia and regalia that had metaphysical significance.

Eventually, there were a great number of different tribes in the Great Plains, all of them speaking different languages and different dialects of those languages. There were many competitive and unfriendly factions among these people. In general they avoided each other — briefly forming various alliances and then breaking them off, staying within the bounds of a fairly confined territory, which they ranged from season to season. Because of a lack of cover, the foot-bound hunters did not favor

A hide painting, depicting a Sun Dance ceremony at the top. (Denver Art Museum)

the open grassland, and so they tended to travel along the forested margins of the Plains. Then Indians began to capture and break the horses that had escaped from the Spanish invaders of Mexico and roamed freely northward through the rich grassy flatlands. By the 1800s, with the acquisition of the horse, an immense population of Indians began to come down into the Plains to hunt. Suddenly the desolate grasslands were filled with nomadic hunters: Arapaho, Arikara, Blackfeet, Cheyenne, Crow, Mandan, and several bands of Dakota (Sioux) in the north;

Kansa, Omaha, Oto, Pawnee, and Ponca in the central Plains; and Comanche, Kiowa, Missouri, Osage, and Wichita Indians in the south.

The life cycle on the great prairie was shaped both by the season and by the terrain. In the summer, during the time of the hunt, the people tracked animal herds and were constantly on the move. Small hunting bands joined with one another, becom-

Warrior of the Plains, Chief Four Bears of the Missouri River Mandans, painted by George Catlin in 1832.

ing a substantial nomadic community. The people lived in tipis that were easily dismantled and dragged from encampment to encampment by dogs or, eventually, by horses. In the winter, when much smaller groups settled by themselves in isolated areas, Plains Indians tended to take shelter in earthen pit-houses (or lodges) built near streams and rivers. They lived on dried meat and fruits as well as whatever prey was available.

Hunting and warring were intricately interconnected among the Indians of the Plains. There have been many cultural and psychological reasons offered to explain the warlike nature of Plains tribes. Probably one of the most realistic causes of intertribal strife comes from the fact that the people of the Plains were relative newcomers who were thrown into a "frontier world" of which they had little previous experience in terms of dealing with the land and dealing with each other. Water and tinder were scarce in many areas, and there was much competition for preferred encampments and hunting grounds. Yet, as Norman Bancroft-Hunt has pointed out, while such factors explain the almost perpetual strife of the Plains, "they do not in themselves give sufficient reason for the pervasiveness of a 'war philosophy' in Plains culture. A small elite body of warriors could almost certainly have acted as a strong enough deterrent to protect the interest of band or tribe ... but instead every man was a warrior to a greater or lesser extent: if not an active one he was either an adolescent trying to achieve this status or an elderly man whose social position was largely based on his previous war record." Victories in battle were crucial to a man's position in the tribe, and recounting — in words or in paintings — various honors won in war was a central device both for providing the prestige of men in Plains Indian society and for keeping tribal history. "This suggests that the causes of war were complex and deeply rooted, and not wholly attributable to immediate material motives.... As tribes followed their own nomadic movement and their territorial claims expanded and contracted, the balance of power between them constantly shifted. Tribe pushed against tribe.... These tensions were played out over the entire space of the Great Plains, and also affected marginal groups that entered the grassland on periodic hunts or to trade.... Because the band system created similar tensions within the societies, flux and motion were expressed both internally and externally. Factionalism might cause tribal splits, with explosive movements away from the original tribal center of power." (Bancroft-Hunt) Now, as in the past, it has

A Cheyenne hide painting, depicting a horse raid.

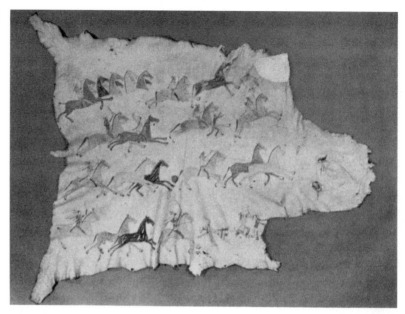

been exceptionally difficult to identify true centers of Indian leadership. Alliances were unstable, with tribal associations changing periodically from friendly to hostile. Leadership was based on different roles: religious, military, social, and so forth. And the notion of the all-powerful Indian "chief" is largely a product of European romance. As a matter of fact, factionalism was probably a very constant basis for changing centers of power within bands and tribes on the Plains. Part of this political instability doubtlessly grew from the fact that the bands within a tribe were fiercely independent. Often one band within a particular tribe would declare as an enemy a certain group that the other bands of the same tribe considered an ally. The psychology of warfare was built upon all of these attitudes and circumstances. Even war was largely an activity of the individual seeking glory and not the unified and highly stratified effort it was among Europeans.

The methods of warfare were drawn almost entirely from the ancient techniques of hunting: ceremonial preparations and procedures, achievements drastically affecting social status, a high degree of individuality both in effort and reward, as well as the use of decoys, ambush, and other devices and tricks of the Indian hunter, which amounted to "guerrilla warfare." Fundamentally, a great deal of masculine bravado was associated with hunting and warring.

Detail of hide painting: armed with the white man's gun in pursuit of the white man's horse.

Curiously, from earliest times, most Plains Indians identified war with gambling. "Gambling was a term used to refer to any act or undertaking that involved risk of a loss of any kind — material or even prestige or status — and which does not have the limited and rather negative implications that it has in European society today. The Plains Indian spoke of war as gambling and gambling as war, linking the two on the basis that superiority had to be established as proof of a person's worth through a form of rivalry that always involved potential risk. . . . War and gambling are also connected with hunting traditions (because hunting was also seen as a challenge and was intimately associated with survival) where spiritual powers are invoked to bring success. . . . To give him protection in battle and the ability to achieve his objectives, the warrior sought a vision in which power was granted. Horse effigies were often used as War Medicines to gain success on horse-raiding expeditions, when they were taken into combat strapped on the visionary's back. A degree of psychological power could also be gained over invisible or dangerous forces by representing them in visible form. It was believed that this protective power was absorbed by the owner of the object provided that he observed certain ritual restrictions. In the case of the [painted] shield, the warrior's most sacred and valued possession, a taboo forbade it ever touching the ground." (Bancroft-Hunt)

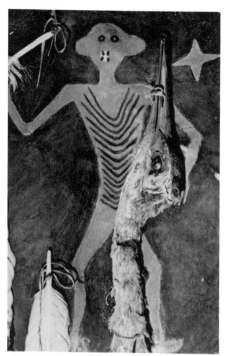

Detail of the visionary image of a shield painting, belonging to Chief Arapoosh of the Crow Indians of Montana. The design depicts the Moon, who came to Chief Arapoosh in human form.

The vision quest resulted in revelations given by various animal spirits, and were the means by which Plains Indians attained spiritual power and social status. The quest was a highly individualized rite: the supplicant went out into the wilderness as he or she approached adolescence, fasted, remained isolated in a desolate region, prayed for vision, and humbled himself or herself before the revered forces of nature. The vision quest could also be used by adults in their search for spiritual power. Dreams were a major source of revelation. The creator of the world in the Blackfeet genesis, a figure called Napi, was explicit in his advice to his people about dreams: "Now," he said, "if you are overcome, you may go and sleep, and get power. Something will come to you in your dream that will help you. Whatever these animals tell you to do, you must obey them, as they appear to you in your sleep. Be guided by them. If anybody wants help, if you are alone and traveling, and cry aloud for help, your prayer will be answered. It may be by the eagles, perhaps by the buffalo, or by the bears. Whatever animal answers your prayer, you must listen to him. That was how the first people got through the world, by the power of their dreams."

The lessons of the visionary almost always became manifest as painted images. Men exclusively produced compositions depicting life forms as well as supernatural beings. Males were the representational artists. Women, on the other hand, traditionally made abstract, geometric compositions. This specialization persists in a general way even today.

Comanche camp life in Texas: woman preparing buffalo hides, by George Catlin, 1834.

The most influential Plains art form was the narrative composition, which was created to tell a story, often heroic or highly personal, celebrating a deed of courage. These representational works were generally drafted by a group of men — often the individuals who had performed the deeds being recorded — who drew on untailored hide robes and tipi liners made of skins or canvas. The paintings usually filled the entire surface. Often they were conceived from time to time as separate pictorial vignettes, which documented specific actions and events. In relationship to each other, these vignettes suggest a continuous narrative. The images superficially resemble stick-figures. The figures are scattered on the surface, though most hides and tipi linings tended to be painted with a sense of centrifugal composition, without top or bottom, suggesting that they were painted to be shown on the ground surrounded by viewers.

Sioux horse effigy, probably carried in ritual dances. The carved holes marked in red depict wounds, probably of an honored horse wounded in battle.

The earliest known hide paintings (circa 1700), like the emblems painted on horses, shields, and other tools of hunting and warring, were highly individualistic and were often revealed to the artist through vision quests and dreams.

"Winter Counts," which were calendrical records, were unique to the Teton Sioux and the Kiowa of the Plains; however, they eventually had a lasting influence on the narrative style of Indians who were thrown together in so-called Indian Territory, now Oklahoma, as well as in the prisons like Fort Marion, Florida. The "counts" were composed of a continuous series of

Comanche and Kiowa Indians painting history on a buffalo robe in Indian Territory (Oklahoma), 1875.

simple images, each image representing an important event in the tribal history for the year. Subjects for the annual "counts" were chosen in council or by common agreement and were then added to the rawhide history of the tribe. The "counts" were mnemonic symbols organized in strict chronological sequence. They were not truly decorative or expressive in an artistic sense, but they did give rise to a formative pictorial tradition among Plains Indians. These tribal and individual drawings are precious because they, along with oral history, are the most decisive chronicles we have, produced from the viewpoint of Indians themselves.

The narrative intent of hide and tipi painting culminated in ledger drawings made by Indians displaced by imprisonment or removal, who nostalgically recreated the traditions of their homelands in ledger books provided by their white guardians. The history of these ledger books is fascinating. Ledger art was almost entirely invented by Indian prisoners-of-war; particularly those inmates of Fort Marion in Florida, where seventy-two Indians were interned in the 1870s. The young men's jailer, Captian Richard H. Pratt (who later founded the Carlisle Indian School in Pennsylvania), recognized his wards' strong interest in painting as a way of keeping historical records. And so he provided them with paper, pencils, and colors, and suggested that they create art for sale to whites. More than a third of the Indians imprisoned at Fort Marion participated in Pratt's art program, resulting in more than six hundred ledger drawings and paintings. The ledger drawings were made on paper and usually outlined in pencil and colored in crayon or watercolor.

It is debatable whether they were created specifically for the white public or for the artists themselves. It is possible that the art impulse sprang from defiance and nostalgia, a recollection of the old days and a protest against the process of assimilation. They were not made for tribal display like the hide narrative paintings, nor for utilitarian purposes like the "counts." They were private expressions of "artists" who were adrift in a world no longer Indian and not yet white.

Some of the drawings are anonymous, but many undoubtedly are consciously autobiographical. Gradually a distinctive style began to develop among specific Indians whose works were either "signed" by a symbol applied by the artists themselves or with "signatures" executed by white jailers or teachers. Among the most interesting of these artists were Buffalo

Bear's Heart: "The Cheyenne Among the Buffalo."

Bear's Heart: "The Church at Fort Marion."

Blackfeet camp, circa 1883, Moose Jaw, Canada.

Meat (a Cheyenne), Etahdleuh Doanmoe (a Kiowa), Howling Wolf (a Cheyenne), Paul Zo-Tom (a Kiowa), and the Cheyenne named Bear's Heart.

THE LIFE OF Bear's Heart provides a firsthand view of the tragic history of Plains Indians in the nineteenth century. And so it is appropriate that his story concludes our historic journey through the native land. (Burt Supree recounted these events in the life of Bear's Heart in a handsome little book of 1977, for which I wrote an afterword.)

Bear's Heart was born in 1851 and grew up among the Cheyenne in the Southern Plains. During his childhood, Indians were still wandering freely throughout an immense territory, hunting the countless buffalo that came together in huge herds during the grass-rich Plains springtime. The whinny of Indian horses and the bellow of the great shaggy bison filled the days. Bear's Heart and his people were contented.

Then the Cheyennes were forced to live within the confines of a reservation in western Oklahoma. The white men who were in charge of the reservation wanted the Indians to give up hunting and become farmers. But the Cheyenne had a very old tradition that regarded the hunt as an essential way for a male to prove his worth. So Bear's Heart and his people did not want to become farmers. Time and again the Cheyenne ran away from the reservation and searched for a land where they could live their own lives in peace. And time and again the soldiers were sent to force them back to the reservation.

Bear's Heart was unhappy. He felt as if he had been born into a world in which his ambitions and dreams no longer had a place. He was a good hunter and warrior, but the white men would not let him hunt and threatened to punish him if he went to war. And so Bear's Heart became angry and unhappy.

Then one day his father died, and Bear's Heart dutifully unbraided his long black hair and painted his face black and began to chant a song of mourning. His young friends came to him and said: "We must make a raiding party and attack the Utes." For it was traditional among the Indians of the Plains to mourn the loss of a beloved person by attacking an enemy tribe. Now, however, it was forbidden to go on such raids. Bear's Heart could not disgrace the memory of his father, and so he joined a small party of young Cheyennes and rode off into the mountains of Colorado to fight the Utes. When the white soldiers found out that a Cheyenne raiding party had killed some Utes, there was an investigation, but Bear's Heart was not found out. Thrilled by his daring exploit, he decided the next summer to go on horse raids into Texas, where enemy tribes had many fine mounts. Again he was not apprehended.

Life on the reservation got worse every day. The men felt helpless and dishonored, for they were forbidden to prove themselves either as hunters or as warriors. As their supply of food disappeared, they silently watched their families go hungry. There were no provisions from the government, although food and supplies had been promised by treaties with the United States. Then, in the summer of 1874, many Indians fled the reservation. Bear's Heart was among them. Everywhere in the Southern Plains, Indians escaped into the open grasslands: Cheyennes, Comanches, Kiowas, and Arapahoes.

Almost at once, soldiers were ordered into the field and told to drive the Indians back onto their reservations and to keep them there. The tribes desperately evaded the military, hiding in little valleys, surviving on meager provisions, and traveling by night. But the soldiers were undaunted and continued to hunt down the Indians throughout the summer and cruel winter of 1874 and 1875.

The leader of the band to which Bear's Heart belonged was a clever man named Medicine Water, and through his cunning the people were able to evade the cavalry. Then one day late in

Plains Indian skin painting, circa 1890.

August, Bear's Heart and his people encountered six surveyors near a town in Kansas called Lone Tree. Surveyors were detested by the Cheyenne, for they were associated with the railroads that scarred the land and brought to the West many settlers who pushed Indians out of their hunting grounds. In a rage, Medicine Water ordered his braves to attack the white men, and they killed all six of them.

Despite the fact that the band of Medicine Water was now hunted mercilessly by the outraged cavalry, his warriors continued to take revenge on any party of white people they encountered. One evening, Medicine Water led his braves into a ravine where John German and his family were camped. In the early morning the Indians attacked, killing the husband and his wife and three of their young children. They took the other four girls as hostages. It was not until many months later that soldiers finally freed the children. No one knows if Bear's Heart was one of the assailants. The anger of the whites was great, but Bear's Heart and his people once again evaded the troops and escaped.

Now there was utterly no food. The people were starving. The soldiers had driven them so hard that many of their horses had been lost. Time and again the soldiers would discover the temporary camps of the Cheyenne, and when they attacked, the Indians had to leave everything behind in their anxiousness to escape. Soon there was nothing left: no weapons, no food, no horses, no shelter.

Miserably, the Indians began to return to the reservation. Bear's Heart was among them.

It was on the desolate reservation that a fellow-Cheyenne named Big Moccasin accused Bear's Heart of being a member of the band that had killed the six surveyors and the family of John German. At once Bear's Heart was arrested and put in the guard-house.

The government announced that hostile chiefs and warriors were to be sent to prison in a place very far away in the East. All the accused prisoners were lined up and then four Indian leaders as well as ten warriors and one women (the wife of Medicine Water) were arbitrarily picked. An additional eighteen men were also selected at random — making a total of thirty-three persons. Then all of the captives were chained together and put in wagons and taken to Fort Sill in Oklahoma.

The final destination of these prisoners would be a sad building in St. Augustine, Florida, called Fort Marion — a place many miles from their beloved homeland. The Indians were taken to the nearest railroad station, which was 165 miles from Fort Sill. Great congregations of relatives and friends assembled along the route, wailing and protesting, weeping and shouting in anguish as loved ones were taken away in chains. All together, there were seventy-two Indian prisoners in the caravan. They peered out as the wagons carried them away, seeing the stricken faces of people they loved vanish from sight. They could not believe that the soldiers were taking them halfway across the United States to a prison. They were certain that all of them would be killed.

Eventually the prisoners were taken from the wagons and put on a train. They wanted to leap to freedom when the terrible machine began to hiss and roar, but they were still in shackles and could not escape. As the train began to move, many of the people were so fearful that they crouched on the floor and covered their heads with their blankets.

Gradually, as the days passed and they made their way toward Florida on a difficult month-long journey, the prisoners began to realize that perhaps they would not be killed after all.

Standing Rock Sioux camp, circa 1870.

At each station along the route, crowds of white people rushed forward to get a look at the "wild Indians." In St. Louis, Indianapolis, Louisville, Nashville, Atlanta, and Jacksonville there were hundreds of curious people who behaved as if they were at a circus, shouting and pushing and peering at the prisoners. Finally, at Jacksonville, the Indians were transferred to a steamboat that took them up river to the town of Tocoi, where they boarded the St. John's Railway for the last fifteen miles of their long journey to Fort Marion.

Lieutenant Richard Henry Pratt was in charge of the prisoners. The first thing he did was have their chains removed. Then he gave them drawing books and colored pencils. It was at this time that Bear's Heart began to make his remarkable drawings — vivid recollections of the good life of Indians on the Great Plains — the drawings were fragile memories of better days that brought a measure of contentment to Bear's Heart.

In an effort to teach the Indians something of the ways of the white world, Lieutenant Pratt decided to introduce them to Western commerce. He brought them "sea beans" — gray seeds with hard shells that washed ashore along the beaches of Florida. He gave the prisoners money for polishing these beans so they could be made into souvenir jewelry for tourists. The Indians soon grasped the nature of the tourist trade, and began to make and sell little bows and arrows.

For three years the prisoners were required to live like soldiers at Fort Marion. Their traditional clothes were replaced with army fatigues. Every day they were awakened at dawn and put through very strict military inspection. Then they were drilled like soldiers. They went to church and to school, where they were persistently taught the importance of work and the values of a "good Christian life." Lieutenant Pratt ordered that every Indian male must have his hair cut short, but the prisoners would not tolerate such disfigurement. Eventually, however, Pratt won over most of his wards by demonstrating that he meant them no harm and only wished to help them adjust to the white man's world. He sent the guards away and organized an Indian police force. One by one the Indians consented to having their hair cut. Bear's Heart was one of the first to sacrifice the marvelous locks of which he was so proud.

Lieutenant Pratt believed that it was essential for Indians to learn to speak English if they were to live in the strange new world of the United States. Most of the prisoners did learn English, and it became the universal language of the prison. Indian inmates from different tribes that spoke entirely different languages were able to understand each other for the first time.

In 1878, after three years of imprisonment, the Indians were finally given their liberty. Most of them were sent back to their reservations, but Bear's Heart wanted to continue his education in the white man's schools, and so he and sixteen other Cheyennes and Kiowas entered the Hampton Institute in Virginia, a training school founded by General Samuel Armstrong for the education of blacks.

Bear's Heart worked hard at his lessons, learning carpentry and also taking classes in English, arithmetic, and reading. It was during these days at Hampton that Bear's Heart apparently came to believe in the superiority of the ways of the world of white people. Then, as if to consecrate his conversion to an alien world, in March of 1879, he entered the chapel of the Hampton Institute and was baptized a Christian.

It is ironic that of all his heroic efforts to be an achiever in the dominant society of America, it was only in his drawings that Bear's Heart produced something memorable and important. These drawings are more than art. Everywhere in his pictures is the subtle influence of his white educators and captors. No rage or resentment is found in his bright, enchanted pictures, in much the way that there is no torment in the drawings of the children of Terezin concentration camp. There is, instead, a steadily growing interest, delight, and belief in the power, culture, and values of white America.

Bear's Heart: "The Train Takes the Prisoners to Fort Marion, Florida, 1875."

Paul Zo-Tom painted this exterior view of Fort Marion, Saint Augustine, Florida, where the Indians were confined, in 1877.

Bear's Heart: "The Prisoners Are Transferred from the Train to the River Boat."

Paul Zo-Tom: "A Class of Indians at Fort Marion, with Their Teacher (Mrs. Gibbs)," with the original signatures of Zo-Tom and Making Medicine.

Bear's Heart stayed on at Hampton for three years. In May of 1880, he spoke before a large audience in the school auditorium. His educators apparently saw in this young Cheyenne unmistakable proof that "savages" could be civilized and turned into useful human beings. A correspondent from the *Boston Journal* reported on May 24, 1880:

"He is a tall, unpleasant looking fellow of thirty-four years [he was actually twenty-nine], with high cheek bones, and he spoke in imperfect English, which he supplemented now and then with gestures.... He spoke with hesitation and nervousness, but straight on, without repetition or any doubling back on his course.... There could scarcely have been a more unpromising subject [for education] than this hard-featured young brave, fresh from waging war on the white when he was taken to St. Augustine [Fort Marion]."

This extraordinary speech of Bear's Heart was taken down and printed in the school's newspaper. It is a very rare and sad account, the autobiography of a buffalo-hunting nomad who was never confined to a reservation, recorded without the interventions of interpreters, and seen sharply with the memory of youth and not through the vague recall of old age and the unconscious compromises of partial assimilation which mark so much of the narrative of Indians whose words were published in subsequent years.

WHEN I WAS A LITTLE BOY, I got out of bed, maybe six o'clock every morning. I got out Wigwam, wash face, go back in Wigwam. My father comb my hair and he tie it then he paint my face good. Then my father said you go shoot; my little friend come and I said to him let us go and shoot. When finish cooking, my mother say "Come here, Bear's Heart, breakfast." Then I told my friend after breakfast you come again we go shooting again. I had buffalo meat just one [?] for breakfast. I will tell you how my home look, Indian bed just on ground. My father and my mother have a bed one side of the Wigwam; I and my brother other side, and my sister another side, and the door on one side. The fire is in middle. My people sit on bed, and my mother she give us a tin plate and cut meat, we have one knife no fork hold the meat by hand, eat with knife. After breakfast I go shooting with my friend. I eat three times every day. Sometimes two times when not much meat. All the time meat, that is all. I no work, I play all the time. After

a while I big boy. My father he said, "Bear's Heart you try kill buffalo now." I say "Yes." When Indians went buffalo hunting I go too. One time I shoot twice and kill buffalo. I skin buffalo and put skin and beef on my horse. I took to my Wigwam. My father he say "Bear's Heart, how many times you shoot?" I say: "One time." He say "Good." When I big boy my father give me gun and I shoot deer. All the time I shoot. I done no work. When my father died I was "a bad man" [designates a person with a depth of sorrow from the loss of a relative that traditionally required pacification by taking a life]. By and by about twenty Indian young men went to fight Utes. I told my mother I want to fight too, and she said "Yes." I go and fight all day first time, we killed one Ute and four Cheyenne. Sundown we stop. In Texas I fight again. In Texas all time fight no stop,

February 1887: Indian children at the Carlisle Indian School with their hair cut, their bodies thoroughly scrubbed, and their traditional dress exchanged for the uniforms of the school founded by the same Lieutenant Pratt who was warden of the Indian prisoners at Fort Marion in 1875.

Indian children learning how to wash clothes at Riverside Indian School.

some fight, some take horses. In the summer I fight, in the winter no fight. I fight then I got tired, I say my two friends: "Lets go back to Agency." My friends they say "Yes." We sent to Agency [tribal headquarters created by government supervisors], the Captain [talk] to us, he say, "Bear's Heart what you want to do, fight or stay here?" I said "Stay here." "All right," say he, "go to Wigwam." About one month after, Cheyenne chief he tell agent Bear's Heart had been fighting so he is bad, then the Captain put me in the guard house. By and by the Captain he sent my two friends to tell all Indians to stop fight and come to Agency. All Indians come back then. Cheyenne chief he look at all Indians and told Captain what Indians fight. The Captain put bad Indians in guard house, and colored soldiers put chains on their legs. One man he got mad and run, the soldiers shoot but no kill him. By and by good many soldiers come from Fort Sill and took us to Fort Sill, where I saw Captain Pratt. Good many Kiowas, Comanches, and Arapahoes, Cheyennes all together with soldiers and Captain Pratt take us to Florida. When I ride to Florida all the time I think by and by he kill me. When I been to St. Augustine some time and womans and mans come to see me and shake hand, I think soldiers no kill me. After awhile Captain Pratt took off all Indian chains, but not too quick. Captain Pratt he see boys no have money. He got sea-beans, he say "Make sea-beans shine." He told us how and when we make sea-beans good we take to him, he give us money. First time we made sea-beans, then bow and arrows, then paint pictures. By and by teacher she come with pictures of dog, cat, cow, and tell us every day nine o'clock morning we go to school stop at twelve o'clock, afternoon just make sea-beans. Before Indians went to school, Captain Pratt he gave Indians clothes just like white men, but Indians no want hair cut. Sunday Indians go to church St. Augustine: down from head, Indians same as white men; but head, long hair just like Indians. By and by after Indians go to church, they say I want my hair cut; my teachers very good. Two years I stay at St. Augustine, then come Hampton School. At Hampton I go to school and I work. I don't want to go home just now. I want learn more English, more work and more of the good way. When I finish my school here, I go home to teach my people to work also, I want my mother and sisters to work house, and I and brother to work farm. When they put chains on me to take me from my home, I felt sorry, but I glad now, for I good boy now.

THE HISTORY OF traditional Plains Indian life ends with this tragic soliloquy. Few traces remain of the "legend days." The most vivid residue of the good days of nomadic freedom and individualism is found among the pictorial records made by hunters, scribes, storytellers, and prisoners-of-war in the eighteenth and nineteenth centuries. Bear's Heart was such an "artist" before there was a name for art among his people. He was a keeper of pictorial history — a tradition so old and pervasive among Plains Indian males that they did not possess a name for it.

In April of 1881 Bear's Heart returned to the reservation of his people. His hair was short, he wore white man's clothes, and he carried his carpentry tools in one hand and a Bible in the other. He was a misfit, though he believed he had come back to his tribe as someone better than he had been when he was taken away six years previously. His people, however, did not agree. As Burt Supree sadly recounts, "The leaders of the tribe were not interested in the ideas Bear's Heart had brought from back East. The Indians' experiences had not given them a good opinion of white men or their ways."

In September of 1881, Bear's Heart had an accident while unloading a wagon train. In January of the next year, he died. He was still a young man, about thirty years of age.

Only the pictures of Bear's Heart remain. They are touching depictions of the great days of the warriors of the Plains. They are shadows of a lost world. But they are also reminders of what all of us have lost in this ancient land newly named America.

Petroglyphs of the Anasazi, the cliff dwellers of the American Southwest.

Acknowledgments
Bibliography
Index

Acknowledgments

My hope of presenting a television series on the cultural history of pre-Columbian American civilizations dates from 1979. The story of how that aim became a reality is so complex, so fraught with drama and farce, and involves such a large cast of villains and heroes that it is best saved for an autobiography. Though I intend at some future time to tell the whole story, there are a few appreciative notes on the realization of *Native Land* that can't be neglected now.

Executive producer Alvin H. Perlmutter was the driving force behind the production of *Native Land*. For four years, he and his excellent associates worked closely with me on the conception and the visualization of the program. Their names appear in the production credits, but they are more than just names because television is a true collaborative form. The interplay of words and images, of sound and music, of photography and editing necessitates a challenging exchange between artists and technicians, which at its best results in a unique kind of experience for the audience. I was fortunate to work with people who persistently gave their best efforts. In John Peaslee I found a producer/director with whom I shared the kind of artistic sensibility that is essential among collaborators. His contributions to the visual realization of the program were so perfectly suited to my vision of the project that it is now difficult to recall where my ideas ended and his began — which is to say that he was exceptionally important in the shaping of *Native Land*. The elegance and remarkable beauty of the photography of Joel Shapiro must be immediately apparent to anyone who has seen the television program. The excellent contribution of audio/video artist Kay Armstrong is equally apparent. And the persistent insights and keen professionalism of assistant director and editor Judd Pillot were essential to the realization of our project. Less visible in the National Public Television broadcast is the work of coordinating producer Douglas P. Sinsel, whose many years of network experience have made him a master in his field. Another important behind-the-scenes collaborator was associate producer Lisa Zbar, whose attention to detail is everywhere in evidence in our program. And finally, I had the marvelous cooperation of a number of excellent dancers, whose artistry and skill were an indispensable element in our efforts to create a new kind of documentary program.

With the strong encouragement of John Wicklein and the assistance of Donald Marbury and Ron Hull of the Corporation for Public Broadcasting (CPB), as well as the sage advice and financial support of Suzanne Weil of the Public Broadcasting Service (PBS), *Native Land* took its first stumbling steps toward prime time. Additional grants, underwriting, and coproduction resources were eventually provided by the Museo del Banco Central of Ecuador and the stations of the Public Broadcasting Service (PBS).

I have had the privilege of writing, hosting, and staging this program, but without both the creative and financial assistance of these and many other people, *Native Land* would still be an idea in the bottom drawer of my desk.

Books that are based on television programs are often transcriptions of the broadcast scripts. I have chosen a different approach: to write a book that elaborates upon the original program. I decided upon this course because television is not only remarkably powerful, but it can also be very frustrating to the writer. It is powerful, of course, because of its persuasive images, which reach a vast audience; and frustrating because it is a visual medium, which often prevents us from saying as much as we want to say about fascinating and complex subject matter. And so it is especially gratifying to be able to reinstate the countless notes and pages of script that I had to relinquish necessarily as part of the "reductionist" process of producing for television. This book also permits me to offer a brief, selected Bibliography, for readers who wish to explore our subject far more than this general survey allows.

Finally, I am deeply grateful to Roger Donald of Little, Brown and Company for his long-standing belief in our project and to editor Michael Mattil for his immeasurable assistance in making this book possible.

JAMAKE HIGHWATER
Cuzco, Peru, 1986

**NATIVE LAND
PRODUCTION STAFF**

Produced by The Primal Mind Foundation
in association with
The Native Land Foundation
and
Alvin H. Perlmutter Associates

Executive Producer
ALVIN H. PERLMUTTER

Writer, Narrator, and Choreographer
JAMAKE HIGHWATER

Producer/Director
JOHN PEASLEE

Coordinating Producer
DOUGLAS P. SINSEL

Assistant Director/Editor
JUDD PILLOT

Associate Producer
LISA ZBAR

Location Coordinator
BRYAN THOMAS

Director of Photography
JOEL SHAPIRO

Audio/Video
KAY ARMSTRONG

Camera Assistant
JOHN ROBINSON

Researcher: North America
JOHN WILLIAMSON

Researcher: South America
CECILIA VICUNA

Musical Director
JAMAKE HIGHWATER

Dancers: Ecuador
NELSON DIAZ, DIEGO GARRIDO, MARIA LUISA GONZALEZ,
PANCHO LOPEZ, WILSON PICO, HUA LAN SCREMIN, MAISCREMIN,
KLEVER VIERA, AND FAUSTO VILLAGOMEZ

Performers: Peru
CARLOS BARRIENTOS AND WALTER MACHICADO (CUZCO)
THEATRE GROUP YUYACHKANI (LIMA)

Costume Designers
LOUANNE GILLELAND AND ELENA PELLICCIARO

Paintbox Graphics
TODD RUFF AND SHARON HASKELL

Mask Designer
SILVA CHAVEZ TORO

Production Secretaries
HELEN BUTLER, ELEANOR STICHWEH, AND JOHN FARINET

Special Thanks
MUSEO NACIONAL DE ANTROPOLOGIA Y ARQUEOLOGIA, *Lima*
INSTITUTO NACIONAL DE CULTURA, *Cuzco*
INSTITUTO CULTURAL PERUANO NORTEAMERICANO, *Cuzco*

Major funding for the program Native Land
was provided by
THE CORPORATION FOR PUBLIC BROADCASTING.

Additional funding was provided by
STATIONS OF THE PUBLIC BROADCASTING SERVICE (PBS)
and
THE BANCO CENTRAL OF ECUADOR

Bibliography

ANGIER, NATALIE. "A 'Lost City' Revisited." *Time* magazine, February 11, 1985.

BANCROFT-HUNT, NORMAN. *The Indians of the Great Plains.* New York, 1981.

BANKS, GEORGE. *Peru Before Pizarro.* Oxford, 1977.

BELTRAN, MIRIAM. *Cuzco: Window on Peru.* New York, 1970.

BENNETT, WENDELL. *Ancient Arts of the Andes.* New York, 1954.

BERNAL, IGNACIO. *Mexico Before Cortez.* Garden City, 1975.

BLISH, HELEN H. *A Pictographic History of the Oglala Sioux: Drawings by Amos Bad Heart Bull.* Lincoln, 1967.

Book of the Chilam Balam of Chumayel. Translated and annotated by Ralph L. Roys. From first edition by the Carnegie Institution of Washington, D.C., 1933. Norman, 1967.

BURLAND, COTTIE. *North American Indian Mythology.* New York, 1965.

———. *Peoples of the Sun.* New York, 1976.

CANBY, THOMAS Y. "The Search for the First Americans." *National Geographic,* vol. 156, no. 3 (September 1979).

CASO, ALFONSO. *The Aztecs: People of the Sun.* Norman, 1958.

CASSON, LIONEL, ROBERT CLAIBORNE, BRIAN FAGAN, AND WALTER KARP. *Mysteries of the Past.* New York, 1977.

CASTRO LEAL, MARCIA. *El Juego de Pelota: The Ball Game.* Mexico City, 1973.

CIEZA DE LEON, PEDRO DE. *The Incas.* Translated by Harriet de Onis; edited, with an introduction, by Victor Wolfgang von Hagen. (Original publication: Seville, 1553.) Norman, 1959.

CLAIBORNE, ROBERT. *The First Americans.* New York, 1973.

COE, MICHAEL D. *The Maya.* London, 1980.

——— . *Mexico.* London, 1962 (revised 1984).

DOUGLAS, FREDERIC H., and RENÉ D'HARNONCOURT. *Indian Art of the United States.* New York, 1941.

DUNN, DOROTHY. *Plains Indian Sketch Books of Zo-Tom and Howling Wolf: 1877.* Flagstaff, 1969.

FARB, PETER. *Man's Rise to Civilization.* New York, 1968, 1978.

GALLENKAMP, CHARLES. *Maya: The Riddle and Rediscovery of a Lost Civilization.* New York, 1976.

GOODMAN, JEFFREY. *American Genesis.* New York, 1981.

GRAHAM, JOHN A. (ed.). *Ancient Mesoamerica: Selected Readings.* Palo Alto, 1981.

GUAMAN POMA DE AYALA, FELIPE. *Letter to a King: A Peruvian Chief's Account of Life Under the Incas and Under Spanish Rule.* Translated, arranged, and edited by Christopher Dilke from *Nueva Coronicay Buen Gobierno,* written 1567–1615; original manuscript held by The Royal Library of Copenhagen. New York, 1978.

GUMERMAN, GEORGE J., and EMIL W. HAURY. *See* Ortiz, Alfonso.

HABERLAND, W. *The Art of North America.* New York, 1964.

HAGEN, VICTOR W. VON. *The Aztec: Man and Tribe.* New York, 1958.

——— . *Realm of the Incas.* New York, 1961.

HAINES, FRANCIS. *The Plains Indians.* New York, 1976.

HALL, ALICE J. "A Traveler's Tale of Ancient Tikal." *National Geographic,* vol. 148, no. 6 (December 1975).

HEMMING, JOHN. *Machu Picchu.* New York, 1981.

HIGHWATER, JAMAKE. *Arts of the Indian Americas: Leaves from the Sacred Tree.* New York, 1983.

——— . *Journey to the Sky: The Rediscovery of the Maya.* New York, 1978.

——— . *The Sun, He Dies.* New York, 1980.

JENISON, MADGE. *Roads.* New York, 1948.

LANNING, EDWARD P. *Peru Before the Incas.* Englewood Cliffs, 1967.

LATHRAP, DONALD W. *Ancient Ecuador: Culture, Clay, and Creativity — 3000–300 B.C.* Chicago, 1975.

LEONARD, JONATHAN NORTON. *Ancient America.* New York, 1967.

LEON-PORTILLA, MIGUEL. *Time and Reality in the Thought of the Maya.* Boston, 1973.

McINTYRE, LOREN. *The Incredible Incas and Their Timeless Land.* Washington, D.C., 1975.

MEYER, KARL E. *Teotihuacán.* New York, 1973.

NICHOLSON, IRENE. *Mexican and Central American Mythology.* New York, 1967.

ORTIZ, ALFONSO. (ed.). *Handbook of North American Indians: Southwest.* Vol. 9. Washington, D.C., 1979.

OSBORNE, HAROLD. *Indians of the Andes: Aymaras and Quechuas.* London, 1952.

————. *South American Mythology.* New York, 1968.

PETERSON, KAREN DANIELS. *Howling Wolf.* Palo Alto, 1968.

————. *Plains Indian Art from Fort Marion.* Norman, 1971.

Popol Vuh: The Great Mythological Book of the Ancient Maya. Translated and with an introduction by Ralph Nelson. Boston, 1976.

Popol Vuh: The Sacred Book of the Ancient Quiche Maya. English version by Delia Goetz and Sylvanus G. Morley from the translation of Adrian Recinos. Norman, 1950.

PRESCOTT, WILLIAM H. *The Conquest of Mexico* [1843]. Republished, New York, 1943.

PROSKOURIAKOFF, TATIANA. *An Album of Maya Architecture.* Norman, 1963.

RENFREW, COLIN. *Before Civilization.* New York, 1973.

RUZ LHUILLIER, ALBERTO. *La civilización de los antiguos Mayas.* Mexico City, 1963.

SEJOURNE, LAURETTE. *Burning Water: Thought and Religion in Ancient Mexico.* San Francisco, 1976.

SILVERBERG, ROBERT. *Mound Builders of Ancient America.* Greenwich, 1968.

SODI MORALES, DEMETRIO. *The Maya World.* Mexico City, 1976.

SOUSTELLE, JACQUES. *The Olmecs: The Oldest Civilization in Mexico.* Garden City, 1984.

STUART, GEORGE E. "Who Were the 'Mound Builders'?" *National Geographic,* vol. 142, no. 6 (December 1972).

STUART, GEORGE E., and GENE S. STUART. *Discovering Man's Past in the Americas.* New York, 1969.

————. *The Mysterious Maya.* Washington, D.C., 1977.

SUPREE, BURTON. *Bear's Heart: Scenes from the Life of a Cheyenne Artist.* New York, 1977.

SWANTON, JOHN R. *The Indians of the Southeastern United States.* Washington, D.C., 1946.

————. *Indian Tribes of the Lower Mississippi Valley and Adjacent Coast of the Gulf of Mexico.* Washington, D.C., 1911.

TAMARIN, ALFRED, and SHIRLEY GLUBOK. *Ancient Indians of the Southwest.* Garden City, 1975.

THWAITES, REUBEN GOLD (ed.). *The Jesuit Relations and Other Documents.* Vols. 75–78, "Travels and Explorations of the Jesuit Missionaries in New France — 1669 to 1737." Cleveland, 1901.

TILLETT, LESLIE. *Wind on the Buffalo Grass.* New York, 1976.

TRIGGER, BRUCE G. "Cultural Unity and Diversity" in *Handbook of North American Indians: Northeast.* Vol. 15. Washington, D.C., 1978.

VAN SERTIMA, IVAN. *They Came Before Columbus.* New York, 1976.

WARING, JR., ANTONIA. *See* Ortiz, Alfonso.

WAUCHOPE, ROBERT. *Lost Tribes and Sunken Continents.* Chicago, 1962.

WEAVER, MURIEL PORTER. *The Aztecs, Maya, and Their Predecessors.* New York, 1972.

Index